ECONOMIC POLICY IN THE CARTER ADMINISTRATION

ECONOMIC POLICY IN THE CARTER ADMINISTRATION

Anthony S. Campagna

Contributions in Economics and Economic History,
Number 171

GREENWOOD PRESS
Westport, Connecticut • London

Library of Congress Cataloging-in-Publication Data

Campagna, Anthony S.
    Economic policy in the Carter administration / Anthony S.
Campagna.
        p.   cm.—(Contributions in economics and economic history,
    ISSN 0084–9235 ; no. 171)
    Includes bibliographical references and index.
    ISBN 0–313–29568–9 (alk. paper)
    1. United States—Economic policy—1971–1981.   2. United States—
Politics and government—1977–1981.   3. Carter, Jimmy, 1924– .
I. Title. II. Series.
HC106.7.C34   1995
338.973′009′047—dc20   95–22981

British Library Cataloguing in Publication Data is available.

Library of Congress Catalog Card Number: 95–22981
ISBN: 0–313–29568–9
ISSN: 0084–9235

First published in 1995

Greenwood Press, 88 Post Road West, Westport, CT 06881
An imprint of Greenwood Publishing Group, Inc.

Printed in the United States of America

The paper used in this book complies with the
Permanent Paper Standard issued by the National
Information Standards Organization (Z39.48–1984).

10 9 8 7 6 5 4 3 2 1

For Alena,
A Father's Joy

Contents

Tables and Figure

Preface

Whatever else may be said of the Carter administration, one thing is incontrovertible: Carter took office at an inopportune time. The economy was floundering, and the political atmosphere was contentious. The nation was in the grip of stagflation, and the mood of the public was gloomy. Having just emerged from a sharp recession, the economy did not appear to be growing strongly enough, and unemployment was still hovering around 7.5%. At the time, no one seemed to be able to manage the economy, and forces beyond our control seemed to be in command.

Carter also faced a shifting political scene. Unwilling to emulate the presidential style of his predecessors, particularly Richard Nixon, he opted instead to go out of his way to differentiate himself from prior presidential models. His cabinet-style government, his organization of the White House staff, and his relationship with the bureaucracy testify to the desire to do things differently. He ran as an outsider, willing and able to clean up the mess in Washington, and this called for, so he thought, a reorganization of government starting at the top. Still, he surrounded himself with the Georgia mafia, who had little or no experience in Washington politics or in foreign affairs. On the job training might be admirable in some circumstances but is disastrous in the arcane world of Washington politics.

At the same time, Congress was asserting its independence and was less coherent and consistent, while party unity was further withering. Buoyed by its success against Nixon and Ford, Congress was not about to relinquish its new-found power and was searching for its new voice in national affairs. Thus, the Congress that Carter faced was a much different institution from the one faced by his predecessors.

To make any progress, therefore, Carter would have to mold his concept of the presidency at the same time as adapting to the changing congressional configuration. It would take a great deal of effort to devise a strategy to achieve success under such circumstances, an effort that Carter, the outsider, was unwilling or unable to make. So in the early years of his administration, Carter seemed inept in his relations with the Washington establishment and uncompromising with respect to his legislative program. He would do what he thought was right and not worry about the political consequences. He had no real interest in politics as usual—the give and take, the horse trading, the camaraderie—and it made him appear remote and cold. Many concluded that he basically distrusted politics and the normal games associated with it. His was an engineer's approach: One saw a problem, devised a solution, and then expected it to be considered on its merits. Modifications and compromises seemed unnecessary, and even damaging; political niceties seemed superfluous and expendable. This attitude was not likely to foster inspiration for those who worked so diligently on his behalf. He set high standards, too high perhaps, and expected those around him to be as faithful to them as he was.

This early approach ensured that he remained a Washington outsider, unable to manage his agenda through the establishment. As hard working and dedicated as he was, Carter needed the cooperation of Congress to achieve his goals. He presented too many programs too quickly to Congress, and members complained that he failed to indicate which should receive priority. He alienated members by his failure to consult with them, by his unwillingness to compromise or consider risks for members, and by his inability to regard political lobbying as necessary. He seemed to lack a political philosophy and had difficulty explaining his ideas and programs to those who did. After a considerable learning period, Carter and his staff did learn the rules of the game, but by that time his performance in office may have already been judged, and many were looking beyond him.

It is not our purpose to describe in detail the operations of the White House staff nor to examine the political style of the Carter administration. Indeed, many have subjected the Carter administration to microscopic analysis in order to understand the flaws in its procedures. We are more concerned with his economic program and how it fared from conception to execution. Along the way, the political process will be introduced as it influences economic policy-making, of course, but the flaws, if any, in the manner in which it was introduced and managed through Congress are better left to political scientists and more knowledgeable observers. Yet, it is useful to remind ourselves of the constraints Carter faced, both of his own making and otherwise, as a prelude to the examination of his approach to economic policy-making.

Now may be a good time to reassess the last Democratic regime that occupied the White House, for after twelve years of Republican rule, the presidency was returned to the Democrats in 1993. I do not intend to conduct a lengthy comparison of Clinton vs. Carter, nor to compare campaign strategies, the initial days in the White House, or relations with Congress. Rather the book concerns the economic problems, mainly macroeconomic ones, faced solely by the Carter administration and what it did about them.

Curiously in this regard, the Carter administration has been neglected, and overall evaluations of its performance are lacking. Is that due to his one-term presidency so that no lasting effects are discernible? Is it because the problems his administration faced were uninteresting, or have they been solved subsequently and made prosaic? Or is it the man himself who left office under a cloud of ineptness, making his administration unworthy of serious study? Whatever the reasons, this book will attempt to answer some of these questions and account for the lack of interest in the Carter years. However, my primary aim is not to determine why others have not found the Carter years inspiring but to correct the situation. Carter occupies a unique position in the nation's recent history, and this position should be explained and analyzed. Wedged between Republican administrations, he seems in retrospect to have been placed by history in a rather awkward position. It is, therefore, essential to understand his contribution and influence with this circumstance in mind; he cannot be ignored. One purpose of this book is to remedy the relative indifference to which his administration has been subject.

To account for some of the questions raised above and reach a better understanding of his administration, the book naturally partitions itself into some rather broad segments. Part I is devoted to the macroeconomic problems and solutions of the Carter administration. Chapter 1 summarizes the economic situation that the Carter administration inherited. Carter came to power following the Nixon/Ford administrations and was forced to deal with any leftover problems from those regimes, as well as the new ones that time inevitably brings. Therefore, it is necessary to provide some background of the economic conditions facing the new administration when it assumed responsibility for the nation's economy.

It would also be interesting to compare the economic policies advocated by Ford and Carter in the presidential campaign of 1976. What approaches were suggested for the prevailing problems, and how did the public react to them? Which problems were recognized by the two candidates, and which ones were considered important enough to stress during the campaign? Chapter 2 outlines the economic issues in the 1976 campaign and suggests the role of economics in general in the election.

Having won the election, the Carter administration became responsible for the management of the economy. Whether or not it inherited serious problems or past mismanagement of the economy, it now had to propose solutions. Chapter 3 analyzes Carter's immediate economic plans that followed from his campaign pledges and his overall vision of where he wanted to take the nation. Chapter 4 reviews the problems faced and the policies followed in the first two years of the administration, and Chapter 5 does the same for the last two years. In addition to criticisms of these policies suggested in both chapters, Chapter 6 provides a summary and critique of the administration's macroeconomic policies. Economic plans and grandiose visions always appear to conflict with reality, with legislative resistance, and with unforseen events that disrupt the most well-structured plans. In this chapter, I will try to sort these things out, paying particular attention to how the Carter administration reacted to changing conditions it could not control and to those it could. Indeed, the success of this or any other administration can often be found in the manner in which it confronts disappointments and disruptions to its intentions.

Part II then deals with other economic facets of the administration's program. Chapter 7 concerns the international trade situation combined with energy matters. In this period, the two areas are closely connected and so their combination is not as strange as it might appear at first glance. Clearly, energy concerns played a major role in shaping the administration's policies in many areas; indeed at times, it was almost preoccupied with energy concerns. Chapter 8 will evaluate the administration's success at reforming various institutional obstacles to efficient management of the economy. In the campaign, Carter spoke often of the need to make government more efficient, which of course called for reforms of various kinds that would enable it to become more efficient. Some of these problem areas included tax and budget reforms, welfare reforms, health reforms, government reorganization, and regulation. With due respect to space limitations, the administration's success in these areas will be evaluated.

Part III is concerned with Carter's legacy. Chapter 9 continues the assessment of the Carter years by reviewing the economic issues in the presidential campaign of 1980. What were the president's economic plans for a second term, and what role did the state of the economy play in the defeat of the president? In Chapter 10, we look at the Carter legacy. From the administration's handling of the economy, what lessons were learned, if any, and what did it bequeath to the new administration? Finally, with the benefit of hindsight, some conclusions are possible with respect to an evaluation of the Carter administration's performance while in office, and to some provisional judgments of Carter's place in the historical record.

Part I
Macroeconomic Policy-Making

Chapter 1

The Economy in the Early 1970s

Political administrations do not begin with a fresh slate, free of what went before. That should be obvious enough, but it is still necessary to remind ourselves that the world does not start over with the advent of a new presidential administration, despite all the political rhetoric to the contrary. Whatever may be said of other areas of public affairs, in the economic sphere it is particularly evident that economic conditions do not conform to political cycles. It follows that any new administration must confront the economic realities it inherits whether it wants to or not, and if it is lucky, it may be able to embark on programs to change that reality; if it is unlucky, economic events may simply prevent the introduction of new approaches and the implementation of whatever innovative ideas the new administration brings with it.

Clearly then, it is necessary, even essential, to understand the economic world that the Carter administration inherited. We would then have some idea of what problems the new administration faced, and what, if anything, had been done about them by previous administrations. Only in this way can we begin to appreciate the economic program that the administration planned, and only in this way can we measure how successful it was in accomplishing what it set out to do. With full awareness of the barriers it faced at the outset, a better assessment of its successes and failures is at least possible, if not easy.

The purpose of this chapter is to provide, in summary form, the state of the economy when Carter took office.[1] After this background is in place, we can examine the economic measures proposed by both sides in the campaign of 1976 in chapter 2, and the economic plans of the Carter administration as they were amended in chapter 3.

THE NIXON YEARS

The decade of the 1970s was not a good time for the economy or for economists. Political and economic events sorely tested our ability to recognize and deal with the economic problems they created. The 1970s started out familiarly enough, at least in retrospect, and while the economy seemed in disarray, it also seemed manageable.

The economy was suffering from the economic conditions created by the Vietnam war, but they were recognizable ones. Inflation, after all, accompanies any war, and Vietnam was no exception. The Johnson administration resisted cuts in government spending, trying in vain to preserve the Great Society, but it failed to raise taxes sufficiently and in a timely manner to pay for the war as well as the planned social spending. The inevitable result was an overheated economy with prices rising and unemployment falling. Table 1.1 provides some summary statistics to illustrate the immediate effects of the overheated economy and other useful data for the period under review.

Table 1.1
Selected Economic Series, 1964–76

Year	% Change in CPI (Dec. to Dec.)	Unemployment rate	% Change in real GNP (1972 $)
1964	1.2	5.2	5.3
1965	1.9	4.5	6.0
1966	3.4	3.8	6.0
1967	3.0	3.8	2.7
1968	4.7	3.6	4.6
1969	6.1	3.5	2.8
1970	5.5	4.9	−0.2
1971	3.4	5.9	3.4
1972	3.4	5.6	5.7
1973	8.8	4.9	5.8
1974	12.2	5.6	−0.6
1975	7.0	8.5	−1.1
1976	4.8	7.7	5.4

Source: Economic Report of the President, 1982.

The economic effects of the Vietnam War are easily seen in the increase in inflation following the build-up in 1965, and the decrease in the unemployment rate, which fell below the socially acceptable rate at that time of 4%. What the table does not show is the change in expectations that was developing: that these trends, especially the inflationary ones, would continue. The public had observed the Johnson administration's response to inflation and its lack of success.

For example, monetary policy was relied upon to reduce inflationary pressures, but it only created two credit crunches in 1966 and 1969. These credit crunches only served to push the economy into slowdowns and recessions; just a glance at the GNP data in Table 1.1 reveals the slowdown in 1967 and the recession in 1970. These episodes of monetary contraction played havoc with the economy without solving the underlying problems. Once the pain of recessions and rising interest rates began to be felt, the monetary authorities quickly reversed their policies.

The Johnson administration pretty much abandoned fiscal policy and Keynesian economics and liberalism along with it. Taxes could not be raised because the war would have been called into question, and federal spending could not be cut because the Great Society would have been made vulnerable. The futility of macroeconomic policy was not lost on the public, and a growing cynicism about the ability and the willingness of government to influence economic matters was developing. In fact a growing distrust of government was apparent owing to the record of promises and deceit in the Vietnam war and to the distrust of Johnson as a leader. The election of Richard Nixon did little to assuage these doubts.

THE NIXON ADMINISTRATION

This then is the economic world that Nixon was able to exploit in the campaign, but one with which his administration had to face upon taking office. When Nixon took office in January 1969, the unemployment rate was 3.3%, the inflation rate (CPI) was about 4.8%, and the economy (real GNP) was growing at a rate of about 6.4%. These data, in hindsight, scarcely warranted any hysteria, and the Nixon administration was not inclined to overreact.

Thus, the first response to these inherited conditions was a policy that has come to be known as "gradualism." Here the aim was to reduce inflation and let unemployment rise to socially acceptable rates over time without causing a recession or other undue repercussions—hence the term *gradualism*. The socially acceptable rate of unemployment was 4%, a target set during the Kennedy administration. The Council of Economic Advisors (CEA) considered the 4% rate as too low, given the changing composition of the labor force, but still this rate would do until the public had been educated to the gradually rising natural rate of unemployment. (The natural rate of unemployment is the rate of unemployment that results when the level of output is in equilibrium given the state of technology, the supply of productive factors, and other institutional factors.)

Accordingly, there seemed to be room for the gradual cooling of the economy before serious problems set in. Monetary policy was again given the job of providing the major restraint, but the worry was that it would tighten too much and cause a recession. In fact, monetary growth did slow significantly in 1969, causing another credit crunch and high interest rates and eventually the recession of 1970. The restrictive monetary policy was reversed when the recession became obvious, and the pain politically unacceptable. It was apparent that the policy of gradualism was not going to work as planned, as unemployment crept up (to around 6%) beyond what was acceptable while inflation did not abate. Throughout 1970 and until the summer of 1971, the administration was involved in an internal debate over the efficacy and promise of more direct controls over the economy—some form of incomes policy.

Nixon, ever mindful since his loss in 1960 of the political damage caused by recessions, but wary of direct wage and price controls presumably from his experience in World War II, was being pulled both ways by his advisors. The political arguments, bolstered by the economic views of Arthur Burns, his old friend and now chairman of the Federal Reserve Board, won out, and on August 15, 1971, the administration announced to everyone's surprise that a system of direct wage and price controls would be instituted to control the economy. John Connally, secretary of the treasury, played an important role in the conception of a plan that would appear to control inflation so that the election that was just around the corner would be ensured. He urged the president to follow his advice and give the appearance of a forceful and decisive leader willing to take dramatic measures to control the economy.[2]

Since controls were always popular with the public, and since Congress had already given the power to impose them to the executive branch (not anticipating their use in practice), the controls were greeted with approval by the public, labor, and management. Of course, the longer they were in existence, the less popular they became, but the initial reaction was surprisingly positive. This gave the Nixon administration the opportunity to achieve its goals without public protest; it was able to control wages and prices while at the same time free to pump up the economy just in time for the forthcoming election. Without fear of exacerbating inflation, the administration could stimulate the economy and look resolute in the process. After the election was won, the policies could be reversed, with the loosening of controls and the imposition of restrictive monetary and fiscal policies.

The political business cycle surrounding the election year 1972 is now well recognized and established and provides a clear exception to the statement that economic conditions do not obey political cycles. Many political scientists and economists have found the evidence convincing that the economy was exploited for political ends.[3] Without dwelling on the evidence, we can summarize the conclusions quickly: Both fiscal and monetary policies were used to pump up the economy prior to the election of 1972. Once the election was over, these policies were reversed, leading to a recession.

One analysis of this period by Alan Blinder showed, for example, that fiscal policy influences on real GNP swung from –$21 billion (i.e., restrictive) in 1971I to $63.6 billion in 1973I, an $84.6 billion reversal that probably increased the growth rate of GNP from 4.7 to 7.3%. Blinder concludes, "In other words, fiscal stimulus transformed 1972 from a year of healthy growth into an unsustainable and inflationary boom."[4]

The same conclusions were reached for monetary policy. Blinder fitted an exponential trend to the monetary sources that yields the same real growth over the period as the actual policies but smoothes them out. Thus, deviations from this trend show the bulges that are due to abrupt changes in policy. Monetary influences were restrictive until 1972, when they begin to deviate positively from the trend. After the election of 1972, the monetary influences become more restrictive. This is what you would expect, if the hypothesis that the economy was manipulated for political reasons was correct. Blinder concludes that "without tremendous support from the Federal Reserve, the 1971–1972 economy would have been much weaker."[5]

Blinder's methodology is but one way to present the evidence of macroeconomic policy shifts that verify the supposition that the Nixon administration used the economy to gather votes. Others have used other methods to reach similar conclusions. While Blinder suggests that this could have happened, in the end he reserved judgment; others are less reluctant to accuse the administration of political machinations, if not at the time, then certainly in retrospect.

This cynical attempt to manipulate the economy for political purposes was successful if viewed from the political perspective. Viewed from an economic perspective, the success of the controls system is debatable. After all, the controls were imposed when the rate of inflation was hovering around 5%, and they were removed when the rate of inflation had doubled. It is generally agreed, however, that the controls succeeded in the beginning but became less and less effective the longer they were in effect. However, the evaluation of the controls system is not our primary concern here. It was successful in achieving its political purpose, but as an economic policy, its success was limited by its design (it was poorly conceived), by its operation (it was inflexible and regularly denounced by its administrators who stressed its temporary nature), and by disinterest once the political objective was secure.

The Nixon administration's system of controls did manage to discredit direct controls as a viable tool to control the economy. Despite the flaws in its design and operation, the failures were taken as proof that direct controls over the economy could not work. The controls also created more distrust of and cynicism about political leaders, their motives, and their ability to manage the economy for the public good. The manipulation of the economy for political purposes did not escape the public, and belief in the institutions that were designed to promote the public welfare was severely shaken. Even the Federal Reserve System was tarnished in this period as it succumbed to the pressures from the executive branch.

The administration was also successful in achieving changes in the international area as it forced the rest of the world to adopt flexible exchange rates. Unable to persuade the international community to switch to flexible exchange rates from fixed exchange rates, it resorted to strong-arm tactics. By unilaterally declaring the Bretton Woods agreement void by closing the gold window, and by threatening to increase import duties, the administration was able to force the rest of the world to comply with its views on international exchange matters. Not many of our trading partners were happy with these tactics, and much good will was squandered by them.

In any event, the administration achieved what it set out to: win the election of 1972 and force the adoption of a flexible exchange rate system. In the end, the system of wage and price controls was not really a domestic economic program; the controls system was a smoke screen for political goals and international trade considerations. To view it solely as an economic program is to miss the point, and to judge it solely as an economic program is a mistake.

THE POSTCONTROLS ECONOMY

After the controls were lifted, everyone expected a bulge in prices and the return of inflation. Their expectations were not denied. Without direct controls, policymakers were left with the usual method of constraining prices—recession. Now the postelection restrictive monetary and fiscal policies could do their job without fear of political repercussions, and the economy dutifully responded and produced a recession. The recession began in late 1973 and lasted until March 1975. As will become evident, this was a rather sharp recession, complicated by many unusual factors and accompanied by unusual political upheavals.

Looking at the unusual factors first, there were several shocks to the economy, each leading to the expectation of further inflation. First, there was the shock caused by the removal of price and wage controls. Prices that were suppressed over the controls period could be expected to rise now that the pressure was released. Second, in October 1973, the Arab members of the Organization of Petroleum Exporting Countries (OPEC) placed an embargo on oil exports to the United States, presenting the nation with a severe oil shortage and, of course, higher energy prices for this vital input that would be transmitted to all sectors of the economy. Third, similar, though less dramatic, inflationary problems were presented by the poor food harvests in 1972 and the disappearance of anchovies off the coast of Peru that are used for cattle feed. These events, combined with the sale of "surplus" grain to the Soviet Union, meant higher feed costs and eventually higher meat costs. Added to these price shocks was the political shock caused by the Watergate scandal that created much uncertainty and distrust at the time of political leaders and their motivations. Indeed, economic concerns of the Nixon administration seemed to slip into the background as it tried to defend itself and became preoccupied with its survival.

It is against this background of price shocks, foreign policy repercussions, and domestic political upheavals that macroeconomic policies of the period must be gauged. Economic policy-making does not take place in a vacuum after all, and these events at the time seemed momentous.

Yet, even allowing for these factors, monetary policy was overly restrictive in this period and appeared to be overly concerned with inflation. The money supply actually declined in the first year of the recession, and of course, interest rates rose. Economists of all stripes were unhappy with the Federal Reserve's (the Fed) performance over the course of this business cycle. For example, the rate of growth of the money supply as defined by M1 (currency and demand deposits) fell in the latter part of 1973 and continued to fall in 1974; interest rates for the interest-sensitive housing market rose to over 8% in August 1973 (from over 7% a year earlier), and continued rising until reaching nearly 10% in August 1974. Similar increases in other interest rates followed the same pattern. Prices, too, began their steady rise, with the CPI rising at double digit rates in 1974.

No doubt the conduct of monetary policy was complicated by the unusual behavior of the demand for money and by inflationary expectations that are difficult to reverse, but still, the monetary policy of the Fed in this period seems perverse and clearly did not inspire confidence. The economy was allowed to slide into a recession. Real GNP growth fell from a rate of 9.5% in the first quarter of 1973 to 2.3% in the last quarter and then turned negative throughout 1974. As might be expected, the unemployment rate crept up from 4.9% in December 1973 to 7.2% in December 1974. Fiscal policy, too, was restrictive in 1973. The full employment budget showed a deficit of –$10.3 billion in 1972, which rapidly turned to a surplus of $7.7 billion in the second quarter of 1973 and grew to over $30 billion by the third quarter of 1974.

There seems to be little question that the Nixon administration deliberately reversed economic policies following the 1972 election and forced the economy into a recession. One may quarrel over the precision of the numbers or the timing of the actions taken, but such endeavors miss the main point: The economy was misused by the Nixon administration. By this time, however, the administration and the nation were thrown into a constitutional crisis caused by the Watergate scandal and the pending impeachment of Nixon, and more attention was paid to the political crisis than to the economic one. Remarkably, the political crisis was solved without unduly upsetting the governance of the nation or disrupting the economy. The transition must have astonished the rest of the world not so accustomed to such political stability. Yet in short order, the nation would be headed by two unelected officials to the highest posts in the land.

THE FORD ADMINISTRATION

Whatever the political ramifications brought on by the Watergate affair, the economy did not wait to discover them; it continued on the path set for it by the outgoing administration. For Gerald Ford, Nixon's successor, it was not a good time to be responsible for the economy. The nation was embarking on the period known as the great stagflation. Prices were rising as was the unemployment rate; interest rates were rising, and real GNP was falling; fiscal and monetary policy were on their restrictive courses; and the whole society was shaken by effects of the oil embargo and the price and supply of energy.

Specifically, when Ford took office in August 1974, real GNP was falling at an annual rate of –1.9%, prices (CPI) were rising at an annual rate of about 14%, the unemployment rate was rising and stood at 5.4%, and the prime rate of interest was 11.6%. It was not a happy time for either the nation or the economy and certainly no time for a new administration.

The consensus among Ford's economic advisors was that the economy would deteriorate further in 1974, but that unemployment should not rise much beyond 6%.[6] In September, Ford assembled a group of leading economists to consider policies to combat inflation, and they dutifully produced an array of opinions. Accordingly, the new administration felt secure in fighting inflation instead of worrying about recession. Ford pronounced inflation public enemy number 1 and introduced a voluntary program labeled "whip inflation now" (WIN). This WIN program was deservedly lampooned, but accompanying it was a real inflation-fighting program that included increasing taxes and reducing expenditures. These measures may not be wise or appropriate in times of a recession, but the conservative administration was determined to ignore the possible consequences of its actions and pursue its primary goal of reducing inflation.

The economy, however, did not cooperate and deteriorated much faster and further than anyone had anticipated. By the last quarter of 1974, real GNP was falling at an annual rate of –9.1%, the unemployment rate was 7.2% and rising, and the CPI was increasing at double digit rates. The recession was deepening and becoming evident to all; it was time to admit it and call for a turnaround of policy.

The traditional signs of economic trouble were indeed evident, but the remedies were not. Policies to combat stagflation were not easy to implement or politically acceptable. Direct controls over the economy or any other incomes policy could not even be considered following the Nixon administration experience, nor could policies that were directed at the use or abuse of economic power. Restraints on the ability of firms to pass on price increases so readily or of organized labor to bargain for higher wages in response to price increases were not considered, if even acknowledged. Antitrust laws were poorly designed to prevent the former, and staggered union contracts prevented the coordination of wage demands (as in Japan) for the latter. Rationing of energy supplies would also have helped to prevent the shortages from manifesting into price increases, while ensuring an equitable distribution of supplies to all households. To manage supply-side problems and supply-side price shocks, something along these lines was necessary in order to forestall the wage-price spiral that was developing and permeating the economy. Temporary price shocks, if left alone, would easily wind their way through the economy and become less and less recognized as temporary. Unchecked, the nation would witness rising unemployment and rising inflation, in other words, stagflation.

Instead of examining less orthodox remedies to the problems of the 1970s, the administration reverted to more familiar policies. Unfortunately, these were demand-side remedies, and demand-side solutions to supply-side problems were bound to be inefficient or ineffective. In January 1975, the president reversed his call for higher taxes to fight inflation and proposed a tax reduction for individuals and business that was designed to stimulate the economy. The tax proposal called for a tax rebate equal to 12% of 1974 tax liabilities, up to a maximum of $1,000. The estimated total rebate was $12 billion, which the administration hoped would stimulate consumer spending. The administration argued that inflation had pushed households into higher income brackets (bracket creep) and forced them to pay higher taxes. The transfer from the private to the public sector presumably curtailed consumer spending, while pushing the federal budget into unplanned restraint. This increase in inflation-induced tax liabilities generated much discussion among professional economists about indexing the tax code for inflation, but nothing was done about this notion.

For business, the tax proposal increased the investment tax credit to 12% for one year in the hopes of reducing the tax bills of business by some $4 billion in 1975. The administration did recognize that there would be lags in response to the tax reduction; investment plans cannot be altered as quickly as consumer plans. Still, increased investment, whenever it took place, was desirable.

The administration's energy policy was designed to discourage consumption and encourage domestic production by increasing the price of energy. Accordingly, it devised a series of tax increases, import duties, and conservation measures. It proposed the decontrol of oil and gas prices, a windfall profits tax on crude oil, an import fee of $2 per barrel of imported oil, the creation of an oil reserve, the encouragement of alternative fuels, and a tax deduction for homeowners who installed energy efficient equipment. Households would pay only part of the energy bill, since low-income allowances were increased, and tax credits introduced. Still, the higher energy bills of households would offset some of the stimulus of tax reductions proposed earlier.

As for fiscal policy, the administration called for a moratorium on new spending programs and a reduction in federal spending of some $17.5 billion on existing programs. Monetary policy, it was hoped, would accommodate the administration's program by easing credit conditions and lowering interest rates.

Monetary policy was basically accommodating, if somewhat erratically, over the duration of the Ford administration. Monetary growth rates were somewhat below the rates needed to furnish the liquidity for the projected rate of GNP growth, but the demand for money was behaving erratically, and targets were difficult to set. In May, the Fed set the target growth rate range for M1 at 5–7½% and 7½–10½% for M2 (M1 + time deposits). Liberal economists berated the Federal Reserve for choosing lower rates of money growth than they deemed necessary, and monetarists were dissatisfied because the Fed did not choose to follow their prescription of a steady rate of growth of the monetary aggregates. Both M1 and M2 behaved erratically during 1975, falling below their ranges in the early months, rising above in the middle months, and then falling again in the later months. Almost everyone was unhappy with the Fed's performance in the period, but what effect did monetary actions have on economy?

After a thoughtful examination of monetary policy in this period, Blinder concludes with this assessment, "If I was forced to summarize the influence of the Fed on the Great Stagflation in a few words, I guess I would stress how *little* difference it made rather than on how *much.* . . . It seems to me unlikely that monetary policy was a major cause, never mind *the* major cause, of the Great Stagflation."[7] Still, it must have been disconcerting to have the monetary aggregates fluctuating, while economists debated whether shifts in the demand for money were temporary or not. If the monetary authorities could not control the money supply, what happens to inflationary expectations and to confidence in the ability of the Fed to manage financial conditions? The Fed's record in this period is not impressive, even if it eventually made little difference as Blinder suggests.

The Fed, of course, continued to be concerned about inflation over the period and drove some real interest rates into the negative zone. Money interest rates fluctuated during the recovery period, but the general trend was downward. Both of these trends were unusual for a recovery period, but when inflationary expectations (downward) are considered, they become more understandable. The administration had reason to be cautious in evaluating the monetary policy it received, even if others were not so constrained.[8] It was, after all, a very confusing period.

Congress went beyond the president's tax program and, in the Tax Reduction Act of 1975 passed in March, enacted a $23 billion reduction instead of the requested $16 billion. Most of the tax reductions went to individuals in the form of a one-time $8 billion rebate on 1974 taxes, $12 billion in the form of a one-time $30 credit for each taxpayer, increased standard deductions and low-income allowances—the earned income credit—and a one-time payment of $50 to each Social Security recipient. In general, the tax reductions were geared toward lower-income recipients.

Corporations received an increase in the investment tax credit to 10% for an estimated benefit of $2¾ billion, but taxes were increased because of curtailments of depletion allowances and other limitations on foreign income deferrals.

In total, tax receipts were lowered by some $42 billion at annual rates, but by the end of the year, the tax cuts that remained in effect were on the order of $15 billion at annual rates. The drop in receipts was temporary, since the tax cuts were largely temporary. Clearly, fiscal policy was expansionary in 1975. The budget deficit on a calendar year basis rose from −$11.7 billion in 1974 to −$73.4 billion in 1975, with tax receipts falling by $5 billion and expenditures rising by about $57 billion during 1974. Transfer payments and defense spending accounted for the increase in federal spending, and the tax cuts obviously accounted for the tax receipts decline.

The full employment budget also registered the expansionary fiscal policy. In the first quarter of 1975, the budget recorded a surplus of $15 billion at annual rates; in the second quarter, the surplus changed into a deficit of −$33 billion—quite a turnaround. The recession ended in March 1975, and the economy began to recover. By year's end, real GNP was growing at an annual rate of 5.4%, the CPI was increasing at about 7%, and the unemployment rate stood at 8.3%, down from the peak of 8.9% recorded in May. This is how the economy fared as the nation entered into the election year of 1976.

THE ECONOMY IN THE ELECTION YEAR OF 1976

The administration intended fiscal policy in 1976 to continue the stimulus provided in 1975. This did not happen. The budget deficit on a calendar year basis decreased from −$71 billion to −$58 billion; the full employment budget also showed restraint as the deficit there fell as well. Fiscal policy was apparently showing unintended restraint as the economy was recovering. What went wrong?

In the first place, government expenditures did not grow as forecast. Transfer payments fell in the recovery, defense expenditure delays and lower rates of inflation combined to produce less government spending than anticipated. Unfortunately for Ford, the major portion of the short-fall, which was only about $3 billion, was concentrated in the second quarter of 1976 and contributed to a sputtering of the economy in the summer of 1976. The overall increase in government spending fell to 8.7%, down from the 10% increases of a year earlier. The administration did not anticipate any changes in spending for 1977 due to the shortfall in 1976.

On the taxation side, the Tax Reform Act of 1976 merely extended some of the provisions of the 1975 tax acts, and as a result, the tax stimulus provided for in 1975 began to fall in 1976. Taken together, fiscal policy was moving toward restraint in this second year of the recovery.

Monetary policy as measured by the growth of monetary aggregates was again erratic. M1 growth fell in the first and third quarters and rose in the second and fourth. For the year, the growth of M1 was below the targets set by the Federal Reserve, while M2 was less deviant as a whole. Again, the demand for money was causing some concern as the velocity fell back to the 3% range. As indicated earlier, monetary policy in this period was erratic at best and incomprehensible at worst.

Interest rates, however, continued their general decline. Once again, this is not the norm in a recovery period. Inflationary expectations must have again played a role in the decline, for if expectations were for continued decreases in inflation, real interest rates would not have declined as much as nominal ones.

As a result of these conditions, real GNP rose by 6.2% for the year but declined in the latter part of the year and by the final quarter was rising at an annual rate of only 3%. The economy was slowing down in the latter part of 1976, partly as a result of the slowdown in government expenditures, partly due to the early build-up in inventories and partly due to decline in real investment. The slowdown is also seen in the unemployment rate, which declined early in the year to 7.6% but at the end had increased to 7.9%. The inflation rate as measured by the CPI continued to decline to about 5% for the year. Declines in the prices of food and energy accounted for most of the observed change. The same trend is observable for real wages. While real hourly earnings rose slightly for the first time in two years, by 1.4%, the rate of increase for the more comprehensive measurement—compensation per hour—was high in the first part of the year and then began to decline, and actually was lower in 1976 than 1975.

Ford was not successful in getting his energy program through Congress. His aim to decontrol prices of oil and gas met with great resistance by a Congress that feared the adverse effects on inflation and the recovery. An accord on gradual decontrols was finally reached in December, after Congress insisted on price reductions on crude oil. As a result, energy prices fell in 1976 but so did production; of course, imports had to rise as energy usage rose in 1976 following declines in 1974–75. Lacking any viable substitute for oil, reliance on imports was growing rather than declining, even as OPEC raised the price of crude from $2.59 per barrel to over $12 per barrel. Postponing further discussion of energy problems, it is only necessary to observe here that a coherent energy policy had yet to be developed.

CONCLUSION

This rather brief overview of the economy in the early 1970s is sufficient to indicate the state of affairs as the nation prepared to elect a new president in 1976. Ford chose to run and hoped to be elected in his own right.

This brief summary should be enough also to convey the idea that the nation was experiencing some unusual events in the economic realm and by no means had learned to adjust to them. From the cynical economic policies of the Nixon administration, to supply-side shocks, to energy shortages and double digit inflation, to declines in real wages, a severe recession, and a period of stagflation, the nation was rocked by events it could not or would not control.

The public responded to these events as it learned to distrust government from Nixon, to doubt government actions from Ford, and to question government's ability to manage things from fluctuations in the economy. Solutions to our problems seemed beyond our ability to deal with them, and a general uneasiness, born of bewilderment and disorientation, permeated the society. It is in this atmosphere that the campaign and election of 1976 took place.

NOTES

1. For a more detailed account see, Anthony S. Campagna, *U.S. National Economic Policies, 1917–1985* (New York: Praeger, 1987). This chapter owes a great deal to the analysis in that book. See also *The Economic Consequences of the Vietnam War* (New York: Praeger, 1991). These books contain much more economic and political details than can be reproduced here.

2. For an insider's view of this period see, Herbert Stein, *Presidential Economics*, rev. ed. (Washington, D.C.: American Enterprise Institute, 1988), 150–156. Stein supplies a valuable account of the events leading up to and culminating in wage and price controls.

3. For example see Edward R. Tufte, *Political Control of the Economy* (Princeton, N.J.: Princeton University Press, 1978); and Douglas A. Hibbs, *The American Political Economy: Macroeconomics and Electoral Politics* (Cambridge, Mass.: Harvard University Press, 1987).

4. Alan S. Blinder, *Economic Policy and the Great Stagflation* (New York: Academic Press, 1979), 145.

5. Ibid., 183.

6. Stein, *Presidential Economics*, 212. Stein was leaving the CEA but attended this meeting along with his successor, Alan Greenspan.

7. Blinder, *Economic Policy and the Great Stagflation*, 200, 201.

8. See the *Economic Report of the President, 1976*, 35–39.

Chapter 2

The Role of Economics in the 1976 Campaign

James Earl Carter, Jr. ("just call me Jimmy") began running for president almost immediately after the crushing defeat of George McGovern in 1972. Having met most of his potential rivals from both parties, he concluded that he was as good as or superior to them, both in competence and in morality. In his autobiography, *Why Not the Best?*, he met "other presidential hopefuls, and I lost my feeling of awe about presidents."[1] Thus began one of the most remarkable crusades for a public office ever witnessed in the United States. For the next several years, a carefully designed strategy was developed to elevate an obscure governor of the relatively small state of Georgia to national attention and recognition.

As governor of Georgia from 1971 to 1974, his record alone would have been insufficient to warrant recognition for national office, except perhaps at the cabinet level. What earned him any consideration was a statement in his gubernatorial inaugural address: "I say to you quite frankly that the time for racial discrimination is over. . . . No poor, rural, weak, or black person should ever have to bear the additional burden of being deprived of the opportunity of an education, a job, or simple justice."[2] This apparent liberal view astonished his audience, for Carter's record on civil rights was mixed, as was the case for many politicians in the South at the time.[3] Still, he attracted national media attention, and they began to tout him as a leader from the new South.

Even so, the notion that he was a serious contender for the presidency in 1972 and 1973 must have seemed preposterous, especially when such well-known rivals as Edward Kennedy, Scoop Jackson, Morris Udall, Birch Bayh, George Wallace, Frank Church, Hubert Humphrey, and Jerry Brown had indicated an interest in the job. So, the task was to establish his credentials with his peers and, at the same time, to gain name recognition with the public. His appointment by the Democratic National Committee, headed by Robert Strauss as chairperson of the Democratic Campaign Committee, helped him achieve these goals. This position entailed giving speeches on behalf of Democratic candidates all over the country. Carter eagerly accepted; such a position would enable him to meet and get to know party officials at every level of government, and more important, they would get to know him.

His selection for membership into the Trilateral Commission as a representative from the new South helped to solidify his ties with the powerful "eastern establishment" and with the ruling elite of both the United States and abroad. "The Trilateral Commission is a private international organization composed of wealthy, powerful and well-connected individuals from the advanced capitalist 'trilateral' world—North America, Western Europe, and Japan . . . to plan solutions to the ideological and programmatic problems facing the capitalist state."[4] Carter not only had connection to the powerful through this appointment, but he also had the opportunity to claim more knowledge of foreign affairs than his previous positions would have allowed. Many of his presidential appointments would be made from the list of members of the Trilateral Commission— Walter Mondale, vice-president; Zbigniew Brzezinski, national security advisor; Cyrus Vance, secretary of state; W. Michael Blumenthal, secretary of the treasury; Harold Brown, secretary of defense, and many others for lesser posts. Ties to such powerful individuals as Nelson Rockefeller tended to belie his claims of populism.

To reach the public, he was urged to write a book describing his history, beliefs, and progress. Accordingly, he wrote his autobiography in which he described his humble origins, his development, his sources of inspiration, his career as a naval officer, his entrance into political life, and his experience as governor. He also carefully weighed his assets and liabilities as a presidential candidate and declared immodestly that he was able to lead a government that was competent, honest, decent, and compassionate. Many of the themes and ideas developed in his autobiography found their way into campaign speeches and eventually into the party platform.

Carter was also fortunate to have the help of a close-knit family and loyal associates to plan and promote the type of campaign needed to win the support of the general public. Family members actively campaigned in all his pursuits of public office and were seasoned campaigners by this time. Also, a young and committed loyal staff, headed by Hamilton Jordan and Jody Powell, gave him valuable advice and were tireless in their efforts on his behalf.

THE CANDIDATES

After a long and grueling campaign, Carter saw his rivals withdraw, and he eventually won the Democratic nomination for president. His phenomenal rise to the top is quite a story but is of more interest to political scientists than economists and has been adequately covered elsewhere.[5] Our interest lies with the economic issues of the presidential campaign.

According to most observers, the 1976 campaign was an issueless one that degenerated into passionless debate over issues of character. Many agree with Roger Mudd of CBS, who characterized the campaign as "vapid and egocentric" and felt that the voters had been cheated. Mudd blamed this situation on Carter, who ran mainly on a platform of trust and integrity to which Ford responded defensively.[6] If this was the case, it is necessary to digress to character issues before turning to the economic issues involved.

It would be plausible to assume that if character traits were the main issues then the public would be well acquainted with the candidates by the end of the campaign. That was not the case, for Jimmy Carter remained an enigma, and Jerry Ford remained a caricature.

Those more sympathetic to Carter agree with the characterization of Haynes Johnson that "Jimmy Carter's life was a testament to belief in all the cherished virtues—thrift and frugality, hard work and integrity, self-improvement and decency. Perhaps more than any other president in a lifetime, he believed in, and was motivated by, a kind of mystical faith in the People."[7] Indeed, Carter stressed these virtues in his autobiography. Following close behind the Nixon presidency, such virtues as decency, trust, and integrity would likely appeal to voters. But there were also other assessments: "a certain toughness, deviousness, flexibility and capacity for maneuver" (Patrick J. Buchanan); behind the talk of love there was "a thoroughly tough, opportunist politician, who comes into almost any competition with his elbows out" (David Broder); or "He is a mean, hard-eyed sort of fellow who tolerates nobody who opposes him" (R. Murphy).[8]

The ambiguity about his character found echoes in his political philosophy. Conservatives found him a fellow conservative; liberals found him to be a liberal; and centrists found him perfectly acceptable. Clearly, either his message was universal or, as his critics asserted, he tailored his message according to the audience, or spoke with such ambiguity and vagueness that no one could be certain what he was saying. Often, he seemed to be on both sides of controversial issues, and his discussions of them were recorded as flip-flops instead of hair splitting.

So, on the one hand he was tough, determined, confident, and re-solved, but on the other hand, he was also gentle, kind, and humanitarian. He was a man of science (a nuclear engineer) and reason but also a born-again Christian, a Baptist, and very religious. He made no attempt to hide either his scientific background or his religious beliefs and denied any possible contradiction between these two areas. Nor did he think religion would interfere with his administration, using another Baptist for an example, Harry Truman, whom he admired a great deal.

Carter remained an enigma right up to the election. Appealing to all groups may be a good campaign strategy, but would it make for effective governing? Can trust and integrity, the issues that won him the presidency, substitute for well-considered and articulated positions on the affairs of the day? Did the voters know what to expect when they elected him? Did they care?

Perhaps the final word belongs to one of his biographers, James Wooten, who wrote,

And so it was that Jimmy Carter found friends and foes on both sides of America's ideological aisle. . . . He was not an ideologue. He was a pure pragmatist who had raised utilitarian politics to a new American art form. He had promised never to lie and never to mislead and if his credibility was eventually questioned, he had nevertheless therefore cornered the market on honesty early in the race. But he had never promised to rid the world of enigma. If his public image was clouded, his conscience was clear.[9]

THE ECONOMIC ISSUES

No presidential campaign can entirely escape the economic issues even if they are not crucial at the time. In reviewing those issues of the Carter campaign, it is possible to gain some insight into the economic views that might have become important in the campaign, and in the case of Carter, some notion of what to expect when he took office, as well as some guidelines by which to measure his eventual successes and failures.

In Carter's stump speech, which he repeated sometimes word for word, there was little to indicate his economic views or personal philosophy. However, there were position papers on economic matters, personal interviews, and parts of other speeches that can be utilized to reveal the thrust of his convictions. In an important speech before the National Press Club in 1973, he identified the mood of the country as basically conser-vative, a mood with which he apparently identified. In his view, conservatism meant "a higher valuation of the human being, of individuality, self-reliance, dignity, personal freedom; but I also think it means increased personal responsibility, through governmental action for alleviating affliction, discrimination, and injustice. . . . Conservatism does not mean racism, . . . [nor] resistance to change, . . . [nor] callousness or unconcern about our fellow human beings." This viewpoint might be labeled benevolent conservatism.

Elsewhere, Carter identified himself as a populist by which he meant deriving political support, advice, and concerns directly from the people, not from special interest groups or powerful intermediaries. Taken together, these views would be difficult to translate into practical politics and most certainly would lead to confusion in interpreting his positions on various issues. Yet, he rejected the stereotypes of liberalism or conservatism, preferring to believe that "good government is not a matter of being liberal or conservative. Good government is the art of doing what is right."[10] It is little wonder that he often appeared to be on both sides of controversial issues. It is also not surprising that he remained a complex man, difficult to characterize or understand; in a word, enigmatic.

Carried over to economics, Carter's philosophy indicates fiscal conservatism. His emphasis on a government with competence and compassion appears to be consistent with fiscal conservatism in principle, but offers quite a challenge in practice. Perhaps to avoid misinterpretation, it is best to let his own words reveal how his political philosophy was to be translated into economic philosophy.

In April 1976, Carter released his position paper on the economy entitled, "An Economic Position Paper for Now and Tomorrow." The following outline summarizes his goals for the economy, along with some specific recommendations on how to achieve them.

1. Rapid reduction in unemployment
   a. with the current slack in the economy, an expansionary fiscal and monetary policy could reduce unemployment without igniting inflation.
   b. providing incentives to private industry to hire the unemployed through subsidizing training costs, special incentives for unemployed youth; meeting female needs for flexible hours, and providing public training programs for private jobs.
   c. governmental programs for public service jobs, improving employment services, providing for summer jobs, training programs, and expansion of the Comprehensive Educational Training Act (CETA).

2. Curbing inflation without recession

   a. recognizing supply-side, not demand-side, factors as causes of current inflation, there is the need to concentrate on improving productivity growth, ensuring better demand and supply relationships, and establishing food reserves.

   b. reform government regulations and enforce antitrust legislation to increase competition.

   c. adopt a monetary policy to encourage low interest rates.

   d. monitor wage and price increases in specific sectors of the economy. Favor stand-by controls that the president can apply selectively.

3. Better coordination between fiscal and monetary policy

   a. the president should be given power to appoint his own Federal Reserve chairman who would serve a term coterminous with that of the president.

   b. to ensure better planning, both government and private, the Federal Reserve should be held more responsible for stating its objectives clearly and informing the public on its outlook for the future to ensure consistency with other branches of government.

4. More effective budgeting

   a. recognizing the need for unbalanced budgets due to special needs and circumstances, the rule should be to balance the budget over the business cycle.

   b. budget planning has too short a horizon. The budget should allow for long-range planning, for example, over a three-year cycle that rolls forward each year. Planning by everyone would be facilitated with a longer planning horizon.

   c. implement a zero-based budgeting technique to control government programs.

5. Better government planning and management

   a. government must plan ahead just like any business. Economic goals must be established and clearly enunciated so that programs can be developed within a planned, orderly context.

   b. the Council of Economic Advisors (CEA) should be expanded to include coordinated planning to deal with long-range planning problems of individual sectors fitted into an overall economic plan for the economy as a whole, as well as to deal with considerations of supply, distribution, and performance in individual industries.

This set of goals and aims constitutes the heart of Carter's position on economic matters important to him. In June 1976, most of his concerns found their way into his platform proposals to the Democratic Party as

"A New Beginning" and found their way into the party's platform as well. Later in September 1976, Carter issued a statement, "The Economics of Stagnation: A Study of the Republican Years, 1969–1976," condemning the opposition on past economic performance. This statement documents all the pertinent economic data on inflation, unemployment, budget deficits, and so on that reveal the extent of the mismanagement of the economy, and this indictment can be read in conjunction with his positive statement of remedies. Issued just prior to the election, this document simply reported the economic data in a succinct format without any concurring discussion of how these mistakes would be reversed.

In addition to these economic matters, Carter also mentioned other areas of concern that interact with the economic ones. He frequently characterized the tax system as a disgrace and vowed to change it. He favored a system that would tax income only once, treat all income the same, be progressive, and be simple to understand. He believed that the nation was ready for a comprehensive tax reform proposal and was eager to tap this sentiment.

Another of Carter's favorite goals was to make government more efficient. By reducing the bureaucracy—for instance, the number of departments—he hoped to make the government more efficient and less costly. This was his experience as governor of Georgia, and he pledged to do the same for the federal government. During the campaign he stressed that he was an outsider to Washington and pledged to clean up the mess if he were elected. Despite the fact that every president has tried to reduce the bureaucracy and failed, Carter was determined to succeed and made it a high priority for his administration.

Not far behind making government more efficient was another goal— creating an energy policy. Basically, Carter sought to reduce the nation's reliance on oil, particularly in light of the recent OPEC embargoes. Greater usage of the abundant coal reserves was the short-run solution, but over time, the nation must look for alternative sources of energy. To this end, he favored more research and development into solar energy with nuclear energy as a last resort. Of course, he urged conservation of all kinds of energy by everyone, some changes in the rate structure of electric companies, and limited deregulation of natural gas. In a speech to the National Press Club in July 1975, he outlined many conservation measures, including mandatory auto efficiency, speed law enforcement, efficiency standards for appliances, improvements in building insulation, and so on. He also called for an international conference on energy to discuss this worldwide concern. Carter, the nuclear engineer, could think of many issues that should be addressed in such an arena, many of them scientific and technical ones.

Finally, there were many issues touched upon during the campaign that had economic effects and repercussions. These issues, however, were not developed to the extent that a firm position could be inferred from Carter's speeches or responses to questions put to him. He was a firm believer in the value of education, for example, and even proposed a cabinet-level Department of Education to coordinate all matters pertaining to education issues. As always, more federal funding seemed necessary. The same was true for day care facilities, welfare reform, health care, urban problems, and low-income housing inadequacies. In general, this fiscal conservative was willing to increase expenditures for unmet social needs provided they met the test of need and efficiency. Campaign rhetoric, however, is not a substitute for plans of action, and many of the social ills that Carter excoriated had been around for some time. It would not be an easy task to remedy them, and much more concrete proposals would be required before they could be considered.

Enough has been presented to convey the tenor of Carter's economic plans and ideas. Politicians state many positions during a political campaign, some with clarity and some with vagueness. Campaign pledges and admonitions must be regarded with a high degree of caution and a healthy dose of skepticism. This may always be true as far as economic issues are concerned, but was particularly true in this campaign when such issues were not always in the forefront.

GERALD FORD

Gerald Ford was also considered to be a warm, decent, honest man. His pardoning of Richard Nixon cost him some degree of trust, and more was lost when Carter coupled his administration with Nixon's, as in the Nixon-Ford administration, but basically he was regarded as a well-meaning, steady person. From those who knew him best and worked with him come the following descriptions: "He was not a Lincoln or a Washington or a Roosevelt or a Truman or an Eisenhower. He was and is a regular guy—a decent, honest, hard-working, God-fearing, patriotic, and proud American who really believed such shibboleths as 'right makes might' and 'my country, right or wrong.' "[11] Others found him, "warm, thoughtful, open-minded, and eager to learn."[12] The love and respect he generated appeared again and again among his supporters and political foes alike. There was no question that he enjoyed wide popularity among the Washington establishment.

Ford was the ultimate insider, having served in Washington for decades in various roles in the House. He knew his way around Washington, knew how the bureaucracy worked, and knew the nation's leaders. He was certainly well prepared to assume the duties of a higher office. His dream of becoming Speaker of the House was never realized, of course, but being selected as vice president by Nixon upon the resignation of Spiro Agnew and then elevated to the presidency when Nixon resigned, should have made up for any disappointment.

Why then was he not regarded as equal to the job? First, he was not very articulate, and his speeches were either less than inspiring or delivered poorly. This made him appear bumbling. Second, thanks to a few stumbling episodes and a few wayward golf shots, he appeared to be clumsy, although ironically, he had been an all-American football player and had been offered a pro contract, and was an excellent golfer and skier. The press and comedians had a field day ridiculing him and, in the process, created a poor image that he was not able to reverse. Third, he was self-effacing and modest, which led to the perception that he was incompetent. Those who knew him well disputed these perceptions but to no avail.[13]

Not to belittle the importance of the public's perception of the man, our concern is more with his political and economic philosophy. We are not concerned with why or how he won or lost elections but with what goals he had and what motivated him to use or not use government for achieving them. Public service was important for him, but for what?

He was, according to two observers, a pragmatic conservative relying on experience rather than formal doctrines, one who held the more or less traditional Republican orthodox beliefs in "meritocracy; putting restraints on the federal government; allowing free enterprise to harness private initiative; and permitting local and state governments to make their own decisions."[14] Under Ford, there would be no inspiring new programs to treat social ills, no drive for political or economic reforms, no visions of a great society. He simply did not believe that government had the answers to the nation's many social problems and agreed with the doctrine that the best government was one that governed least.[15] With this philosophy, let us see what economic issues surfaced in the Ford campaign.

ECONOMIC ISSUES IN THE FORD CAMPAIGN

In Chapter 1, we reviewed the economic record of the Ford administration. Toward the end of Ford's tenure, the economy was emerging from a recession and appeared to be improving. However in the summer of 1976, the economy seemed to stall again. It is in this context that we review the Ford campaign.

The economic plans for a sitting president are different from those of a challenger. The challenger must present an agenda different from the current administration. It must offer a new vision. An incumbent is forced to defend or explain his past performance and still indicate plans for future improvement. He cannot stress the latter for fear of compromising the former. Thus, a comprehensive economic plan may not be explicit but must be inferred.

At least that was the case for Ford. He did not think in terms of dramatic changes or comprehensive overhauls for the economy and was philosophically opposed to grand designs for government involvement in the economy. His main goals for America were explicitly stated, however, in a speech at the University of Michigan in September 1976. He listed the following goals and his record and plans for achieving them:

1. Americans want a job with a good future. Tax cuts that encouraged production are desirable using the free enterprise system to do the rest.

2. Americans want homes and decent neighborhoods and schools where our children can get a quality education. Keeping interest rates low, reducing down payments, and using federal guarantee programs to lower monthly payments will encourage home ownership for every American family that wants one and will work for one.

3. Americans want physical security, safety against war and crime, safety against pollution in the water we drink and in the air we breathe. Implied is the plea for a strong national defense but strivings for peace, for stronger law enforcement, and mandatory sentences.

4. We want medical and hospital care when we are sick at costs that will not wipe out our savings. Recommended protection against catastrophic illness for aged and disabled, along with consolidation of federal health care programs.

5. We want the time and opportunity to enlarge our experience through recreation and travel. Expansion of the national park system was the main suggestion.

These goals are laudable, and most of the public would subscribe to them, but they are hardly inspiring or innovative. They do not excite the imagination nor stir the hopes of the electorate.

So Ford was inevitably put on the defensive about his past economic achievements. In countless speeches, he proudly reviewed his past record at holding down government spending, a policy he intended to continue if re-elected. He claimed to have saved the public $9 billion by his vetoes of sixty-six bills. Anyone listening to these claims would have been assured that no further expansion of government spending would be tolerated in a new Ford administration.

When government spending is held down, taxes can be reduced. Again, he was proud of past tax reductions and promised another as the first order of business if re-elected. An increase in the personal exemption, a decrease in tax rates, and other provisions would amount to a tax reduction of some $28 billion. In a message to Congress in July 1976, he outlined his legislative priorities and urged action on these items. From these items, it is possible to ascertain what his priorities were; all of them were mentioned at some time in speeches across the country.

1. *Tax reductions combined with spending restraint.* In addition to the foregoing he wanted to increase the exemption on estate taxes. He also wanted a job creation act to encourage jobs by allowing for more rapid amortization of capital.
2. *Crime control.* Included in this category were mandatory sentencing for serious offenses and for drug-related crimes, the banning of cheap imported guns, and the establishment of a permanent office of special prosecutor.
3. *Restoring the integrity of the Social Security System.* Increase taxes and correct calculation flaws were the main ideas.
4. *Catastrophic health care protection for those covered by Medicare.*
5. *Restrictions on forced, court-ordered busing.*
6. *Revenue sharing and block grants.* Continue revenue sharing program and consolidate block grant programs for education, Medicaid, and child nutrition.
7. *Regulatory reform.* Review all regulatory practices and remove or revise regulations in aviation, trucking, and financial institutions.
8. *Energy.* Deregulate natural gas, encourage synthetic fuel research, encourage conservation, improve operations of utilities, encourage electric power construction, and revise automobile emission standards.
9. *Completion of national defense program.*
10. Many other programs on environment, higher education reform, and agricultural issues.

This legislative program was never fully presented in the campaign, but parts of it were announced to various audiences, and bits and pieces of it can be found in speeches, comments, and responses to questions. Ford pursued a rose-garden strategy for some time, staying in the White House to look presidential. He held press conferences in the White House or gave interviews instead of campaigning to a larger audience. Whether or not this hindered the presentation of his agenda for the future is problematic, and the question is left to others.

At any rate, the foregoing provides some indication of the major themes emphasized by Ford in some forum or another. The themes are presented in summary form in order to establish the tenor of the economic campaign without getting bogged down in details. Stepping back temporarily and viewing the economic elements in the campaign, it becomes clear that economic issues were not given prominence, and after reading the speeches of both candidates, when such issues were discussed, they must have elicited little enthusiasm.

Before looking at the presidential debates, one more observation is suggested. In economic matters, there was not much to separate the candidates. In very broad terms, their economic philosophies and economic plans were not that different. It is little wonder then that other issues dominated the campaign, whether by design or accident.

THE DEBATES

The last chance for the candidates to clarify their positions on economic matters was in the national debates. Whether or not they did so is debatable, since the debates have been heavily criticized; they have been called boring, a rehash of their campaign speeches, a joint press conference, or a joint interview session. It would be difficult to contest any of these characterizations. Studies suggest that those who were predisposed to one candidate or another remained so and thought their candidate "won" the debate.

Furthermore, for those who followed the campaign, there was nothing new emanating from the debates—just a repeat of memorized positions carefully constructed from notebooks. Thus, the participants appeared not to answer the questions put to them directly but to resort to prepared responses. Politicians are well trained to avoid direct answers by using oblique language and to evade questions to which they do not wish to respond. For those who did not follow the campaign, perhaps some idea of the character of the candidates was possible, with the issues being less informative. In fact, most people and the press were concerned with who won rather than the substance of what was said. (Ford was declared the winner in the first debate.) Accordingly, most people, including the press and the participants, did not believe that the debates were overly successful. The evaluation of the debates is not the purpose of this section; this task has been adequately covered by others.[16]

Still, it might be useful to review briefly the debate on economic issues. The first debate covered domestic and economic matters. As might be expected, the topics of unemployment, taxes, the size of government, and budget deficits received major attention. Surprisingly, inflation did not receive much attention nor did the other domestic social problems—civil rights, busing, abortion, and women's issues.

Concerning unemployment, Carter again emphasized the need for government help in reducing unemployment, but his answers lacked the specificity of his earlier positions. Ford insisted that the private sector is the place to look for job creation and tax cuts would do the trick of promoting economic recovery, thus providing additional jobs.

On taxes, Ford pushed for his latest tax cut proposal for the "middle class," combined with keeping the lid on government spending. Carter accused the Republicans of giving tax breaks to the corporations and using low-income people to pay the taxes. Carter repeated his characterization of the tax code as a disgrace and outlined loopholes that could be easily closed.

On government spending and deficit, Carter responded to the question of how he could advocate additional government spending on jobs, health care, welfare reform, and child care and still balance the budget by claiming that the economic recovery and additional employment would produce enough revenue to finance the additional spending. Carter pointed out the huge deficits created by the Republicans since the Johnson administration and promised the budget would be balanced by fiscal year 1981. Ford suggested that any surplus that did emerge should be returned to the taxpayers and not spent on additional government programs. Ford also promised to balance the budget by fiscal year 1978.

On the question of the size of government, Carter again insisted that he could follow the example of his experience in Georgia to reorganize the executive branch of government and cut back on the bureaucracy and thus promote efficiency. Ford protested that the actual experience in Georgia was not as Carter claimed and government employment actually increased while the programs suffered a loss of efficiency.

Clearly this was old stuff to educated viewers who were familiar with the candidates and their positions. It is interesting to note, however, that the issue of jobs and unemployment had some effect on voters. The difference between the candidates on these issues was clarified and was increased after the debate by 17–29%; still other studies showed no impact, and another showed the candidates were about the same on these issues. It also became evident that Carter clearly differentiated himself on the issue of government reorganization. On the spending issue, only

Republicans saw Ford as more conservative, while on tax reform, both candidates were perceived as favoring it *after* the first debate.[17]

Frankly, beyond these observations, it is difficult to avoid the conclusion that the debates did not contribute very much to the economic knowledge of the general public, nor did they clearly differentiate one candidate from the other. Differences did emerge, of course, but they were not the dramatic ones that might clearly distinguish them in the public mind.

By now we have sufficient knowledge of the economic positions taken by the candidates from both their campaign promises and from the debates. To repeat, campaign pledges and positions must always be scrutinized and viewed with some skepticism. This chapter reviewed campaign positions on economic issues not so much to evaluate them but to ascertain to what extent the candidates actually differed from each other. This procedure is necessary in order to examine a hypothesis, proposed later, about Carter's position in the general swing of the nation toward conservatism. For this reason, some knowledge of what he and Ford were proposing to the American people is required. Carter's actual performance in office must now be examined to reveal how much of his campaign platform was followed, how much he changed in office, and more important, how he fit into the changing economic and political climate of the country.

NOTES

1. Jimmy Carter, *Why Not the Best?* (Nashville, Tenn.: Broadman Press, 1975), 137.

2. Ibid., 106.

3. Many have commented on the apparent hypocrisy of Carter on some issues, and the flip-flops on others. He often seemed on both sides of a controversial issue in an attempt to please all factions. Civil rights was one such issue, along with abortion rights, the Vietnam war, campaign ethics and funding, and right-to-work laws. While probably no worse than any other politician, Carter's transgressions were subject to more scrutiny, since he insisted on truth from office holders—"I'll never lie to you," he said—and made honesty a major issue in his campaign. This gave critics of Carter, as well as some supporters, grounds for attacking every misstatement, every ambiguity, and when they grew tired of his self-righteous moralizing, probably overstated the case against him. For a critical appraisal of Carter and his administration, see Victor Lasky, *Jimmy Carter: The Man and the Myth* (New York: Richard Marek, 1979); and Laurence H. Shoup, *The Carter Presidency and Beyond* (Palo Alto, Calif.: Ramparts Press, 1980).

4. Shoup, *The Carter Presidency and Beyond*, 43, 44.

5. Martin Schram, *Running for President 1976: The Carter Campaign* (New York: Stein and Day, 1977).

6. Quoted in Lasky, *Jimmy Carter: The Man and the Myth*, 308.

7. Haynes Johnson, *In the Absence of Power* (New York: Viking Press, 1980), 286.

8. Quotations from Lasky, *Jimmy Carter: The Man and the Myth*, 237, 192–193, 114.

9. James Wooten, *Dasher* (New York: Summit Books, 1978), 38.

10. Address at the Town Hall Forum, Los Angeles, August 23, 1976.

11. Robert T. Hartman in *The Ford Presidency*, edited by Kenneth W. Thompson (New York: University Press of America, 1988), 92.

12. Leo Cherne, in *The Ford Presidency*, 52.

13. For more on Ford, see his biographers, such as Jerald F. terHorst, *Gerald Ford and the Future of the Presidency* (New York: The Third Press, 1974); and Edward L. Schapsmeier and Frederick H. Schapsmeier, *Gerald R. Ford's Date with Destiny* (New York: Peter Lang, 1989).

14. Schapsmeier and Schapsmeier, *Gerald F. Ford's Date with Destiny*, 165.

15. See terHorst, *Gerald Ford and the Future of the Presidency*, 58.

16. See Sidney Kraus (ed.), *The Great Debates: Carter vs. Ford, 1976* (Bloomington, Ind.: Indiana University Press, 1979); and U.S. House of Representatives, Committee on House Administration, *The Presidential Campaign 1976*, Vol. 3, The Debates (Washington, D.C.: United States Government Printing Office, 1979). This same committee reproduced the campaign speeches of both candidates, devoting volume one (in two parts) to Carter and volume two (in two parts) to Ford.

17. David O. Sears and Steven H. Chaffee, "Uses and Effects of the 1976 Debates: An Overview of Empirical Studies," in Kraus, *The Great Debates*, 235, 223–261.

Chapter 3

The Launching of the Carter Administration: Beginning Initiatives

Carter and his running mate, Walter Mondale, won the election by the rather slim margin of 50.1% to 48.0%, and while the number of votes cast broke a record by some 4 million over the 1972 election, the turnout rate at 54.4% was the lowest since the 1948 election. As might be expected, Carter carried the South and East, while Ford captured the West and Midwest. These data help to reinforce the supposition that this presidential campaign elicited little excitement and lacked the type of issues that would galvanize the public to express its preferences definitively.

As further evidence, the Gallup polls indicated in September 1976 that respondents saw inflation as the most important issue, over 68% said as much; followed by government spending, 57%; unemployment, 56%; crime, 56%; and tax reform, 54%. In October, only 47% ranked inflation as the most important problem, with 31% ranking unemployment first. From these data, one would expect that economic problems played a major role in determining the outcome of the election. Yet when asked why they voted for Carter or Ford, of those voting for Carter only 1% mentioned their belief that he would get inflation under control, and 5% believed he would help the unemployed; only 4% liked his general economic policies. For Ford, only 2% thought he could bring down inflation, and 9% liked his general economic policies (the unemployment problem was not indicated specifically).

So, on what basis did voters make their selection? For Carter, 33% said a change in administration was the reason, while 14% just liked him, and 12% liked his general policies. For Ford, 43% favored his experience, 16% did not like the other choices, and 12% just liked him. Clearly, personal characteristics played an important role in this election, and while economic problems appeared more important to the voters before the election, they cast their votes on other bases. Unfortunately for Mr. Ford, whenever voters indicated their concern for economic matters, it was always the Democrats who were seen as better able to deal with them.

It would not be wise to place too much faith in these data or in polls in general. They are inserted here to help support the idea that the campaign was not terribly enlightening, nor did the voters respond to the visions or plans of either candidate. As such, whoever won would have a difficult time getting his policies accepted, particularly so in the absence of a mandate for dramatic change.

CONSTRUCTING AN ADMINISTRATION

The tone of Carter's administration was probably set in his inaugural address. Among the usual generalities, one paragraph stands out and is quite revealing:

We have learned that "more" is not necessarily "better," that even our great nation has its recognized limits, and that we can neither answer all questions nor solve all problems. We cannot afford to do everything, nor can we afford to lack the boldness as we meet the future. So, together, in a spirit of individual sacrifice for the common good, we must simply do our best.

What are we to make of this less than inspiring prospect? Why set this pessimistic and negative tone at a time when the nation longed for reassurance? It is a lesson in constraints, of course, but the suggestion that the nation cannot solve all problems is neither original nor profound. Here at the outset, Carter reveals himself as an uninspired leader who has more regard for the truth than for invention.

This reserve, this conservatism, would be found later in many of Carter's programs and policies. Here is the engineer's passion for problem solving pitted against the cold reality of impossible and impractical pursuits. The rational response may be to withdraw, but the daring spirit would want to continue the fight. "We cannot afford to do everything," he said, "nor can we afford to lack boldness." But boldness in the face of the unknown requires taking chances and exposing the nation to risks; Carter had almost laid the foundation for the opposite by stressing limitations and caution. Moreover, the call for individual sacrifice for the common good would come back to haunt him as a contradiction in a society that stresses individualism.

All in all, this was a curious paragraph to insert into a speech that was designed to set the tone for the new administration. In retrospect, it was a significant statement, for it accurately forecast the administration's philosophy while in office.

More signs of the administration's probable direction were evident in Carter's appointments. He had promised to appoint more women and minorities and to tolerate a diversity of views. In keeping with his outsider image, his White House staff choices included young Georgians (with one exception) who had previously worked for him. Loyalty to associates is an admirable trait, but their lack of experience with the Washington establishment would prove damaging in the introductory phase of this untried administration. There was no chief of staff, but Hamilton Jordan served as chief aide. Carter elected to follow the example of Franklin Roosevelt's White House model—the spoke-in-a-wheel concept—wherein cabinet members were to have relatively free access to the president without the intercession of someone who would clear the necessity.[1] Carter claimed that he always used such a model—in his business and as governor of Georgia—and saw no need to change to the more hierarchical structure favored, for instance, by Nixon. Yet Carter's model was to prove a prescription for chaos, with the president spending too much time on details and managing the staff.

The poor White House structure may have been responsible for the early administrative problems, but other problems surfaced as well. One observer suggests that competent people were put into the wrong jobs. Hamilton Jordan was admittedly not an administrator; Frank Moore, as congressional liaison, did not have any experience in dealing with Congress and learning on the job had unfortunate consequences for legislative actions. Less tangible but equally plausible was the clash of cultures between the Georgia mafia and the Washington establishment with different values, and possibly a hostile press added to the perception of disarray.[2] James Fallows, a White House speech writer, later concluded "that Carter and those closest to him took office in profound ignorance of the possibilities and more likely pitfalls. They fell prey to predictable dangers and squandered precious time."[3] The spoke-in-the-wheel structure adopted by the administration also ensured the insularity of departments; members were boxed-in by the structure and did not stray into another's area, thus limiting the sharing of information and advice. Carter defended the appointment of cronies to his staff, maintaining that loyal and well-known associates would inspire mutual confidence and limit backbiting.[4]

Carter's unwillingness to emulate the presidential style of his predecessors testifies to one characteristic of those who run as outsiders to Washington: the perceived need to do things differently. In this case, it was the reorganization of government, starting at the top. Yet, there is a price to pay for being an outsider, and whatever the merits of his reorganizational plans, Carter did not include adequate provisions for dealing with the Washington establishment. Specifically, the administration failed to recognize that Congress was changing, asserting its independence and becoming less coherent. Party unity was withering, and the whole political atmosphere was becoming more contentious. Buoyed by its success against Nixon and Ford, Congress was not about to relinquish its newfound power and was searching for its new voice in national affairs.

Thus, the Congress that Carter faced was a much different institution from the one faced by his predecessors. To make any progress, therefore, Carter would have to mold his concept of the presidency at the same time as adapting to the changing congressional configuration. It would have taken a great deal of effort to devise a strategy to achieve success under such circumstances, an effort that Carter, the outsider, was unwilling or unable to make.

It is not our purpose to describe in detail the operations of the White House staff nor to examine the political style of the Carter administration. Indeed, many have subjected the Carter administration to microscopic analysis in order to understand the flaws in its procedures. We are more concerned with his economic program and how it fared from conception to execution. Along the way, the political process will be introduced as it influences economic policy-making, of course, but the flaws, if any, in the manner in which it was introduced and managed through Congress are better left to political scientists and more knowledgeable observers. Yet, it is useful to remind ourselves of the constraints Carter faced, both of his own making and otherwise, as a prelude to the examination of his approach to economic policy-making.

ECONOMIC POLICY-MAKING AND IDEOLOGY

Carter described himself as a conservative in fiscal matters and a liberal in social policy. He clearly identified himself with the liberal causes of justice and equity, but at the same time, he worked for a limited and efficient government. He also described his concept of populism as the following: "The Southern brand of populism was to help the poor and the aged, to improve education, and to provide jobs. At the same time the populists tried not to waste money, having almost an obsession about the burden of the excessive debt. These same political beliefs—some of them creating inherent conflicts—were to guide me in the Oval Office."[5]

This then must pass for his ideological precepts. The search for a more profound commitment beyond these broad generalizations is likely to prove fruitless. He seemed almost unaware of or impatient with the tensions between equity and efficiency. Moreover, economic issues, particularly macroeconomic issues, were basically incompatible with his manner of addressing problems. Often in the solution of macroeconomic problems, there is no clear best option, no easy solution, and this inconclusiveness conflicts sharply with the engineer's methodology of identifying and solving problems.[6] He saw issues in moral terms that often conflicted with his perfectionist attributes. Of course, no leader wants to be presented with options that are all unpleasant, but that is not what is meant here by the incompatibility of economics with Carter's leadership style. The assumption that a solution was possible prevented Carter from confronting macro issues from the proper perspective. Besides, Carter was more amenable to microeconomic issues. Macroeconomic issues simply did not offer the possibilities of solutions that micro issues did, and most presidents seem to have difficulty with the ambiguous macro options presented to them. Charles Schultze testified that Carter "had to work at macro [as opposed to micro issues]. He seemed on the one hand fighting for it and on the other hand almost resisting it."[7]

Ideology in Transition?

Carter's ideology seemed to reflect the nation's wavering beliefs. Most people wanted economic justice and greater equity in economic affairs, and most wanted economic growth and opportunities but were skeptical about government's ability to achieve them. People wanted the government programs that promised help to those who needed it but did not want to pay for them. Carter had to deal with the distrust of government that he inherited from presidents Johnson and Nixon. Liberalism suffered under Johnson, and conservatism suffered under Nixon; both were under suspicion. So there were confusing elements of liberalism and conservatism running through the national psyche in some schizophrenic way.

As might be expected, such ideological confusion was carried over into the economic sphere and was reflected in Carter's economic program and in his administration's entire approach to economic problems. He took office not knowing exactly what he wanted to accomplish, and the public had not signaled its desires either. Consequently, he would be pushed and turned by economic events he could not control and appeared to vacillate among several goals. He could not satisfy the traditional liberal wing of the Democratic party, either because he was philosophically opposed to their agenda or because economic events caused him to choose policies that were antithetical to their beliefs. On the other hand, the conservatives in the Republican party promoted more drastic actions than he would have assented to in order to reduce government involvement in the economy.

While these tensions always exist in American politics, they were particularly evident in this period. Faced with problems such as stagflation, where easy solutions were not possible, Carter had to make choices that necessarily alienated both camps. Inflation and energy problems that haunted the Carter administration did not offer the possibilities of leadership without pain and criticism.

So the Carter administration can be divided into two phases: the first two years in which it fostered stimulus and active government, and the latter two years when it retreated. We may also characterize them as liberal and conservative phases. But in the first phase, Carter did not go far enough for liberals, and in the second phase, he did not go far enough for conservatives. He thus pleased neither camp and, lacking an economic philosophy to guide him, resorted to pragmatism that was labeled irresolution.

However, before considering the Carter administration's economic program, it might be useful to take a closer look at the administration's economic advisors. Looking at these cabinet choices, we find more liberal views than is found in the other cabinet appointments. W. Michael Blumenthal was chosen as secretary of the treasury. Blumenthal, a specialist in international trade, brought both academic credentials and wide business experience to the post. He was an ardent free trader and was willing to entertain progressive social initiatives and government planning. Thomas Bertram (Bert) Lance, a Georgia banker, was selected for Office of management and budget (OMB). Lance, a close personal friend of the president, had helped him reorganize state government in Georgia. Juanita M. Kreps, a labor economist, was appointed secretary of commerce. A liberal economist, she was interested in women in the labor force, income distribution, and consumer affairs. She also brought considerable business knowledge to the job. F. Ray Marshall, another labor economist, was selected for secretary of labor. His specialty was in manpower problems, with particular emphasis on rural and minority employment problems. Joseph A. Califano, Jr., was appointed as secretary of health, education, and welfare (HEW) and brought with him extensive experience in shaping government programs under Johnson; he appeared well suited to lead the attack on government reorganization. Patricia Roberts Harris, the only black in the cabinet, was Carter's choice to head the department of housing and urban development (HUD). Criticized for being inexperienced in the field, Harris had to learn on the job, but she received both praise and disapproval as the right person for the job.

Finally, for the Council of Economic Advisors (CEA), Carter selected a well-known Keynesian economist, Charles L. Schultze, as chairman. Schultze, from the Brookings Institution, served in the Kennedy/Johnson administration as director of the budget bureau. The other posts went to Lyle B. Gramley, the research director of the Federal Reserve System, and William Nordhaus, professor of economics at Yale. All three were considered liberal economists who could be expected to favor government intervention into the economy.

This then is the team that would be active in the economic sphere and that would be advising the president on economic matters. Together with some idea of how the administration was constructed, we have the basic framework of the administration. It is now time to look at the early economic initiatives.

FORD'S PARTING STRATEGY

When Carter assumed responsibility for the economy, it had begun to stall in the spring and summer of 1976. The unemployment rate had risen from 7.3% in May to 8.0% in November, before ending the year at 7.8%. The rate of growth of real GNP fell from 9.2% in the first quarter of 1976 to 3.9 and 3.0% in the last two quarters of 1976. The economy was recovering from the recession of 1973–75 but at a much slower pace than previous recoveries. There was considerable slack in the economy as manufacturing firms were operating at 80% of capacity. Finally, with the absence of price shocks that hit the economy in the early 1970s, the rate of inflation was in the neighborhood of 7% in January 1977, down from double digit rates but still above the rates previously found in economic recoveries.

The failure of the economy to grow at a rate similar to past growth rates at this juncture in the recovery (about a 5% shortfall) was attributed to the decline in real investment, housing, some consumer durables, and government spending that fell short of the budget by $11 billion and to the deterioration in the stimulus of the tax policies adopted during the downturn.[8] In the absence of any discretionary actions of government, the economy seemed destined to limp along with high unemployment rates and slow growth.

In response to this forecast, the Ford administration was entertaining another tax reduction to accompany some spending reductions and reallocations. Permanent tax reductions of some $10 billion for individuals in calendar year 1977 would have come from increasing exemptions, increasing low-income allowances, and reducing some tax rates. Corporate tax rates equal to $2.5 billion in 1977 would come about as a result of reducing the tax rate to 46% from 48%. Ford also proposed an increase in the Social Security tax rate and called for an integration of the corporate and personal income tax structure. Federal spending would rise by 12% in calendar year 1977, and thus, the full-employment surplus would decline by $13 billion, indicating more stimulus in the economy. Monetary policy was considered to be consistent with this expansion. The Congressional Budget Office (CBO) estimates that this program would have produced a very modest stimulus, adding just $5 billion to real GNP and reducing unemployment by 0.1 percentage point.[9]

Yet, these data conceal the thrust of what the Ford administration had in mind when it proposed its final budgets. The budget for fiscal year 1978 reveals that further tax reductions were in store for the economy right up to 1982, presumably to counter inflationary tax receipts and return power to the private sector. Federal expenditures were to decline steadily with the reductions coming at the expense of state and local grant programs and benefit programs to individuals, while increases in spending for national defense would continue. The real growth in spending would be on the order of 1% in FY78 and zero in FY79. Thus, the Ford proposals would have shifted the budget to defense and away from welfare programs and reduced the extent of government in the economy.

As a result of these policies, the federal deficit would fall from $ −57.2 billion in FY77 to $ −11.6 billion in FY79, and to a surplus of $13.4 billion in FY80. Together with the rosy forecasts for 1977 of inflation (5.1%), unemployment (7.3%), and economic growth (5.2%), these budget projections were fictitious. The spending cuts would never have been accepted by Congress, as similar proposals were rejected in the past; cuts in these social programs, in the income security areas, simply were not likely. Other budgetary shifts and tax proposals would certainly have faced strong opposition as well.

But Ford did not win the election, and his final budget must be viewed as either an exercise in wishful thinking, or as a hurdle for the new administration to overcome. By proposing tax and spending decreases that were fanciful, was he setting up the new president for failure when the economy did not perform as forecast by his administration, or was he building expectations for a conservative shift that could not be satisfied by any administration?

CARTER'S EARLY INITIATIVES

In February 1977, Carter had his chance to respond to and amend Ford's budget. In a sharp reversal, he submitted a stimulus package that was designed to revitalize the economy and reverse some of the spending trends indicated in Ford's fanciful budget. Specifically, he presented a package of tax decreases and spending increases that would cost $15.5 billion in fiscal year 1977 and $15.7 billion in fiscal year 1978. This two-year budget program of $31.2 billion was designed to stimulate the economy quickly by providing a one-time $50 rebate on 1976 taxes payable in the second quarter of 1977; a permanent increase and simplification in the personal standard deduction that would be only partially reflected in FY1977 but be more effective in FY1978; and finally a business tax cut that would similarly affect tax receipts—less in 1977 and more in 1978 when the tax would be fully effective.

When the immediate effects of the tax stimulus wore off in 1978, spending increases were designed to provide continued stimulus. Additional spending on public works and public service employment were designed to stimulate the economy over a longer period but could be reversed if the economy improved. Thus some flexibility was built into the overall plan.

In addition the stimulus package was purposely made rather modest so as not to prevent the attainment of a balanced budget by 1981. Permanent tax and spending provisions were avoided to ensure flexibility in response to economic changes that could not be foreseen at the time of the submission of budgetary changes. As is easily seen, this philosophy of economic management is far different from that held by the Ford administration. While hardly radical, it represents a departure from the more conservative approach.

For a quick summary of the stimulus package, Table 3.1 provides the data presented by the administration. The $50 rebate program, available to nearly everyone, was to provide immediate stimulus and cost $11.4 billion. This rebate replaced the $35 program slated for expiration at the end of 1977. This was a temporary program, and the administration expected the proceeds to be spent quickly. The other proposal for individuals was to simplify tax calculations by substituting a flat standard deduction for the current one that required percentage calculations; single taxpayers would be able to deduct $2,400 and married couples, $2,800. These standard deductions, along with personal exemptions, could easily be built into the tax tables thus simplifying tax preparation. The flat deductions that replaced the percentage-of-income deduction would clearly benefit lower income groups more with about 65% of the tax reduction going to those with incomes below $10,000.

To stimulate business and aid in the economic recovery, the administration proposed giving business a choice. Each business could choose, for

Table 3.1
Budget Cost of the Stimulus Program (in billions)

	Fiscal Year	
	1977	1978
Rebate and Social Security Program		
$50 per capita rebate		
Reduction of tax	8.2	—
Refunds in excess of liability [refund		
exceeded tax liability in 1976]	1.4	—
Total	9.6	—
$50 payment to Social Security and railroad		
retirement beneficiaries	1.8	
Total rebate program	11.4	—
Simplification and reform program		
Replace standard deduction with flat		
deduction	1.5	5.5
Business tax reduction program	0.9	2.7
Total tax program	13.8	8.2
Expenditure programs		
Increased countercycle revenue sharing	0.5	0.6
Public service employment	0.7	3.4
Public works	0.2	2.0
Expanded training and youth programs	0.3	1.6
Total expenditure programs	1.7	7.6
Total administration proposals	15.5	15.7

Source: U.S. House of Representatives, Committee on Ways and Means, *Tax Aspects of President Carter's Economic Stimulus Programs*, 95th Congress, 1st session, February 1977, 26.

a five-year period, between (1) a refundable credit of 4% of the employer's share of Social Security payroll taxes (then 5.85% of taxable payrolls); or (2) an additional 2% investment tax credit (mainly from 10 to 12%). The former was instituted to benefit labor-intensive businesses and nonprofit organizations; the latter would benefit capital-using industries by reducing the cost of capital.

The countercyclical revenue sharing program was increased by $1 billion and the formula for activation of the program was changed. Of the additional $1 billion for the program, only $500 million was expected to be spent in 1977 with the remainder in 1978. The program was given a four-year authorization, and the trigger point for when the program would be activated was changed from an additional $62.5 million for every half percentage point of unemployment over 6% to an additional $30 million for every one-tenth of a percentage point of unemployment over 6%.

For job creation, the administration raised the number of federally funded public service jobs from 310,000 to 600,000 by the end of 1977, and to 725,000 during 1978. These jobs would require additional spending of $700 million in 1977 and 3.4 billion in 1978. These public service jobs under the Comprehensive Employment and Training Act (CETA) were designed to create opportunities in areas not likely to be provided for in the private sector: repair and renovation projects, conservation, rehabilitation of blighted urban areas, parks and recreation programs, and hospitals. Particular attention was to be given to Vietnam war veterans, largely by subsidizing large private corporations to hire and train these veterans.

For youth programs, the administration planned to provide 72,000 positions in 1977 and another 82,000 in 1978. The cost was set at $1.5 billion for the two-year period. In addition, the Job Corps was to be expanded by 8,000 slots in 1977 and another 14,000 in 1978. The increase of 22,000 slots (on a base of 22,000 slots) would cost $342 million over the two-year period and bring the total number of jobs in the program to 44,000.

This was the administration's original plan for economic stimulus. It would have entailed a budget deficit of $68 billion in 1977 and $57 billion in 1978, about $10 billion higher each year than Ford's original estimates for these fiscal years. With the plan in place, the expected economic impact on the economy was thought to be an increase in the growth rate to 5¾–6% for 1977 (up about 1½ percentage points over the previous half year), a decrease in unemployment to 6.7–6.9% in 1977 (down from the 7.7% of 1976) and to nearly 6% by the end of 1978, and little or no effect on the inflation rate.

Congress adopted the tax program on March 3, 1977, but added $2.8 billion for 1977 to the stimulus package (making it $17.5 billion for 1977), largely by increasing the amounts spent on outlays for jobs and for local assistance. After these changes were considered, the CBO estimates for economic growth, unemployment, and inflation were still in line with administration estimates.[10]

EARLY CRITICISMS OF CARTER'S ECONOMIC PLANS

While the administration received wide support in Congress for its economic program, critics found fault with various aspects of it. The attacks came from many sources: labor, industry, and, of course, economists. Some said it went too far in terms of stimulus, and others felt that it did not go far enough; some objected to more government involvement, while others wanted government to become more involved. These objections are to be expected and can even be anticipated when the reversal of direction is involved as it seemingly was in 1977. Hence, there is little to be gained by rehashing familiar philosophical disputes.

Instead, we can summarize the more cogent arguments against the Carter economic program that were made at the time.[11] In this way, it will be possible to consider these objections in more detail later and in the light of actual experience.

1. *Stimulus package.* Some form of stimulus package was acknowledged by most as necessary, although more conservative observers did not seem overly enthused about it and worried more about the inflationary effects. More liberal observers thought the package necessary but were concerned that it was too small. The total stimulus provided was about 1% of GNP, while in the most successful stimulus experience in 1964, the ratio was over 2%.

2. *Investment tax credit.* Supporters of the investment tax credit were generally from the business world, and their only objection was that it should be enlarged (to 13%) and made permanent. Organized labor saw it as a gift to business that would not do any good anyway. Others, including economists, did not view the credit as very effective, particularly when it was granted to all investments rather than incremental ones.

3. *Employer's Social Security tax rebate (4%).* The effort to increase employment for labor-using businesses was seen as laudable but hopelessly ineffective with this program. The credit of 4% of the existing 5.85% of the employer's share of Social Security taxes translates into a tax credit of 0.234%, hardly enough to encourage employers to hire new workers.

4. *Rebate of $50.* There was considerable controversy over the effectiveness of this rebate. The question revolved around how much *immediate* stimulus would be provided by this temporary tax rebate. In economic theory, a temporary tax cut would more likely be saved rather than spent, since a temporary change does not affect the consumption patterns of households that are based on some notion of their permanent incomes. Not many saw this rebate as a significant fiscal policy tool. Many favored the phasing out of the rebate after some income level was reached; why give a rebate to those who do not need it?

5. *Job creation programs.* Organized labor favored these public works and public employment programs, while businesses were rather cool to the concept. Even supporters of the jobs component part of the package expressed concern over eligibility requirements, duration of the program, and training availability. There was more confusion over these programs than with the other components.

These comments reveal the boundaries of the controversy initiated by the Carter economic plan. They also signal the types of revisions that would be suggested by various factions. For dissenters who did not like the investment tax credit, the payroll tax credit, or the tax rebate, it was clear that a better approach would have been to reduce the corporate income tax directly and/or increase depreciation allowances to stimulate investment spending. For individuals, a permanent tax cut would be more appropriate. For those who basically favored the program, more stimulus was needed and better formulation of the investment tax credit and job creation programs were required.

ALTERATIONS IN THE ECONOMIC PLAN

Even as the administration was proposing its economic plans, the nation was forced to endure a severe cold snap that closed many businesses temporarily, created some temporary unemployment, and forced consumers to reallocate more consumption toward meeting their fuel requirements. Energy prices and food shortages pushed up the CPI by 1% in February alone and threatened to hinder economic growth in the first quarter of 1977. At the time, many were worried about the long-term consequences of this exogenous shock, but by the end of the quarter, conditions had already improved significantly, and the economy resumed its recovery.

Household behavior in this period began to present some difficulties for macro policymakers. Consumption had increased in the last quarter of 1976 and the first quarter of 1977; the saving rate, of course, dropped. Consumption, always difficult to forecast, increased in this period as a result of the resolution of the strike against the Ford Motor Company and the cold weather spending requirements. Additional spending could also have come from the anticipated $50 rebate and perhaps some from a surge due to the inauguration of a new administration (although no increase in consumer confidence was detected, and some confusion over the administration's pending energy proposals was possible). In any case, consumption was rising faster than disposable income and providing stimulus to the economy. The question was would consumption continue in this manner, or would households attempt to restore their previous saving habits; if so, the fall in consumption would hinder the economic recovery.

Meanwhile, government spending was rising rapidly, and businesses were rebuilding their inventories depleted during recession and planning to add to their productive capacity. Retail sales continued strong in March, housing rebounded from the cold weather pause, and in general, the recovery was proceeding without the strong stimulus package planned for 1977. It is under these circumstances that the administration, led by Lance, Blumenthal, and the president, withdrew its $50 rebate in April for individuals and (for the sake of fairness) its investment incentives for business. These parts of the stimulus package, designed to affect primarily 1977, were no longer necessary according to the administration; the jobs programs and public works programs, designed to affect the economy in 1978, were retained.

The administration felt that the part of the economic program for 1977 was no longer needed since the economy was meeting the economic targets without the stimulus: Unemployment had fallen to 7.4% in March, on its way to the targeted 7% by year's end, and real GNP growth was 7.5% in the first quarter of 1977, on its way to its yearly target of 6%. Inflation, however, was rising at an annual rate of 12%, if February increases in the CPI were to continue, and at 10% if the Wholesale Price Index increases were to continue. Therefore, the administration reasoned, the rebate would not induce additional investment but would actually hurt business confidence and create fears of higher interest rates.[12]

The April 1977 revised budget estimates now showed a budget deficit for 1977 of $48.7 billion, down from the original $68 billion. The withdrawal of the rebates and investment incentives accounted for $12.2 billion of the reduced deficit, while reduced government spending (the shortfall again from original estimates) accounted for most of the rest. For 1978, the budget did not change much, and the deficit remained at $57.9 billion; the increase of $3.1 billion in receipts due to the withdrawal of business incentives was matched by an increase of $3.2 billion in spending, largely for farm subsidies and Social Security.

Finally, the administration was forecasting a *decrease* in the growth of real GNP for 1977, to 4.9%, and an *increase* in unemployment for 1977 to 7.2%, along with an increase in inflation. It is difficult to escape the conclusion that the administration was switching its concern from economic stimulus to fighting inflation. How else can the contradiction between its withdrawal of stimulus plans in the face of its own forecasts of economic slowdown be explained? The administration argued that it was just being flexible in the face of changing economic conditions. Flexibility is, of course, to be admired, and allowances have to be made for such things as forecast errors; difficulties in making estimates for some portion of the budgets, such as entitlements, and timing discrepancies between appropriations and actual spending but these difficulties are always present. In this case, the administration seemed overly eager to change directions on the basis of the experience of one or two months.

Before passing judgment on the administration's moves by examining the actual economic outcomes for 1977, it would be wise to pause and point out the political consequences of its policy reversals. Dissenters within the administration warned that the policy reversals would seriously damage the administration's claim for consistency, but Carter overruled them.[13] The policy reversals were unilateral with no consultation with Congress, which had just passed its budget resolution for the totals indicated in Carter's budget. These budget totals remained with their higher budget deficits already approved, leaving open the possibility of all kinds of congressional mischief. In brief, the administration lost a great deal of political capital by the sudden reversal of policy that was neither understood by Congress nor sanctioned by it. In the words of Edmund Muskie, the (friendly) Democratic chairman of the Senate Budget Committee:

These circumstances have created a crisis of confidence and competence for the budget process. It is a crisis of confidence because the Congress enacted the budget process just 3 years ago to avoid the fiscal policy roller coaster which withdrawal of support for the rebate represents. It is a crisis of competence because, if economic conditions in April justify this abandonment of the course we set 2 months ago, Congress has a right to know why those conditions were misjudged in February when the program was proposed. . . . The budget process was not intended to work this way. And it cannot work this way.[14]

Republican members also had a pleasant time berating the administration, and again the public must have suffered some loss of confidence or, at best, was left confused by the policy reversal. This reversal represented a serious and costly political blunder and would haunt the administration thereafter. Carter ran on a platform of competence and trust, but in this episode his administration exhibited neither.

A FURTHER ASSESSMENT OF POLICY-MAKING IN THE EARLY YEARS

The Stimulus Package—Taxes

According to Schultze, a Washington veteran in policy-making and analysis, Carter had difficulty reconciling his personal philosophy with economic imperatives.[15] He more or less was forced to stimulate the economy since the economy slumped just prior to the election and became a campaign issue. After criticizing Ford for not reacting to the situation, Carter had to propose some economic stimulus, which meant decreasing taxes or increasing expenditures, either of which could lead to an increase in the budget deficit. Providing stimulus was easy; accepting deficits was not. This is a recurring problem in macro policy-making, but to a fiscal conservative, the problem is made more acute and more intractable. So, right at the start, the administration was somewhat constrained by the philosophical preconceptions of the person at the top. (Ironically, as Schultze pointed out, Carter was more in tune with the policies of restraint that were followed in the second half of his administration).

Under these circumstances, it is instructive and interesting to see what kind of stimulus program such a hesitant fiscal conservative would tolerate. Would it be possible to construct a program that would do the job but not conflict with Carter's antipathy toward undue government intervention? What elements would such a program contain?

Recall the main features of his stimulus package: the tax rebate of $50 and the change in the calculation of the standard deduction; for business, a tax reduction that would encourage investment; and increased revenue sharing, public service employment, public works spending, and training and youth programs.

It is easy to see why Carter accepted this package. First, there is the overall sense of fairness in its design. The individual tax cuts were designed to benefit the lower income groups, and the expenditure increases were designed to reach the unemployed or unemployable and communities apparently hurt by the past recession. The tax reductions were *temporary*, meant to be spent quickly with no lasting effect on tax revenues. After all, Carter had promised a balanced budget by 1981, and permanent tax reductions would have complicated the attainment of that goal. The flexibility component would also appeal to one not fully committed to countercyclical fiscal policy.

Political awareness is also evident as the administration bowed to congressional demands for additional spending on public works. Spreading around public works expenditures would not only acquiesce to traditional approaches to stimulating the economy and secure votes for the package, but would also indicate Carter's willingness to work with key congressmen and recognize political realities.

According to Schultze, Carter did not like the rebate concept (nor did Congress), and thought it akin to giving someone something for nothing. Schultze was a strong proponent of the rebate and was able to convince the president of its usefulness as a quick and simple way to increase spending.[16] Nor did Carter appreciate spending on public works, but he accepted its inclusion into the program for political reasons. The tax reform proposal that changed the standard deduction was readily accepted as were the public service and training components.

Here at the outset then we have a president reluctantly proposing an economic stimulus package, parts of which he does not really approve, for an economy that does not really need it, as soon became evident. Surely this was not a propitious beginning for any administration, particularly for one that was so ambiguous about its economic convictions. The stimulus package was immediately criticized by nearly every group. Few liked the universality of the rebate (something for nothing), and there was much consternation over public service jobs and training programs, objections that could be anticipated.

Criticisms and Evaluation of the Tax Program

With this recital of the elements of the stimulus program and its background, it is time to conduct a more searching evaluation of the administration's first macroeconomic policy. The first criticism to consider is the size of the stimulus package. Was it too small to do the job? The administration claimed there was sufficient slack in the economy so that inflation was not a particular worry. The CPI was increasing at an annual rate of approximately 4.8% at the end of 1976, while the unemployment rate was stable at 7.8%. Moreover, the gap between potential and actual GNP, calculated at an unemployment rate of 4.9%, was on the order of $90 billion, or about 7% of GNP. On this basis, a $15 billion stimulus package for 1977 (about 1% of GNP) appears too small to close the gap, and too small to affect unemployment seriously. Using a multiplier of 2, the 1977 part of the stimulus package would close only a third of the gap between potential and actual GNP.

It would appear that the administration may have been more concerned with the future prospects of balancing the budget and did not want to sacrifice revenues. Inflation, too, may have been more important than was acknowledged. We know that inflation spurted in early 1977, particularly in food prices, and that may have tempered the degree of stimulus proposed. Yet the administration continued to express its view that there was much slack in the system and that the inflation currently being experienced was due to what Schultze called "momentum inflation," that is, prices are rising today because prices rose yesterday. This wage-price spiral cannot be cured by high unemployment and excess capacity. Only a steady economic recovery can stop this catch-up spiral; the administration thought it had a plan for this steady expansion.[17]

Thus, with unemployment running at 7.8% and manufacturers using only 82% of their capacity, the administration had reason to believe it had room for stimulating the economy and a rationale for doing so. Why then was it so timid? The stimulus package should have been double the amounts proposed and designed better to do the job.

The second criticism centers around the type of stimulus package. Why a tax rebate which surely would generate much opposition from a variety of sources, some even from within the administration, starting with Carter who disliked the idea? Recall that Charles Schultze was a strong advocate of the concept and was able to sell it on the basis of its temporary nature. There would be no sacrifice of revenue that would accrue with a permanent tax cut (and prohibit a balanced budget?); any such permanent tax cut could come later when the time was right.

Still, aside from the moral objection of giving something for nothing, would the temporary tax cut be spent to provide the stimulus, or saved and present an embarrassing gift? The prevailing economic theory suggests that the temporary tax rebate would not be as effective a stimulus as a permanent tax cut. For example, a temporary tax change may be only 50% effective, with 50% of the change being "wasted." With this assumption, one estimate put the increase in GNP one year later at only $12 billion.[18] If the assumption that put spending at 50% of the rebate were correct, then the fiscal stimulus of the tax rebate was certainly not very strong. Treasury secretary Michael Blumenthal, testifying for the stimulus package, countered this argument by asserting that consumers had experienced real income disappointments in the recent past and would consequently spend the rebate quickly to compensate.[19] In more normal times, perhaps, the criticism of temporary tax cuts would have more validity; it follows that the state of the economy must be considered to judge the effectiveness of temporary tax changes. These were apparently not normal times. Unfortunately for Blumenthal's reasonable argument, high energy bills would force households to spend their rebates in ways that would not lead to purchases of consumer goods that might have furnished the desired stimulus.

So the controversy was unresolved, but in either case, the tax rebate was too small to provide the stimulus needed. One additional problem with the temporary tax rebate was not seriously considered: its possible procyclical nature. If the households did spend the rebate quickly, as the administration claimed, then there would be a short boost to the economy. While that was desirable from the administration's view, it could have created a false sense of prosperity in which firms might overexpand in capital goods or inventories. When the rebate ceased, these firms would be left with excess capacity or excess inventories. In either case, the economy might stall once again, and thus the rebate policy would turn out to be procyclical, contributing to a boom and decline.

Changing the standard deduction to flat amounts from a percentage of income was the administration's bow to tax reform, scarcely a radical change to a system that had been declared a disgrace. Changes in the method of calculating the standard deduction, even the elimination of it, had been discussed for some time. In fact, the Ford administration had proposed a similar provision, and thus, there would be little opposition expected to this noncontroversial tax change. Real tax reform was promised at a later date by the administration; this was only the beginning, but still a rather modest start.

Business Taxes

The administration ostensibly offered business a choice of tax cuts for a five-year period: either a 2% increase in the investment tax credit or a 4% credit against Social Security taxes paid. This package was a response to the perceived need to stimulate investment, create jobs, and avoid inflationary policies. The investment tax credit feature was designed to stimulate investment, but it tended to favor capital-intensive industries over labor-intensive ones and in general favored the larger firm. Hence, large industries supported this provision. A spokesman for General Electric, for example, not only supported the credit but wanted to increase it to 13% and make it permanent.[20]

The five-year provision seems unusual given the existence of lags in the investment decision. As a short-run stimulus, it leaves much to be desired. To be effective in the short run, the period of the additional tax credit should have been made even more temporary, perhaps one or two years to encourage firms to make investment decisions more quickly. As a fiscal policy measure meant to get the economy moving quickly, the policy was not particularly effective.

Whether or not the investment tax credit is an effective method to stimulate investment has always been questionable anyway, particularly when it extends to all, rather than incremental, investment over some base. If the *additional* tax credit was meant to stimulate investment, then it should logically apply to *additional* investment over some base amount. In any case, the investment tax credit could make capital-intensive industries even more capital intensive, not a sound policy if job creation is a major goal.

More generally, the investment tax credit was obviously predicated on the perception that a capital shortage was a problem. The question then becomes twofold: was there a capital shortage? If so, was the investment tax credit the best way to remedy it?

Capital requirements are always difficult to estimate. They must be related to the growth of the labor force (and its productivity), the changing product mix of the economy, technological changes, the existing capital stock, and the degree to which the existing stock is utilized. It is often difficult to estimate these influences and conclude that a shortage (or surplus) of capital stock exists.

If one looks at real investment expenditures for producer durables (the ones that would be affected by the investment tax credit) as a percent of real GNP from 1960 to 1976, no discernible decrease is evident; the average is 6% of GNP, and investment spending since 1965 has equaled or bettered that average. True, investment on real producer durables fell in the recession of 1975–76 but so did real GNP. It is also true that the growth rate of investment in producer durables fell to 2.9% over the period 1970–76, down from 4.9% for the 1960–76 period. However, the growth rate of the nonagricultural labor force was about 1.9% and 2.1% over the same periods.

These data are unrefined, of course, but they do indicate that expenditures on producer durables were not far out of line from past relations. Moreover, manufacturers' utilization of existing capacity was below the benchmark year of 1973 of about 87%, averaging 84% in 1974, 74% in 1975, and 80% in 1976. If firms had excess capacity, why invest more unless the period was unusual, or unless they had very favorable expectations of future conditions. Both of these qualifications would appear to be questionable in 1977. Nevertheless, the administration was counting on favorable expectations to induce more firms to proceed with their investment plans.

The Carter administration was apparently more concerned with the experience during the Ford administration. There is at least some evidence, if rather inconclusive, to suggest that more investment was needed. Concentrating on the period from 1973, the Carter administration determined that more investment was needed, since the growth rate of investment (net of pollution equipment) was falling to a rate of 1.9% and the labor force was growing at a rate of 2.2%.[21]

Yet why would the failure of investment to grow at past rates be so surprising in the period 1973–76? The sharp recession and uncertain prospects would account for that. Indeed, it would be surprising if the growth of investment had remained constant. So what else can account for the decline in investment spending?

One argument frequently given for the alleged decline in investment spending was that inflation in capital goods had outpaced inflation in other areas. If true, then firms would be hard pressed to replace their equipment and machinery because they would not have provided enough funds for depreciation; depreciation based on historical costs would be insufficient to purchase the higher-priced replacements. The argument is theoretically correct but would apply in reality only to the years 1974–76. In other years, the GNP deflator was greater than the rise in prices of producer durables. Specifically, the Bureau of Economic Analysis (BEA) of the Department of Commerce has estimated that depreciation based on historical costs and the straight-line method of computation would have been sufficient to replace investment goods up until 1975, when there was a shortfall of $6.6 billion and a shortfall of $10.1 billion in 1976. (See Table 3.2.)

This appears to be evidence that would support the notion that investment could have declined due to inflation. However, these large shortfall

Table 3.2
Shortfall of Capital Consumption Allowances (CCA) to Replacement Costs, Selected Years (in billions)

	1973	1974	1975	1976	1977	1978
Total shortfall of CCA[a]	−7.2	−15.2	−28.3	−35.0	−38.5	−45.9
Domestic Corp. Nonfinancial	6.2 5.6	2.3 1.7	−6.2 −6.6	−10.1 −10.2	−9.0 −9.0	−10.9 −10.9
Sole Proprietors and partners	−1.6	−2.6	−4.3	−4.9	−5.6	−6.2
Other Private Business[b]	−11.8	−14.9	−17.7	−20.0	−23.9	−28.8

[a]Except for farms and other private business, the shortfall is calculated by adjusting depreciation on income tax returns to consistent historical costs and then converting these costs for current replacement costs.
[b]Includes private homes (under rental income of persons) and investment of nonprofit institutions serving individuals.

Source: U.S. Department of Commerce, Bureau of Economic Analysis, *The National Income and Product Accounts of the United States, 1929–82*, September 1986, Table 8.4, 389.

amounts cannot be taken at face value. The BEA converts income tax data to historical costs and applies a straight line method of computing depreciation. But since 1954, various methods of accelerated depreciation have been permitted to provide replacement funds. In fact, these methods were devised to offset the effects of inflation. The lack of funds for replacement investment must therefore remain suspect.[22]

Yet even if it is granted that more investment was required, was the investment tax credit the most efficient way to generate it? As a short-run stimulus measure, the investment tax credit would not be effective unless it were instituted for a very short period—say one year. Firms *might* under these circumstances speed up their investment spending. Still, even here investment spending depends upon many factors, with the cost of capital being only one, perhaps not even a major one.

In any case, there are too many lags in the investment decision to warrant using the tax credit as a useful stimulus in the short run. Evidence on the effectiveness of the investment tax credit, available at the time, suggested that a lag of two to four years was possible. These early studies also concluded that the benefits of the tax credit exceeded the cost, and that firms were more apt to use the tax credit than other means of stimulating investment, such as accelerated depreciation.[23] While all these studies were challenged, their results were available to the administration that chose to employ the credit, hoping either for quick reactions that would stimulate the economy or just including the credit in the stimulus package to appease business interests. If the credit worked and investment was stimulated over the two-to-four-year period, it would still benefit the economy and in addition would be helpful at re-election time.

In early 1978, the General Accounting Office reviewed the literature on the subject and concluded that the investment tax credit, if it was to be used at all, should be directed at the goal of economic growth, should include structures, and should be made refundable.[24] Ever since its introduction in 1962, the investment tax credit has been controversial. Many firms and associations testified that the investment tax credit was the most effective way to stimulate investment, although they expressed a hope that a reduction in the corporation income tax or faster recovery provisions would be forthcoming as well.[25]

Despite all the controversy over the investment tax credit and alternative methods for stimulating investment, one essential fact remains: Investment spending cannot increase unless saving increases.[26] From our national income accounts, it is clear that in the end investment will be constrained unless saving—business, personal, and government—increases.

On the other hand, the payroll tax credit would tend to favor smaller, labor-intensive firms, and make them more labor intensive. This provision was probably inserted to placate small business generally, but its effectiveness, whatever the impetus, was questionable.[27] The credit was so small, 4% on the Social Security rate of 5.85% or .00234%, less than ¼ of 1%, that no one could seriously entertain the notion that the credit would lead to job creation. This provision was also limited to a five-year period, which made it even more questionable. If it worked, the reduction in labor costs would have been anti-inflationary, but it was too insignificant to improve its appeal. Clearly this provision was politically motivated and hastily conceived. Moreover no one pursued the implications of the federal government sharing the costs of Social Security with private employers.

The Tax Measures Actually Passed

As we already know, in April 1977 the administration withdrew the rebate proposal and the investment tax credit from its stimulus package. These provisions were apparently no longer necessary since the economy was improving on its own. The repercussions of this decision have already been discussed, and will be again, and they need not be repeated here.

The other tax proposal for business, the 4% credit against Social Security taxes, was scrapped by Congress in favor of a rather complicated employment tax credit for 1977 and 1978. (It was not extended by the Carter administration when it expired.) Congress wrestled with an employment tax credit that would (1) cover only incremental employment, (2) limit administrative costs, (3) not favor new firms over old ones, (4) discourage part-time employment, (5) favor the handicapped, and (6) consider depressed areas of the country. The end result was a clever policy that attempted to steer through these issues, but was so complicated and finally so limiting that its effectiveness was questionable right from the start.[28]

The employment tax credit (which was not refundable) was set at 50% of the amount by which wages paid exceeded 102% of the wages paid in the previous year. Thus, the tax credit was aimed at incremental employment. However, in an effort to limit administrative costs to the employer, the tax credit was based on only those wages subject to federal unemployment taxes; thus, the 50% deduction applied only to the first $4,200 of annual wages, or $2,100 maximum. To prevent the substitution of part-time workers for full-time workers, the total tax credit could be no larger than the excess of a given year's total wages over 105% of the previous year's wages, and the total subsidy could not exceed $100,000 or 25% of total wages subject to unemployment taxes.

Clearly, these complex rules of eligibility would be difficult to understand and would likely deter many from applying for the tax subsidy. Even for those who might possibly take advantage of the program there were several limitations. First, large firms that paid wages above $4,200 annually would find the wage subsidy fell rapidly, for example, those that paid wages of $10,000 would receive a subsidy of only 21% rather than 50%. Hence, larger firms were not likely to be encouraged by the wage subsidy program. Together with the cap of $100,000, these realities clearly would limit the participation of large firms in the program.

Small and medium-sized firms would benefit more from the wage subsidy, which may have been the aim of the restrictions in the first place. Firms that pay lower wages would receive more benefits, and thus, small firms were more likely to utilize the credit. However, it would still be profitable to employ *additional* part-time workers instead of full-time workers, and then release them later. Another possible consequence of this temporary wage subsidy would be for firms to hire more in the current period when the credit is available and reduce employment in future periods when it is not. Moreover, inflationary wage payments would benefit the firm doing the hiring but affect the inflation rate adversely.

The estimated revenue loss of the employment tax credit program was $2.4 billion, not too different from the original tax cuts for business. The results of the program are difficult to measure. In the words of the CBO, "Tax and expenditure policy changes of only a few billion dollars rarely produce impacts on employment or inflation large enough to be measured with any confidence."[29] The CBO nevertheless estimated that the unemployment effects would be virtually zero—one-tenth of one percent at best.

The administration confirmed its disappointment with this complex program and indicated that it was being underutilized. After a year and a half, only $1 billion of the tax credit was claimed. This result occurred in a period of employment growth, which makes it even more disappointing. Complexity of the program and lack of information were blamed for the failure of the policy to elicit a greater response.[30] As a result, the administration pushed for a new jobs program targeted at the young and the handicapped. This employment tax credit was passed in 1978, providing for a credit of 50% of the first $6,000 of wages in the first year and 25% in the second year of employment. The aim of the policy was to reduce structural unemployment in a period of generally rising employment for disadvantaged persons, particularly for the young between ages eighteen and twenty-four. Other programs under CETA aimed at providing some

510,000 jobs for the disadvantaged. Thus, the administration switched its emphasis to helping the segments of the labor force that were not participating in the overall recovery. For the United States this was a new policy to combat structural unemployment, the success of which would determine future responses to this nagging problem.

Outside the administration, there was general agreement that an employment tax credit of some kind was a useful policy that ought to be continued, eliminating of course the undesirable features of the overly complex first attempt.[31] It was seen as an appropriate method to increase employment without exacerbating inflation and to encourage the growth of small or new firms (or the entry of new firms since the benefits are more pronounced for these firms), promoting competition and thereby once again limiting inflationary problems. While it is true that the administration was not terribly concerned with inflation when it proposed its stimulus package, due to the amount of slack in the economy, it is clear how such a policy to increase employment without stimulating inflation would appeal to it when inflation did become a concern.

Finally, the Tax Reduction and Simplification Act of 1977 also extended some of the provisions of Ford's tax programs of 1975 and 1976. Items such as the personal income tax credit, the 10% earned income tax credit, and the small decreases in the corporate income tax rates were carried over. The change in the standard deduction was also retained.

The Stimulus Package—Expenditures

The expenditure portion of the stimulus package was passed in accordance with the administration's request. Designed more to combat structural unemployment than to promote stimulus within the economy, grants-in-aid to state and local governments totaled $8.2 billion, of which $5.5 billion were allocated to training programs and to CETA. Other grants were awarded for countercyclical assistance of $1.1 billion and $1.6 billion for public works programs. Most of the funds were allocated for 1978, with only $1.2 billion out of the $8.2 billion allotted for 1977. The larger expenditures in 1978 were planned to kick in just as the rebate tax provisions were coming to an end.

Comprehensive Employment and Training Act (CETA)

The economic stimulus program was designed to increase aggregate demand, and it was hoped, employment. Still, this is a roundabout path to full employment. Changes in aggregate demand or increases in the rate of economic growth may indeed increase employment, but not everyone shares in the prosperity. Certain identifiable groups fall behind even as the rest of the nation is prospering. The young, the old, minorities, Native Americans, and other disadvantaged groups are known to lag behind the general population; many never do catch up. In addition, there are always groups that claim special attention and treatment—in this case, the Vietnam veterans.

Thus, the Carter administration became sensitive to the needs of these groups as it fashioned its program to change the CETA. The CETA had undergone many changes since its inception in 1973. As a descendent of the manpower programs and the war on poverty programs of the 1960s, confusion over programs and goals and conflicts arose among Congress, the Nixon/Ford administrations, and the Department of Labor, which was responsible for the actual operation of the program.[32]

Originally, the emphasis of the CETA was on comprehensive manpower programs for the unemployed, underemployed, and disadvantaged persons. Public service employment was to play a secondary role to training and education programs. In FY1975, for example, 41% of the $3.1 billion total expenditures went for comprehensive programs and 31% to public service employment (28% went to other programs).

The Carter administration began to shift the emphasis toward more direct public service jobs and away from manpower programs. Thus, it increased the amounts allotted to CETA to $5.6 billion in 1977, $9.5 billion in 1978, $9.4 billion in 1979, before decreasing them to $8.7 billion when inflation became more important to it and spending on social programs began to decline. Public service employment increased to 50% of the total in FY1977 and to 54% in 1979.

While it is clear that the administration was responding to the needs of selected groups in the society, it is difficult to assess the effectiveness of the whole endeavor and of the CETA program in particular. The original aim of the CETA was to decentralize and return control over the programs to local communities and sponsors who were closer to the problems. The assumptions made by conservatives was that those closer to the problems would fashion better solutions than those emanating from Washington. However, the numerous programs that developed under so many different sponsors make it difficult to make judgments about the success or failure of CETA. There were widespread incidents of fraud and abuse of the funds as control passed to local administrators, some of whom were more interested in the political power that accompanied the ability to dole out funds.[33] Later, controls were tightened and some of the abuses stopped, but the program never really survived its initial negative reputation.

Many of the jobs created were later destroyed when the funds evaporated, much of the training was inappropriate for existing job opportunities, and in the end, the jobs created were not suited for the poor. Moreover, the earning power of the participants was not noticeably improved—somewhere in the range of a few hundred dollars at best.[34] Despite the problems of CETA, there were some successes that ameliorate the negative impressions gained from the abuses and mistakes. Many people found jobs after participating in the program, welfare rolls dropped, women and minorities gained more than white males, income gains were substantial for some participants, and employment did increase as about a third of the participants found permanent jobs.[35]

Was the social rate of return worth the costs of the program? One estimate of CETA training programs put the postprogram earnings gains at $1.14 for every $1.00 invested. Even better returns were found for the Job Corps program, with the return of $1.39 for every dollar invested, and for on the job training programs, with a range of $1.26 to $5.93 for every dollar invested.[36] Thus a positive rate of return would argue for the program's continuance as Levitan and Mangum maintained,[37] but these positive final results were not available in 1981; hence, CETA did not survive the budget ax of the incoming conservative administration, not that it would have been acceptable public policy in any case.

Over time the flaws in the original design might have been corrected, the training programs restructured, the on-the-job training experience developed, and so on, but the Reagan administration was not receptive to the pleas of CETA's advocates. In an era of restructuring industry, global competition, and the need for a skilled labor force, the abandonment of a program such as CETA would be short-sighted and unfortunate. In the 1970s, the global economy was just emerging and the requirements for it might have gone unnoticed. By the 1980s, however, when the program was dismantled by the Reagan administration, such actions are less forgivable. Ideological concerns were overriding and the program was sacrificed, too soon in the view of many knowledgeable people in the field.

Concern for the disadvantaged was not terribly strong in the Reagan/ Bush administrations so that the decision to reduce the efforts on their behalf is not surprising. But the repercussions of an unskilled and untrained labor force go beyond ideological concerns in a world of increasing competition. Whether or not CETA would have fulfilled the need for an upgraded labor force is beside the point because some suitable program might have evolved out of it.[38]

Public Works

Public works programs are always popular with Congress because members can boast of securing public funding for projects that are visible to constituents. Economists are less enthusiastic about such programs, particularly when they are promoted as a remedy for short-run stabilization problems. In the Carter administration Charles Schultze raised objections to public works programs but in the end did not resist too strenuously, since opposition to them would have proved fruitless. Rather, Schultze attempted to keep them as small as possible so as not to present a barrier to the rest of the administration's program.[39] The bulk of the program was devoted to upgrading the nation's infrastructure and to education and might have been worthwhile long-term projects even if they were inappropriate as short-term stimulus efforts. In the past, timing problems of public projects were seen as limiting the use of this vehicle for countercyclical purposes; there are many lags in construction projects, and the fiscal stimulus may occur at the wrong time in the business cycle.

Moreover, the public works program was so small that it was difficult to measure the success or failure of this approach. Data problems abounded as they normally do in the construction area and restricted the ability to estimate the fiscal and employment effects. If employment increased, for example, would it be at the expense of other private projects, and would only selected communities benefit? Would only the more skilled be employed at higher wages, while ignoring the unemployment problems of the disadvantaged, women, and blacks? These and many other issues call into question the efficacy of using public works programs as a countercyclical policy.[40] Other programs directed at those most in need or other monetary and fiscal policies would have been more effective in achieving the desired ends. Schultze's reservations appear to be well founded.

Clearly, this two-year stimulus package was conceived to provide flexibility as well as stimulus. A fiscal policy program that is spread out over two years offers many advantages, particularly in an era when economic conditions were uncertain and changeable. When and if the economic situation changed sufficiently to require amendments to the original plan, alterations could easily be made.

Yet, there are difficulties with this apparently rational plan. The ingredients of this package did not lend themselves to such fine tuning. First, the business tax provisions were temporary anyway and, as previously indicated, were less likely to affect economic decisions than permanent ones. For individuals, more flexibility was available, but more political damage also accompanied any serious change. Second, the expenditure programs could not easily be withdrawn, requiring as they did more formal responses on the part of state and local governments. Finally, the highly vaunted flexibility could also be interpreted as incompetent macroeconomic forecasting and create less confidence in policymakers. Generating uncertainty and confusion over the direction of policy is undesirable at any time but particularly in the early stages of an administration.

Drastic changes to any publicized program would only be acceptable in the light of significant changes in the economic conditions that fostered the plan. Reactions to small events or inconsequential fluctuations would likely engender only bewilderment at first, then distrust, and finally condemnation. In the end, the political risks would likely outweigh the economic ones, and the apparent flexibility would vanish. It is apparent that Carter downplayed the political risks in favor of rationality, which was immense.

Before continuing the analysis of the early economic initiatives, we will pause and review the actual economic outcomes in 1978 and the administration's response to them.

NOTES

1. On the White House staff issue see, Q. Whitfield Ayres, "The Carter White House Staff," in *The Carter Years: The President and Policy Making*, edited by M. Glenn Abernathy, Dilys M. Hill, and Phil Williams (London: Frances Pinter, 1984), 144–164.

2. Ibid., 153–158. For more on the relations with the press see the description by press secretary Jody Powell, *The Other Side of the Story* (New York: William Morrow, 1984).

3. James Fallows, "The Passionless Presidency," *Atlantic Monthly* (May and June, 1979). The quote is from the May issue, page 34. These articles are an insightful analysis of the Carter years in the White House.

4. Jimmy Carter, *Keeping Faith* (New York: Bantam Books, 1982), 41.

5. Ibid., 74.

6. This discussion owes much to two articles by James Fallows, "The Passionless Presidency," *Atlantic Monthly* (May and June, 1979).

7. The interview was published in *The President and the Council of Economic Advisors: Interviews with CEA Chairmen*, edited by Erwin C. Hargrove and Samuel A. Morley (Boulder, Colo.: Westview Press, 1984), 465.

8. Congressional Budget Office, *The Disappointing Recovery*, January 11, 1977.

9. Congressional Budget Office, *Overview of the 1978 Budget: An Analysis of President Ford's Proposals*, January 1977, 6.

10. For example, GNP growth was estimated at between 4.8–6.3% in 1977 and between 3.5–5.5% in 1978; unemployment was estimated at between 6.7–7.4% by the fourth quarter of 1977 and between 5.8–6.8% by the fourth quarter. Congressional Budget

Office, *Overview of the 1978 Budget: An Analysis of President Carter's Revisions*, March 1977, 5.

11. For those interested in more detailed criticisms of the Carter program see the testimony of various individuals and groups in U.S. House of Representatives, Committee on Ways and Means, *Tax Aspects of President Carter's Economic Stimulus Program*, 95th Congress, 1st session, February 2–9, 1977.

12. See the statements by administration officials in U.S. Senate, Committee on the Budget, *Briefing on Proposed Revisions to the Federal Budget for Fiscal Years 1977 and 1978*, 95th Congress, 1st session, April 26, 1977.

13. Carter, *Keeping Faith*, 77.

14. Ibid., opening statement of Sen. Edmund Muskie, 2–3.

15. Hargrove and Morley, *Interviews*, 463.

16. Ibid., 477–478.

17. See the testimony of Schultze in hearings before the U.S. House, *Tax Aspects*, 58.

18. See the statement of Michael K. Evans in testimony prepared for the U.S. House Ways and Means Committee and reprinted in *Panel Discussion on the President's Economic Stimulus Program*, 95th Congress, 1st session, February 4, 1977, 13–43. Numerical data appear in Table 4, page 9. Appearing on the same panel, Walter Heller maintained that the rebate would spark consumer spending as it did in 1975 (p. 47). Still the increase in energy bills would siphon off much of the rebate that might have been spent on other consumer goods and provide the needed increase in aggregate demand. Thus, the situation in 1977 was not comparable to that of 1975, lending support to Heller's basic complaint that the stimulus was unduly conservative.

19. U.S. House, *Panel Discussion*, 21. Schultze also claimed, later, that the rebate would be spent quickly.

20. See the statement of Reginald H. Jones, chairman and executive officer, a member of the panel of experts testifying before the House Ways and Means Committee, U.S. House, *Panel Discussion*, 71.

21. See *The Economic Report of the President 1978*, 157.

22. For a contrary view, see the testimony of Michael K. Evans before the U.S. House of Representatives, Committee on Ways and Means, *Panel Discussions*, 15–21. Some of the confusion about this argument may result from taking *total* investment instead of just the producer durable component. Replacement funds would have been lacking for sole proprietors and partners and other private business (that includes owner-occupied homes) components. See Table 3.2

23. See the estimates of Robert E. Hall and Dale Jorgenson, "Application of the Theory of Optimum Capital Accumulation," in *Tax Incentives and Capital Spending*, edited by Gary Fromm (Washington, D.C.: The Brookings Institution, 1967), 54. Other papers at the same conference are worth examining for those interested in the initial studies on investment incentives. Of particular interest was the paper by Lawrence R. Klein and Paul Taubman, "Estimating Effects within a Complete Econometric Model," in Ibid., 197–242. Klein and Taubman actually sampled firms as to their motivations.

24. General Accounting Office, *Investment Tax Credit; Unresolved Issues* (Washington, D.C.: General Accounting Office, 1978).

25. This conclusion is not based on any systematic survey but on samples taken from testimony given before the House Committee on Ways and Means. See U.S. House, *Tax Aspects*.

26. It is clear that Charles Schultze recognized these relationships. See his discussion in *Memos to the President* (Washington, D.C.: The Brookings Institution, 1992), 256.

27. Schultze, in Hargrove and Morley, *The President and the Council of Economic Advisors*, 477, called it an "idiotic proposition," even though it was mainly his idea as a means to placate small business.

28. For a good summary of the progress through the Congress of this tax provision and its problems, see Emil M. Sunley, "A Tax Preference Is Born: A Legislative History of the New Jobs Tax Credit," in *The Economics of Taxation*, edited by Henry J. Aaron and Michael J. Boskin (Washington, D.C.: The Brookings Institution, 1980), 391–408. See also Orley Ashenfelter, "Evaluating the Effects of the Employment Tax Credit," in U.S. Department of Labor, *Conference Report on Evaluating the 1977 Economic Stimulus Package* (Washington, D.C.: U.S. Government Printing Office, 1978), 1–14, and the subsequent discussion. The discussion in the text owes much to these two works.

29. Congressional Budget Office, *Employment Subsidies and Employment Tax Credits*, April 1977, 32.

30. See the testimony of Emil M. Sunley, assistant of the Treasury for Tax Policy in the U.S. Senate, Joint Hearings of the Committee on Finance and the Select Committee on Small Business, *Jobs Tax Credit*, 95th Congress, 2nd session, July 18 and 26, 1978, 96.

31. Ibid. See the testimony of economists Robert Eisner and John Bishop, as well as representatives from business such as William Anderson, president, Smaller Business Association of New England, Inc.

32. For a history of CETA in operation see, Grace A. Franklin and Randall B. Ripley, *CETA: Politics and Policy, 1973–1982* (Knoxville, Tenn.: University of Tennessee Press, 1984), 18–25.

33. Ibid., 68.

34. Burt S. Barnow, "The Impact of CETA Programs on Earnings," *The Journal of Human Resources* (Spring 1987), 157–193.

35. Franklin and Ripley, *CETA*, 197–198.

36. Robert Taggart, "A Review of CETA Training," in *The T in CETA*, edited by Sar A. Levitan and Garth L. Mangun (Kalamazoo, Mich.: W. E. Upjohn Institute for Employment Research, 1981), 111.

37. Ibid., 90.

38. This is not the place for a full evaluation of CETA even if one were possible. For partial assessments and evaluations in addition to those previously mentioned see, William Mirengoff, Lester Rindler, Harry Greenspan, and Charles Harris, *CETA: Accomplishments, Problems, Solutions* (Kalamazoo, Mich.: W. E. Upjohn Institute for Employment Research, 1982); Bonnie B. Snedeker and David M. Snedeker, *CETA: Decentralization on Trial* (Salt Lake City, Utah: Olympus Publishing Company, 1978); National Commission for Manpower Policy, *CETA: An Analysis of the Issues*, special report 23, (Washington, D.C.: U.S. Government Printing Office, May 1978); Congressional Budget Office, *CETA Reauthorization Issues*, August 1978.

39. From the interview in Hargrove and Morley, *The President and the Council of Economic Advisors*, 476.

40. For a comprehensive discussion of the problems associated with public works programs, see Jeffrey M. Perloff, "Approaches to Evaluating the Local Public Works Program," in U.S. Department of Labor, *Conference Report on Evaluating the 1977 Economic Stimulus Package*, 1978, 21–48.

Chapter 4

Analysis of the Macroeconomic Policies at the Start of the Administration

Forecasts are required in order to formulate macroeconomic policy, but the economic world is not known for behaving according to predictions. All kinds of economic and noneconomic events occur to disrupt the best laid plans and upset the most well-meaning intentions. We have already witnessed how the administration and Congress altered the administration's economic program according to their perceptions of the economic situation facing the nation. Now we will try to understand what actually happened in 1977, after which we can examine the administration's response to reality and what was planned for and achieved in 1978.

THE ECONOMY IN 1977

After the administration withdrew its rebate and business tax credits, the fiscal stimulus for 1977 was reduced by $14 billion. When Congress passed the Tax Reduction and Simplification Act of 1977, the total stimulus turned out to be just over $6 billion ($17 billion for 1978). Included in the tax act were provisions for a flat personal standard deduction, a nonrefundable employment tax credit for 1977 and 1978 that subsidized firms that hired new workers after the firm's wage bill exceeded 2% over the previous year, extensions of some tax provisions enacted in 1975 and 1976 (including a personal income tax credit, the earned income tax credit, and the reduction in corporate tax rates that reduced the rate on income below $50,000), an increase in countercyclical revenue sharing, and some minor changes in the tax code of 1976. In addition, the public works and job-creating programs were approved as submitted.

With these modifications of the administration's original stimulus package, the effects on the economy are shown in Table 4.1. The results are mixed. The 4.9% real growth rate of GNP, while above its long-term rate,

Table 4.1

Selected Economic Series, Calendar Year 1977 (percent change at annual rates except where noted)

| | | 1977 | | | |
	Year	I	II	III	IV
GNP (% change)					
current dollars	10.8	13.2	13.7	10.2	10.7
real (1972 $)	4.9	7.5	6.2	5.1	4.2
Investment (nonres.)	8.8	4.5	1.7	0.9	2.0
fed. gov't expend.	5.1	−0.1	4.2	2.2	0.8
consumption	4.7	1.3	0.4	0.7	1.9
net exports	−33.3	−23.2	−11.3	29.8	−13.1
Price level (% change)					
GNP deflator	5.6	5.3	7.1	4.8	6.2
CPI (seasonally adj.)	6.5	8.8	8.8	5.9	4.6
PPI do	3.1	9.3	10.2	0.4	5.0
Unemployment rate (%)	7.0	7.5	7.1	6.9	6.6
High-employment budget					
(calendar year in bill.)	−24.6	−2.1	−9.0	−35.3	−38.0
Budget totals					
(fiscal year in bill.)					
receipts	$ 356.9				
outlays	401.9				
deficit	−45.0				

Note: Data presented on a national income accounting basis except where noted, that were known at the time, and reported in the *Economic Report of the President, 1978*.

was below the rate hoped for (about 6%) by the administration. In fact, the quarter-by-quarter growth rate shows a steady decline over the year, starting at 7.5% in the first quarter and then falling to 6.2%, 5.1% and 4.2% in subsequent quarters. (See Table 4.1). The first quarter was buoyed by inventory accumulation and consumer spending, and when these sectors returned to more normal levels, the growth rate dropped. Even as government spending picked up in midyear due to the stimulus, it was not sufficient to overcome the fall in consumption, the lackluster performance of fixed investment, and the poor showing of exports. State and local spending that was also supposed to be stimulated by federal programs did not increase until the last quarter of 1977, and for the year by about 1%.

Clearly problems remained. The administration blamed the failure of investment to respond to the uncertainties involved in fluctuating prices, energy problems, exchange rates, and future sales. Capacity utilization in manufacturing rose modestly, and pressure on facilities was not really a factor in explaining investment spending. Exports floundered due to unstable economic conditions abroad, while imports soared because of auto and oil imports. Finally, the high employment budget that measures the effect of government involvement showed a drop in the deficit in the first half of the year, meaning that government was actually contributing to the slowdown rather than stimulating the economy. Later in the year, the spending shortfall was reversed, and for the year, the high employment deficit was about $25 billion, not much different from 1976.

Price level changes were also somewhat of a disappointment. Instead of falling or remaining constant, the CPI rose by nearly two percentage points over the 1976 rate. Energy and food prices can explain the inflation in the first part of the year, but these forces disappeared as the year progressed. In Table 4.1, the bulge in prices can be seen in the first quarter of 1977 in the CPI and in the last quarter in the PPI, and in both instances the administration reacted (too?) quickly to the evidence. The growth of labor productivity fell to about 2% in 1977 (down from 4.1%), while unit labor costs rose by over 12%, and compensation per hour, including fringe benefits, rose by about 9%. If these trends were to continue, further pressures on the price level were inevitable.

Unemployment rates were high for the year at 7% but were falling in the latter part, and by December, the rate was down to 6.4%. Still, the rates for minorities, women, and teenagers remained much higher than for prime males. Meanwhile, the participation rate of all workers was rising to record levels—about 62%. Since the labor force was growing at 2.7% in 1977 along with the growing participation rate, it is obvious that reducing unemployment further would present a severe challenge. In 1977, 3.1 million more people were employed, over 200,000 in public service jobs, but job creation would have to rise by many times that amount to get unemployment down to socially acceptable rates.

With these results in mind, it seems in retrospect that the administration overreacted to the economic conditions in the first quarter of 1977. The economy was experiencing a temporary spurt due to the unusual inventory problems of business and overconsumption by households. Yet when these trends were reversed, as they were expected to do, the economy exhibited too much slack and a below normal recovery from the past recession. The administration, however, discarded these signs in favor of those indicating that inflation was heating up. Yet the major causes of inflation were soon to abate, leaving the underlying rate of inflation (without food and energy prices) rather constant. Still, the administration reduced the stimulus package with an eye toward inflation, and the record shows that no one was pleased with the results of its hedging fiscal policy.

The monetary sphere was not given as much attention as fiscal policy by the administration. Yet money markets were behaving erratically. First, the money supply as defined by M1 (demand deposits plus currency) grew at a faster pace than was targeted by the Federal Reserve. For the year, M1 grew at a rate of over 7.4%, well over the targeted range of 4½ to 6½ set by the Fed for the period. M2, the broader definition of the money supply, grew at a rate of 9.8%, also higher than the targeted range of 7 to 10%, later reduced by half percentage points. In general, the growth of monetary aggregates did not satisfy the aim of monetary policy in 1977, which was to reduce the growth rates of the aggregates in order to reduce inflationary pressures and reverse inflationary expectations. The quarter-to-quarter growth rates often exceeded the rates of growth necessary to achieve the aim of gradually reducing the increases in the money supply to combat inflation.[1]

Despite the "easy" money, interest rates rose sharply over the course of the year with, for example, three-month treasury bills rising from 4.6% in January to 6.1% in December (nearly a one-third increase, and far exceeding the administration's forecast of 4.6% made in April). The federal funds rate rose from 4.6 to 6.6% in the same period. The federal funds rate was above its target for most of the year, forcing the Fed to revise its target rate closer to the actual rate. Long-term rates were more stable, making the yield curve somewhat flatter. The stock market reacted to these rising interest rates by dropping 16% in the Dow-Jones industrial averages over the year.

Finally, there were disturbing signs for the future of monetary policy that were observed in the recovery from the recent recession. The velocity of money, GNP/M1, rose dramatically in 1976 and early 1977 despite the stability of interest rates. The rise was blamed on institutional changes, interest-bearing checking accounts, better money management techniques, and credit cards, but whatever the cause, if the trend continued there would be trouble ahead in controlling the money supply. Shifts in the demand for money would make it more difficult for the Fed to control monetary aggregates. With an unstable velocity of money, rising interest rates could indicate too much money in the system, or not enough, and devising the proper policy would become complicated.[2]

In view of these developments, it is useful to inquire how the administration felt about the monetary policy it was receiving. Was it receiving what it wanted from the monetary authorities, or was it disappointed? The administration certainly took note of the increase in the federal funds rate and worried about the future of interest rates. Also noted was growth of monetary aggregates and the problems that changes in the velocity were causing. Yet, the administration was remarkably sanguine about the monetary policy it was receiving and not terribly concerned about the prospects for 1978. According to Schultze, the administration wanted an accommodating monetary policy in the beginning presumably to avoid conflicts with its fiscal policy. Was this an accommodating monetary policy? If it was, would the excessive monetary growth lead to inflation and thwart its fiscal plans? If not, why did the administration not protest? There were signs that the administration recognized the increasing difficulties of the Fed in controlling monetary conditions, but it might have voiced its concerns more forcefully early in the game as it was forced to do later on.

In summary, the administration acknowledged that the nation had a long way to go to achieve its economic goals. The growth rate was too low, the unemployment rate was too high, capacity utilization was too low, and prices were rising too fast.[3] It did not acknowledge that its own timidity might have added to the difficulty of reaching its goals. Instead, it proposed a new stimulus package designed to boost the economy, thus confirming its mistaken reverses in policy earlier in the year.

PROSPECTS FOR 1978

The increase in fiscal stimulus provided by public works and public employment was considered to be sufficient to overcome the decrease in spending by households on consumption and housing. The outlook for 1978 was for sustained improvement in the economy, but over the longer term, there appeared to be grounds for concern. Higher payroll taxes were slated to begin, and along with inflation and income growth, the total tax bill was expected to rise at the very time that government expenditures would be declining. The higher taxes and diminishing expenditures would act as a drag on the economy and prevent the movement toward the administration's goals. Thus, the outlook for 1978 was not encouraging, and additional stimulus was required to offset the depressing effects of government.

Accordingly, the administration proposed another round of tax reductions. For individuals, the major change would be a tax reduction of $17 billion that would be achieved if the $750 personal exemption and the general tax credit of $35 were replaced by a $240 per capita credit. This proposal would benefit lower- and middle-income taxpayers, since the previous personal exemption benefited higher-income groups more; a tax credit would benefit all families equally. Along with this revision, tax rates would be cut across the board: The first bracket would be reduced to 12% (from 14%), and the top bracket reduced to 68% (from 70%). The rate reductions were again designed to benefit lower-middle-class households. These changes were needed quickly and were proposed to become effective on October 1, 1978.

In addition to these tax cuts, a series of tax reform issues were proposed to make the tax system simpler and fairer. Some personal deductions were eliminated (state and local taxes), some were limited (medical, casualty, capital gains), and new taxes were imposed on unemployment compensation for higher-income recipients.

For corporations, a $6 billion tax reduction was proposed in the form of a permanent rate cut of about four percentage points and a permanent investment tax credit of 10% that was extended to structures. Reform measures would have limited depreciation allowances, curtailed entertainment expenses, eliminated the subsidy for exports (DISC) and the deferral of U.S. taxes of foreign subsidiaries, and changed the taxation of financial institutions. Changes in the tax treatment of municipal bonds was also suggested in a way that would have continued the subsidy to state and local governments but would have avoided giving the wealthy another avenue to escape taxes. Finally, a $2 billion cut in the federal unemployment insurance tax rate from 0.7 to 0.5% effective January 1, 1979, was proposed, along with the repeal of the 4% telephone excise tax effective October 1, 1978.

For 1978, the proposed tax reductions would offset the scheduled increases in Social Security taxes and unemployment insurance, but in calendar years 1979 and 1980, the reductions would exceed the tax increases by some $13 billion. Without spelling out all these proposed changes to taxation, it is clear that the administration was worried that the expansion would run out of steam in the latter part of 1978 and certainly in 1979 without further stimulative actions of government; the private sector needed help.

If the administration's plans were ratified by Congress, the forecasts for the economy in 1978 included a 4½ to 5% increase in real output, an unemployment rate of 6 to 6¼%, an increase in the CPI of 5¾ to 6¼%, and an increase in real fixed investment of 7 to 8%. Housing and net exports were not expected to change significantly nor add to the expansion.

INFLATION PROPOSAL

In 1978, the administration became more concerned with inflation as the major problem facing the U.S. economy. It had already tempered its stimulus policies in 1977, but no progress had been made in the fight against inflation. The inflation rate had apparently stabilized at around 8%, with the underlying rate (excluding food and energy) in the 6 to 7% range. The administration noted that inflation was not accelerating nor was it decelerating. Left alone, the inflation rate would likely continue until the next shock and then be bumped upward.

Thus, there was a need to decelerate inflation and upset the stability by positive action. Accordingly, the administration considered several options to decelerate inflation.[4] It rejected outright controls, claiming that they work only in emergencies; rejected incentive income policies such as TIP (taxed-based income policies wherein the federal government would determine a wage standard and firms and workers would either be penalized for not adhering to it or rewarded for so doing, all through additional or reduced taxes)[5] as being risky and little understood; and by the process of elimination accepted the remaining option—voluntary controls.

The Council on Wage and Price Stability, headed by Barry Bosworth, planned to meet with representatives of labor and industry (presumably those who had received the largest wage and price increases in the recent past) in order to establish the proper means to achieve deceleration that were appropriate in various circumstances. Obviously, circumstances vary by industry, product, and location, and no one standard was deemed possible. This lack of a standard differentiated this type of voluntary program from the wage and price guideposts in the 1960s. Instead, each company was asked to limit its 1978 wage and price increases below the average of the past two years. This vague standard was not very effective from the start, and the real question is why anyone thought it would be.

So in October, the administration switched to a numerical standard and, after some discussion, reached a firm standard in December. Briefly, it called for limiting pay and fringe benefit increases to 7%, and limiting price increases over the next year and one-half to a percentage point below the average annual rate of price increases in the period 1976–77. With voluntary standards, participants who are willing to cooperate may hesitate to do so because they are uncertain that others will follow their example. If others fail to comply with the standards, prices may rise (for this as well as any other reason) and penalize those who did comply. Accordingly, the administration created a wage insurance scheme that guaranteed workers who did comply a tax credit if the rate of inflation exceeded 7%. The tax credit would be calculated as the difference between the CPI and the 7% standard, with a maximum of 3%, and would be applied to the first $20,000 of income. Thus, workers would be protected from inflation as long as the CPI was 10% or below. If inflation rose over 10%, the worker would, of course, lose. The estimated budgetary cost would be $5 billion for each percentage point above 7%.[6]

REVISIONS OF THE BUDGET

On April 11, 1978, Carter signaled the administration's increasing concern for the vexing problem of inflation when he said, "It now has become embedded in the very tissue of our economy. It has resisted the most severe recession in a generation. It persists because all of us—business and labor, farmers and consumers—are caught on a treadmill that none can stop alone. . . . No act of Congress, no program of our government, no order of my own can bring out the quality that we need: to change from the preoccupation with self that can cripple our national will, to a willingness to acknowledge and to sacrifice for the common good." This echoed the southern brand of populism that Carter espoused and that was registered in his view of fiscal conservatism.

The administration was in a difficult situation because it did not want to solve the problem of inflation by creating another recession, while unemployment was still relatively high; it did not want direct controls to do the job for fear of bureaucracies; and it did not want to surrender to energy blackmails while encouraging conservation. In a period when the trade-off between inflation and unemployment was beginning to favor inflation with small gains for employment, making macroeconomic policy was neither easy nor entertaining.

In May 1978, however, the administration acted. It decided to scale back its tax proposals by $5 billion in the face of rapid inflation, and it lowered its goals for economic growth. The tax stimulus was reduced to $20 billion and postponed to January 1, 1979. It included tax cuts of $14 billion for individuals, mainly by lowering tax rates and increasing the personal exemption from $750 to $1,000, and a $6 billion tax cut for business, mainly by decreasing tax rates. The capital gains tax was also reduced. What prompted these reversals?

In April, the producer price index was increasing at an annual rate of over 15%, while the CPI was increasing at about 11%. Food prices alone were increasing at a rate of nearly 20% on an annual basis, and energy was not far behind at about 12%. Even the underlying rate, excluding these items, was rising at an alarming rate at just under 10%. Meanwhile, the unemployment rate was stable or declining slightly to 6.1%, and the capacity utilization rate was climbing by nearly two percentage points to 84%. With productivity continuing to fall, unit labor costs shot up by 15% in the first quarter of 1978 and showed no signs of abating. In short, there were clearly inflationary pressures on the economy that the administration could not ignore.

The target rate of growth of real GNP was lowered to 4% for both 1978 and 1979, down from the 4.5 to 5% originally suggested. Federal outlays were reduced by $4.5 billion, and with the reduction in tax cuts, the deficit was reduced accordingly by $11 billion for fiscal 1978.[7] The administration was clearly bent on reducing government's contribution to the difficulties of the economy as its fiscal policy was becoming more restrictive.

THE ECONOMY IN 1978

The results for 1978 were mixed, reflecting once again the peculiar economic circumstances of the late 1970s. (See Table 4.2.) Unemployment fell to 5.8% at year's end, the lowest rate since 1974. But real economic growth fell to 3.9% for the year, the lowest growth rate in the recovery period. Growth was uneven over the course of the year, being negative in the first quarter at −.1%, strongly positive in the second at 8.7%, slowing to 2.6% in the third quarter, and recovering to 6.1% in the last quarter. Meanwhile, prices continued to accelerate as the CPI increased sharply to 7.7%, up 1.2 percentage points over 1977 (2.4 percentage points from the seasonally unadjusted series from December to December); producer prices also accelerated to 7.8%, up 1.8 percentage points over 1977 (2.6 percentage points from December to December); and the GNP price index rose to 7.4%, up 1.2 percentage points over 1977.

The trends in these key economic indicators were serious enough to cause the administration to retreat from an activist fiscal policy toward more constraint. As already mentioned, it reduced the size of its tax cuts in the face of mounting inflation. Congress went along with the revision and passed the $20 billion tax package. Again, federal government spending increased at a slower rate from the previous year and actually experienced a shortfall in outlays of some $12 billion from the January budget estimates. Since inflation had become the major concern of the administration, no attempt was made to remedy the slower growth of government spending. The shortfall in spending was widely distributed over nondefense items, particularly in the expenditures for additions to the strategic oil reserves.[8] The high employment budget deficit fell to −$12.9 billion in 1978, down from −$24.6 billion in 1977.

Table 4.2

Selected Economic Series, Calendar Year 1978 (percent change at annual rates except where noted)

		1978			
	Year	I	II	III	IV
GNP (% change)					
current dollars	11.6	7.1	20.6	9.6	14.7
real (1972 $)	3.9	−0.1	8.7	2.6	6.1
Investment (nonres.)	7.8	1.0	5.0	0.9	1.3
fed. gov't expend.	−1.1	−2.3	−4.1	3.4	2.9
consumption	3.9	−0.4	1.5	1.0	1.7
net exports	−9.5	−6.5	289.7	−18.6	19.6
Price level (% change)					
GNP deflator	7.4	7.2	11.0	6.9	8.1
CPI (seasonally adj.)	7.7	7.1	10.9	9.7	8.4
PPI do	7.8	−19.2	10.7	7.0	10.1
Unemployment rate (%)	6.0	6.2	6.0	6.0	5.8
High-employment budget					
(calendar year in bill.)	−12.9	−29.5	−9.0	−7.9	−5.4
Budget totals					
(fiscal year in bill.)					
receipts	$ 401.9				
outlays	450.8				
deficit	−48.8				

Source: Economic Report of the President, 1979.

Monetary policy was erratic over the course of the year, as monetary aggregates grew at an uneven pace. The Federal Open Market Committee (FOMC) operating ranges for the growth of monetary aggregates were set at 4 to 6% for M1 and 6½ to 9% for M2.[9] In the first quarter of 1978, the growth of monetary aggregates was within the ranges set. In the second quarter, however, the growth of M1 (at 9.9%) accelerated and far exceeded the set ranges; M2 was generally within its range. In the third quarter, the growth of the aggregates continued strong, but in the last quarter, there were significant reductions in both monetary aggregates, with M1 falling to near zero growth and M2 falling to 4.5%, about half its former rate.

Partly as a result of these trends, interest rates rose rapidly in 1978. Three-month treasury bills, for instance, rose from 6.5% in January to 9.1% in December, with the increasing trend more pronounced in the latter half of the year. Over the same time period, mortgage interest rates rose from 9.2% to 10.0%; the prime rate rose from around 8% to 11.5%, and the federal funds rate rose from 6.7 to 10.0%. Moreover, in the last quarter of 1978, short-term rates rose above long-term rates, as the yield curve became inverted. Clearly, monetary policy was also moving toward restraint as the year progressed. For the next year, the growth of monetary aggregates was expected to slow with the growth of M1 expected to be in the 2 to 6% range and M2 in the 6½ to 9% range.

The Fed was keeping one eye on inflation, with concern for how its actions would affect economic growth, and the other eye on the foreign exchange value of the dollar. The trade-weighted value of the dollar had declined sharply in October, and the Fed was anxious to increase the value of the dollar by monetary restraint.[10]

Two institutional changes promised to complicate the conduct of monetary policy in the future. Banks and nonbank thrift institutions were allowed to issue six-month money market certificates that paid higher interest rates. While this may have slowed the process of disintermediation, where banks that have interest rate ceilings lose funds to other financial institutions, it would soon make the definition and control of money more difficult. Mortgage funds were less affected when this provision was introduced in June than would have been anticipated from past experience.

The other innovation was the permission given to banks to make automatic withdrawals for their customers from savings to checking accounts (ATS). This procedure would certainly complicate the definition of money, particularly M2, and could confuse the monetary authorities in their efforts to control monetary aggregates. Both of these innovations caused the Federal Reserve Board to react cautiously until their effects could be observed.

It appeared that the administration welcomed the monetary restraint of the Fed. Indeed Charles Schultze revealed that he and Secretary Blumenthal had pressured the Fed (by leaking to the press) to tighten up at the end of 1978.[11] The administration also shared the concern for the falling dollar value in international trade. Thus, it appeared that the administration was getting the monetary policy it wanted and had no real conflict with the monetary authorities.

PORTENTS FOR THE FUTURE

Since inflation was being acknowledged as the most important problem facing the nation, a closer look at it may be helpful before turning to the

Table 4.3
Inflation Components and Wage Costs, 1976–78 (percent change)

	1976	1977	1978
Consumer Prices			
All Items	4.8	6.8	9.0
Food	0.6	8.0	11.8
Energy	7.2	9.5	6.3
All items less food and energy	6.1	6.4	8.5
Producer Prices			
All finished goods	3.3	6.6	9.1
All finished goods less food	5.5	6.6	8.3
Private Nonfarm Business			
Compensation per hour	8.4	8.1	9.4
Real hourly earnings	1.3	1.0	0.6
Output per hour	3.5	1.3	0.6
Unit labor costs	4.7	6.7	8.8
Capacity utilization rate- mfg. (%)			
Federal Reserve Index	80.2	82.4	84.2
Last quarter			85.7
Wharton Series	87.4	90.1	92.8
Last quarter			94.8

Source: Economic Report of the President, 1979 and 1980.

outlook for 1979. Table 4.3 shows the situation facing the administration in January 1979 as it was deciding how to respond to the highly visible and politically damaging problem of inflation.

The price trends in Table 4.3 clearly reveal the acceleration of inflation. As the administration noted, the most worrisome problem was that the underlying rate of inflation, excluding food and energy prices, was increasing rapidly. The high underlying rate of inflation, if it continued, would present a real challenge to policymakers. Even if they could discover the cause of it, formulating policy without severe disruption to the economy would be a test. Food and energy prices presented problems, of course, but often not much can be done about them as far as policy is concerned. They can, however, result in reductions in the living standards of income recipients who try to protect their past consumption habits by demanding more income. Wage earners demand higher wages to try to recover the loss in real income, as do other income recipients, and many begin to build in future inflation in their contracts.

The causes for the increase in the underlying inflation rate can only be tentatively identified. Labor markets were not overly tight in 1978, but the unemployment rate was moving down faster than expected, and the composition of the labor force was changing, making past definitions of tightness somewhat suspect. Another reason can be found in the dismal performance of labor productivity. In 1978, the growth rate of labor productivity was almost nonexistent. The causes of this slow growth were not obvious but probably included the slow growth in investment, the shifts in the age-sex composition of the labor force, increased regulations on business, and the slowdown in research and development expenditures.[12] But compensation per hour for union and nonunion workers was rising rapidly and driving up per unit labor costs. From the point of view of workers, however, their real average hourly earnings were barely increasing and their ability to keep up with inflation was a struggle.

Capacity usage in manufacturing was also approaching the degree of usage that would signal pressure on existing facilities and perhaps short-run price increases before additional capacity could be installed. So both labor and capital were either beginning to experience demand pressures or were about to; at least the administration thought so.[13]

Another contributor to inflation was the depreciation of the dollar. The dollar fell in value by about 9% against the currencies of our trading partners. This decline raised the prices of imports and contributed to the inflation rate by about .5% per year at a dollar depreciation rate of 10%. Imports continued, however, but the outlook was uncertain for the coming years if the prices of imported goods continued to rise. The decline in the value of the dollar started in 1977 and, after a period of stability, declined further in the summer of 1978. In September and October, the fall was pronounced, and the Fed became alarmed at the effect on inflation should the trend continue. Apparently the international community had decided that inflation in the United States was not going to moderate, and the administration's policies were ineffective or inefficient. Accordingly, the Federal Reserve raised the discount rate a full percentage point (to 9½%) and imposed a 2 percent supplementary reserve requirement on large time deposits. In addition, along with Germany, Japan, and Switzerland, the United States contributed $30 billion to the fund to prop up the dollar. Currency markets responded favorably to the move and the dollar appreciated slowly, but failed to return to pre-1977 levels and would not do so in Carter's term. Some currency speculation might have moderated, but faith in the U.S. macroeconomic policy was far from convincing; the administration, however, blamed the entire episode on the breakdown of exchange markets.[14]

OTHER DEVELOPMENTS

Whatever the source, the public was becoming frustrated over the rate of inflation and unhappy with the politicians entrusted to deal with it and the other economic problems that were also surfacing. One manifestation of frustration was the anger that developed over the rising tax burden which manifested itself in the tax revolt that started in California with proposition 13. In this case, rising housing prices and rising property taxes furnished the justification for limiting the amount of property taxes that Californians would have to pay. Whatever the merits of the case, the movement was to spread to other states as well, but the real message was that the public was growing tired of paying higher taxes.

Another example of this retreat from taxation was the proposal of Rep. Jack Kemp (R, NY) and Sen. William Roth (R, Del) to reduce federal taxes drastically—by about 30%—in order to get the economy moving again. Persuaded that high taxes discourage incentives and productivity, the Kemp-Roth tax bill envisioned a spurt of economic activity that would stimulate the economy without damaging fiscal responsibility. In other words, the tax reductions would not increase the deficit very much, if at all, because the increase in economic activity would result in a large feedback of revenues. The proposal received a great deal of attention at the time and was discussed and examined at length by the administration and other organizations.[15] Most observers thought it was too extreme and would not result in the advertised benefits. Later, of course, it would be adopted by the Reagan administration in 1981.

Finally, Congress passed the Humphrey-Hawkins bill that established the commitment to full employment without inflation. It not only established priorities, but it set target dates by which the numerical targets were to be achieved. Full employment was established as the most important goal and was set at 3% by five years after passage of the act in October 1978. Price stability, defined as 3% in the CPI, was also to be achieved by that time, and the act actually set out policies that could be followed to achieve both full employment and price stability. Both the executive and monetary branches were expected to explain their progress to Congress in reaching these goals or state why they could not be achieved. This last escape clause, and numerous qualifications in the act, made it just another declaration of principle by Congress without sanctions if ignored. In reality, the act was mainly a final tribute to the dying Senator Humphrey who had espoused an active government to reach full employment using whatever means available, including real government planning. As a means to establish some general guidelines for policymakers, it might have had some usefulness, but for practical purposes, it was not well designed and was generally ignored.

OUTLOOK FOR 1979

Everyone was expecting a recession in 1979. This was the administration's judgment: "A reduction in economic growth from the rate of the last 2 years is *needed* both because idle labor and capital resources have been cut considerably and because inflation has accelerated. The task for aggregate demand policies will be to provide a climate in which inflationary pressures can begin moderating, but to avoid restraint so severe as to generate a recession."[16] [emphasis added] Thus, there were no new tax cut proposals, and government spending was slated to rise by a small real increase, about 1%. The budget deficit for fiscal year 1979 was thought to be about –$37.4 billion, down from the –$48.8 billion in 1978. Inflation concerns clearly were driving fiscal policy, as price stability took precedence over the full employment goal.

The tax cut of 1978 was expected to be effective in the first half of 1979, but would tail off in the second half. Thus, the growth of real GNP would fall from the previous year to around 2 to 2¼%. All sectors of aggregate demand were expected to decline, with consumption falling to an increase of only 2%, nonresidential investment to about 4+%, and housing to about –9%. The housing market collapse was a result of the forecasted high interest rates, since the Federal Reserve was expected to continue its tight monetary policy.

The growth of labor productivity was anticipated to be about the same as the previous year—the low 0.5%. This low growth rate would increase compensation per hour to over 8%, while leaving the unemployment rate about 6%.

ANALYSIS OF THE MACROECONOMIC POLICIES OF 1978

Once again in 1978, the administration vacillated in its economic policies. The confusion and uncertainty generated in the minds of the public can only be guessed at. Consider that the administration asked for tax reductions to stimulate the economy (and offset bracket creep in the tax collections), while at the same time it was considering inflation-fighting proposals. (The fact that the tax cut was reduced and postponed to January 1979 only added to the confusion). Clearly, the administration wanted to achieve two goals simultaneously that may well have been mutually exclusive. It wanted to continue the stimulation of the economy, while complaining of possible inflationary demand pressures as the labor market tightened and capacity utilization neared critical rates.

The conflicting goals were baffling, but when the administration trimmed its stimulus package and turned to fighting inflation, the bewilderment led to suspicion that the administration did not know what it was doing. While it was clear that the administration was changing its primary goal to fighting inflation, which was applauded by many, equally evident were its unclear goals; its lack of commitment to any one goal subjected the administration to the charges of indecisiveness and ineptitude.

Of course, the administration again risked political capital by supporters, and opponents as well, by appearing irresolute. Carter did not care about playing political games at this stage and preferred to do what was right without regard to political repercussions. Still, there are limits to sudden shifts in policy, for what is the "right" thing to do cannot shift so quickly; flexibility in policy-making is desirable to some extent, but flexibility used too frequently may yield the opposite perception—incompetence.

The administration was shifting its goals and responding to inflationary pressures brought on by accelerating food prices, rising home prices, supply bottlenecks in construction, and the continuing decline in the growth of labor productivity (0.8% in 1978). Yet it is not clear that fiscal and monetary restraint would significantly affect these sectors directly. Reductions in federal government purchases in nondefense areas, reductions in the tax stimulus proposal, and the repeated shortfall in federal expenditures added to fiscal restraint, and monetary policy did likewise, responding in part to the depreciating dollar and in part to fight inflation. Higher interest rates could have restrained the housing market, except that mortgage markets were much less affected this time due to the introduction of money market certificates that shielded the money market from the shortage in the availability of funds, and to some extent higher mortgage rates.[17]

Furthermore, Otto Eckstein's analysis using the Data Resources model revealed that the demand pressures in labor and capital markets were not contributing to overall inflation and apparently were no cause for concern.[18] The costs of labor and capital were indeed rising, giving the core inflation rate of 7.8%, but the administration's anti-inflationary policies would not directly affect the core rate significantly in the short run. Schultze, in subsequent testimony, expressed the view that the stimulus in this period *added* to inflation at a rate of about ½ to 1%, and admitted that the economy continually showed more strength than anticipated.[19]

Evidently the rate of inflation was becoming a problem for the administration, and some response had to be made. It is not clear, however, whether a better short-run response was available. There were not many tools available to fashion a better short-run anti-inflation program. At least this was the claim.

Thus, it is not surprising to find the administration resorting to voluntary wage and price controls. Yet considering the experience with voluntary controls during the Kennedy administration, and the disillusionment with direct controls during the Nixon administration, it is puzzling in retrospect as to why the administration made this move. Having retreated from a tax-based incomes policy (TIP) as an anti-inflationary measure, why did the administration choose voluntary controls instead? Obviously, it was an easy way out to show concern about inflation without antagonizing anyone and thus give the appearance of doing something without the necessity for bureaucratic controls, congressional approval, or costly political battles. Yet there really is a cost should the policy fail to achieve the desired results. Credibility once lost is difficult to regain.

At best, voluntary controls would be minimally effective as was the case with the Kennedy experiment. Economic agents act in their own self-interest and are not accustomed to acting in the national interest, are very wary of compliance by the next fellow, and hence hesitant to comply themselves. Why risk the danger of failure in such a program? Perhaps the voluntary nature of the system appealed to the president and conformed to his personal philosophy. As a fiscal conservative, he would have been eager to fight inflation, especially through voluntary action of the community. Even TIP had some appeal for him.

But the apparent simplicity of voluntary controls could run into uncontrollable or unusual events, as happened in the Carter years, such as the oil price increases, which made controls rapidly obsolete. Any degree of compliance that occurred under these circumstances would be extraordinary. While the lack of cooperation by economic agents would be understandable, the result would make the idea of voluntary controls appear ridiculous. If voluntary controls were not effective, as they turned out to be, more is lost than just the sacrifice of the program. The more the administration officials tried to justify the controls program, the more derisive were the criticisms. Moreover, the administration's other economic policies would suffer as well, as people began to lump this unfortunate experience with all other economic initiatives.

We will return to these issues again, but before attempting a general critique of the administration's macro policies for the first half of its tenure, we will review the economic policies of the second half of Carter's term. A better picture of the overall macroeconomic policies and how the first and second halves are related is possible if the entire record has been discussed.

NOTES

1. See "Monetary Policy and Open Market Operations in 1977," *Federal Reserve Bulletin* (April 1978), 265–78; and Richard W. Lang, "The Federal Open Market Committee in 1977," Federal Reserve Bank of St. Louis, *Review* (March 1978), 2–21.

2. The issue is important in this period but would become more so in the 1980s and call into question the ability of the Fed to control monetary conditions. For more on this period, see *The Economic Report of the President, 1978*, 61–63.

3. Ibid., 60–61.

4. See the testimony of Barry P. Bosworth in U.S. Senate, Committee on the Budget, *First Concurrent Resolution on the Budget—Fiscal Year 1979*, 95th Congress, 2nd session, February 22, 1979, 132–153.

5. For more complete explanations of TIP see, the *Economic Report of the President, 1978*, 150–52; and David C. Colander (ed.), *Solutions to Inflation* (New York: Harcourt Brace Jovanovich, 1979).

6. See the *Economic Report of the President, 1979*, 80–85.

7. See the testimony of Charles L. Schultze in U.S. House of Representatives, Committee on the Budget, *Economic Outlook at Mid-Summer*, 95th Congress, 2nd session, July 12, 1978, 83–90. Space prohibits the inclusion of the testimony of other administration officials and outside economists. For those interested, see also U.S. Senate, Committee on the Budget, *Second Concurrent Resolution on the Budget—Fiscal Year 1979*, 95th Congress, 2nd session, July 1978.

8. These and other data in this section are from the *Economic Report of the President, 1979*.

9. These are long-term ranges that were frequently adjusted by inserting short-term ranges of two-month durations. The Fed continued to stress, however, that long-term ranges were paramount and should be adequate.

10. See the "Record of Policy Actions of the Federal Open Market Committee," *Federal Reserve Bulletin* (January 1979), 51–61; also Richard W. Lang, "The FOMC in 1978: Clarifying the Role of the Aggregates," in Federal Reserve Bank of St. Louis, *Review* (March 1979), 2–24.

11. From an interview quoted in Erwin C. Hargrove and Samuel A. Morley, *The President and the Council of Economic Advisers* (Boulder, Colo.: Westview Press, 1984), 485.

12. For an early discussion of the productivity slowdown, see Edward P. Denison, "Explanations of Declining Productivity Growth," in U.S. Department of Commerce, *Survey of Current Business* (August 1979), 1–21.

13. See the *Economic Report of the President, 1979*, 58–61, for capacity pressures, and pp. 63–65 for labor.

14. For the administration's view of these events, see *The Economic Report of the President, 1979*, 154–159.

15. See, for example, Arthur B. Laffer and Jan P. Seymour, *The Economics of the Tax Revolt* (New York: Harcourt Brace Jovanovich, 1979); and Congressional Budget Office, *An Analysis of the Roth-Kemp Tax Cut Proposal*, 1978.

16. *Economic Report of the President, 1979*, 92.

17. Ibid., 51.

18. Otto Eckstein, *Core Inflation* (Englewood Cliffs, N.J.: Prentice-Hall, 1981), 33. A discussion of the elements of core inflation is too complex to analyze in detail, and all that is inferred in the text is that demand pressures did not appear critical at the time.

19. Schultze interview in Hargrove and Morley, *The President and the CEA*, 483.

Chapter 5

The National Economy in the Second Half of the Administration, 1979–1980

The much heralded 1979 recession did not arrive as predicted. 1979 was not a particularly good year—but the economic conditions that normally would have produced a recession did not do so in this strange period. Consider only a few examples: the Federal Reserve moved toward monetary restraint; real government expenditures remained virtually constant, while taxes increased due to inflation; inflation rates rose sharply; confidence in the economy fell for households and business; real wages fell sharply; and the growth of labor productivity continued to fall. These and other problems should have been sufficient to cause the economy to decline; instead it merely stumbled along in stagnation. Still, the disturbing signs at the end of 1979 caused nearly everyone, in and out of government, to forecast a recession in 1980.

The administration identified three possible reasons for the failure of the recession to appear in the face of these shocks to the economy: First, consumers adjusted to continued inflation by reducing saving and consuming. Inflationary expectations caused consumers to borrow to make immediate purchases, rather than wait for prices to increase further. Second, monetary restraint no longer limited the availability of credit as it once did, since new banking rules, new monetary instruments, and new laws that eliminated usury provisions did not restrict aggregate demand as abruptly as before. Third, the economy was not as imbalanced in terms of inventories and sales as often happened in the past to bring about recessions.[1] We can evaluate these points later when more data have been introduced, but for now, let us set aside these explanations and review the actual results for 1979 and the early predictions and results for 1980.

Table 5.1 reveals that real GNP growth of 2.3% for 1979 was about in line with the administration's predictions. However, the percent change from a year earlier masks the developments over the course of 1979. GNP

Table 5.1

Selected Economic Series, Calendar Year 1979 (percent change at annual rates except where noted)

		1979			
	Year	I	II	III	IV
GNP (% change)					
current dollars	11.3	10.6	6.7	11.9	10.3
real (1972 $)	2.3	1.1	−2.3	3.1	1.4
Investment (nonres.)	5.8	1.2	−0.2	2.6	−1.8
fed. gov't expend.	0.6	1.8	−3.0	−0.7	3.1
consumption	2.6	0.2	−0.7	1.2	1.0
net exports	53.3	31.8	−22.4	52.3	3.0
Price level (% change)					
GNP deflator	8.8	9.3	9.3	8.5	8.7
CPI (seasonally adj.)	11.3	10.5	14.3	13.9	12.2
PPI do	10.9	13.6	10.5	10.7	15.0
Unemployment rate (%)	5.8	5.7	5.8	5.8	5.9
Money Growth (% at annual rates)					
M1	5.5	−1.3	8.1	9.7	5.0
target range		1.5–4.5	same	same	3.0–6.0
M2	8.3	2.8	8.8	11.9	8.9
target range		5.0–8.0	same	same	same
High-employment budget (bill. at annual rate)	9.8	−0.4	14.3	11.5	13.8
Budget totals (fiscal year in bill.)					
receipts	$ 465.9				
outlays	493.6				
deficit	−27.7				

Source: Economic Report of the President, 1980 and Federal Reserve *Bulletin*, January 1980, 112–113.

growth rose slightly in the first quarter, turned negative in the second quarter, rebounded in the third quarter, and then fell back to slow growth in the final quarter. If the quarterly growth rates are averaged over the year, the growth turns out to be about 0.8%, far below what the administration hoped to achieve. Still, at the close of the year, no recession was evident, but again, everyone expected one in 1980.

It is easy to see why. Nearly all sectors of aggregate demand were falling, monetary policy turned restrictive, and the energy problem threatened to get worse. Real government spending was virtually constant, while tax receipts were pushed up due to inflation; the result was a budget deficit that was $10 billion less than anticipated. The high employment budget, in fact moved from a deficit of $11 billion in 1978 to a surplus of nearly $10 billion in 1979. Clearly, fiscal policy was restrictive.

In the private sector, real nonresidential investment fell dramatically, as did investment in the residential sector. Over the four quarters of 1979, real nonresidential investment fell to under 2%, and for the year was 5.8%, down from the 8.4% increase in 1978. New housing starts fell by 14% and personal consumption expenditures also fell (particularly in the second quarter) to 2.6% for the year, down from 4.5% in 1978. Households were apparently forced to cut back due to rising energy costs. Only net exports rose as the dollar continued to depreciate and farm exports rose. The economy seemed to be sagging, just poised to drop off into serious trouble.

The major concern in this stagnation was, of course, inflation, caused primarily by oil supply price shocks and potential shortages. Consumer prices were rising at a rate over 11%, with energy prices rising at over 25%, and housing costs at over 12%. Under these circumstances, it is understandable why aggregate demand was falling; not only were current plans upset by rapid inflation, but future plans were waylaid by the uncertainty created by continuing energy problems. Consider that energy prices were rising at over 62% in the producer price index, a forerunner of price changes that will occur later at the consumer level. Foreign policy setbacks with Iran only served to heighten fears of energy shortages and even greater price shocks in the future. (Energy problems are discussed in more detail in a later chapter.)

Driven by inflationary concerns, the Federal Reserve moved toward further restraint. It established target ranges for monetary growth that were below those existing. For M1, the range was 1.5 to 4.5%; for M2, the range was 5 to 8%. In the first quarter, the growth of M1 was negative, and M2 rose slightly by 2.8%. (See Table 5.1.) During the next two quarters, however, the rate of growth of monetary aggregates was above the established targets, and the Fed's efforts to combat inflation through slowing monetary growth seemed to be thwarted by the institutional changes discussed earlier.[2] As inflation soared, the velocity of money was also misbehaving: The velocity growth of M1 soared to 11.6% (at annual rates) in the first quarter, fell to –1.5% in the second, before returning gradually to 4.8% in the last quarter. For the year, the velocity of M1 was 4.2%, down from 5.8% in 1978, a 27% reduction. Apparently, money market developments were upsetting the normal relations between the growth of monetary aggregates and the federal funds rate that was used to control credit conditions until the last quarter of 1979. New instruments in the money market were also disturbing past relations.

Whatever the cause, the Fed finally gave up trying to manage monetary conditions as it had in the past and turned to controlling bank reserves directly in order to control the money supply, instead of indirectly through the federal funds rate. In October, it adopted the monetarist prescription and Chairman Paul Volker announced that the Fed would change its operating procedures; it would control the growth of monetary aggregates and let the federal funds rate (and hence all interest rates) vary freely. As a result, the growth rates of M1 and M2 fell within the ranges set by the Fed, and these were meant to be restrictive; it also raised the discount rate to 12% to signal its intent to fight inflation. Interest rates, accordingly, rose quickly. Three-month treasury bills rose from 10.1% in September to 12% in December; over the same period, the prime rate rose from 13.5% to 15.5%, and the federal funds rate rose from 11.4% to 13.8%. These sharp interest rate increases only added to the concerns of business firms and all other borrowers already battered by inflation and uncertainty.

The surprise of this period was in the unemployment statistics. The unemployment rate remained about 5.8% during the year as the economy created over 2 million new jobs and even as the labor market participation rate increased. The good news was tempered, however, by developments on the productivity front. The growth in the productivity of labor turned negative in 1979, falling to −1.2%. Since compensation per hour was increasing at a rate of 8.9%, it is clear that labor costs were bound to rise by over 10%. Added to this difficulty was the disturbing fact that once again real wages were falling by about 3% and bound to cause labor unrest in the future. Since consumer prices were rising by over 11% and money wages by about 8%, the decline in real wages was evident. Moreover, since the rise in consumer prices was caused largely by energy prices and housing costs, workers were keenly aware that their real incomes were shrinking; the effects on household budgets was immediate and highly visible.

Finally, a look at the voluntary wage and price standards under the conditions outlined above would be interesting. Recall that the wage standard was set at 7% for the year. Since the adjusted hourly earnings index (adjusted for overtime and interindustry employment shifts) rose by about 8%, it is clear that the standard was exceeded, more by union than nonunion workers. Nevertheless, the administration claimed at least a partial victory in that "the President's program aided in keeping wage rates from accelerating. Estimates . . . developed by the Council as well as others, suggest that wage increases during the first program year were about 1 to 1½ percentage points lower than would be expected."[3]

No doubt there were many dissenters from this sanguine view, but even if correct, an inflation rate of 11% (13% from December to December), if expected to continue, would surely wreck such a voluntary program. Workers were not likely to volunteer to be inflation fighters in the face of such declines in their real wages. In fact, organized labor was opposed to the pay guidelines from the beginning. The AFL-CIO, led by George Meany, instructed the unions to ignore the guidelines. Meany even took the administration to court over the program, arguing that the sanctions against companies that violated the standards constituted a mandatory program, not a voluntary one, and the administration had been granted no authority by Congress to impose mandatory controls. Carter won the case and eventually won over the AFL-CIO and its new leader, Lane Kirkland, by establishing an eighteen-member Pay Advisory Committee that would design the new pay standards for 1980. Labor would be adequately represented by six members to match those from management and the public. The Committee's central function was to recommend changes to the basic program, and it managed to accomplish some modifications by year's end; the basic pay standard, however, was not altered as the year ended. In March 1980, Carter accepted the Pay Advisory Committee's recommendation of 9.5% as the new pay standard. A new price standard was adopted in November 1979 that asked companies to limit their price increases for the next two years, ending September 30, 1980, to the price change for the two years from 1976 to 1977. Alternatively, if the profit standard was followed, price increases were permitted as long as the growth of profits did not exceed 13.5% over the two years and the profit margin was no higher than the average of the best two out of three fiscal years prior to the program. Finally, the real wage insurance program, designed to cushion the blow of inflation on workers who complied with the wage standard, was given scant attention by Congress, and it died in committee without coming to a vote, except in the House Budget Committee, which recommended against it.

THE ECONOMIC OUTLOOK FOR 1980

As the puzzling economic year of 1979 came to a close, there was much uncertainty over where the economy was headed, whether the past trends would continue or whether a sharp break would result. Private spending, which buoyed the economy in 1979, could not be expected to continue indefinitely, since inflation showed no signs of abating. Energy prices were acknowledged to be the main cause of inflation, which was not particularly comforting. With declining real growth, declining real wages, and declining labor productivity, but increasing prices and increasing interest rates, there were reasons enough to worry about the economic conditions that were to carry forward into 1980. There was no mystery, however, as to the administration's (and likely the nation's) main concern: "Fighting inflation must therefore remain the top priority of economic policy."[4]

With 1980 an election year, it is surprising to find this statement in the CEA's annual January report: "There are a number of reasons for expecting a mild recession in the first half of this year." This is a refreshingly honest statement, but likely to prove politically damaging. In any case, it was a first for an incumbent administration seeking re-election.

The administration argued that the forecast of a recession would normally call for fiscal and monetary ease, but this was no ordinary period. Fighting inflation was the priority, and fiscal and monetary ease would only send the wrong signals to the economy and make fighting inflation even more difficult. Moreover, the recession was still only a forecast, and past forecasts had been incorrect. Whether or not the administration was wise in its assessment, it was not a propitious time for forecasters, considering all the disturbing signs in the economy at the time, plus the uncertainties created by pending legislation in energy taxes, real wage insurance, and so on.

THE PROGRAM FOR 1980

Because inflation was top priority, the budget for fiscal years 1980 and 1981 continued the policy of restraint. There were no proposals for changes in tax laws, meaning that inflation would generate increased tax revenues, and government spending would be held down to avoid adding to the inflationary conditions. Total receipts for FY 1980 were estimated at $524 billion and outlays at $564 billion for a budget deficit of about $40 billion. In real terms, however, the proposed increase in outlays was only 2.8% over 1979 using a projected 11% inflation rate. Critics argued, however, that the spending restraint came at the expense of needed social programs. For example, national defense increases remained relatively constant in this period, while spending on education and training and natural resources fell in real terms. Community and regional development fell in both nominal and real terms. Indeed, for programs identified as benefiting the poor, spending increased by 7% in nominal terms, but fell in real terms by about 4%. Many of these programs received only level funding Aid to Families with Dependent Children (AFDC), others increased only marginally (food stamps), and still others fell in both nominal and real terms (CETA).[5]

Administration officials defended these budget items as necessary in view of the world situation in the case of national defense spending, and in view of inflation in all other controversial cases. They expressed regret that some worthwhile programs had to be reduced, but given the current state of the economy, it was impossible to meet and fund all the demands by sincere proponents of favored programs.[6]

The economic assumptions that underlay the administration's budget projections are given in Table 5.2. It is evident that the administration was not only predicting a mild recession, as real GNP was expected to fall by only 0.6% over the year, but also predicting stagflation. Prices were anticipated to rise by double digits again, and unemployment was expected to rise from the 5.8% range to 7.1% for the year. By the fourth quarter, unemployment was forecast to be about 7.5%. The private sector was not expected to help in the downturn as investment and consumption were forecast to fall, and only net exports could contribute to stabilization.

Table 5.2
Selected Economic Series, Calendar Year 1980

	Forecasts 1980	Actual 1980
GNP (% change)		
current dollars	8.3	8.8
real (1972 $)	−0.6	−0.2
Investment (nonres.)	−0.3	−3.4
fed. gov't expend.	3.0	6.5
consumption	−0.5	0.2
net exports	2.0	42.7
Price level (% change)		
GNP deflator	9.0	9.0
CPI (Dec. to Dec.)	10.4	12.4
CPI (year to year)	11.8	13.5
Unemployment rate (%)	7.0	7.1
Budget totals (fiscal year in bill.)		
receipts	$ 523.8	$ 517.1
outlays	563.6	576.6
deficit	−39.7	−59.6

Note: Data presented on a national income accounting basis.

Source: Economic Reports of the President, 1980 and 1981.

Table 5.3
Comparison of Forecasts for 1980

	Real GNP (% change)	Unemployment Rate	CPI (% change)
Commercial Models			
Chase Econometrics	−1.2	7.2	11.5
Data Resources	−1.4	7.1	11.8
Merrill Lynch	−1.8	7.6	11.2
Wharton Assoc.	−0.6	7.1	11.9
Average of 42 Business			
Forecasts	−1.0	7.4	11.0
CBO Forecast	−0.9	7.0	11.3
Administration Forecast	−0.6	7.0	11.8

Note: These are January forecasts with the average of 42 business forecasts taken from *Blue Chip Economic Indicators* Vol. 5, no. 1, January 10, 1980.

Source: Statement of Alice M. Rivlin, director, Congressional Budget Office, in House of Representatives, Committee on the Budget, *Economic Issues for Fiscal Year 1981*, 96th Congress, 2nd session, January 29, 1980, 18.

In a period when forecasts were precarious at best, it might be interesting to compare the administration's forecasts with those made by the CBO and private forecasters. Table 5.3 yields the comparable data. All other forecasters were far more pessimistic than the administration in their estimates of the fall in real GNP and the unemployment rate. Estimates of inflation varied widely, with those of the administration appearing on the high side.

To illustrate the difficulties in forecasting in this period, just one month later private forecasters had changed their predictions to smaller declines in GNP (with the DRI and Wharton models now predicting positive growth) larger increases in the CPI (average of 13.2%), and lower unemployment rates (average of 7.0).[7] As the months wore on, of course, these data continued to fluctuate, but the point here is not accuracy, but difficulty of forecasting in such a period.

MONETARY POLICY

The Fed was more than happy to comply with the administration's desire for restraint. Price stability has always been a prime goal of the Federal Reserve System, and it has felt obligated to fight inflation and provide orderly markets. Since October 1979, the Fed changed its operating rules to concentrate on controlling monetary aggregates, while allowing interest rates to fluctuate freely in response to inflationary pressures. At the end of 1979, as we have seen, interest rates did indeed increase sharply.

The Fed, however, still had difficulty defining the money supply and lacked an explanation for the unstable relationship between monetary growth and GNP. For 1979, the actual rate of M1 growth, 5.5%, fell within the range set by the Fed of 3 to 6%. Still, the predicted rate of M1 growth given GNP, prices, and interest rates should have been 7.8%, meaning that the lower growth of M1 was able to finance a greater increase in GNP than past relations would indicate was possible.[8] Nevertheless, the Fed continued with its monetarist experiment and established monetary growth targets for monetary aggregates. For M1 (now called M1-A) the long-term range for growth was set at 3.5 to 6%; for M1-B that included negotiable orders of withdrawal (NOW) accounts, ATS, credit union draft balances, and demand deposits at thrift institutions, a range of 4 to 6½% was established for the first half of the period and 3.5 to 6% for the second half, slightly above the previous year but well below the anticipated inflation rate of 11%. For M2, which included money market funds and savings deposits at all depository institutions, the range was set at 6 to 9% for the first half of the year and 5.5 to 8.5% for the second half. Interest rates under these conditions were expected to fluctuate more than they had in the past, but the new procedures were not expected to cause many problems over the long term.

ACTUAL DEVELOPMENTS IN 1980

The much heralded recession finally materialized in 1980. The administration was correct in forecasting a mild and short recession, for real GNP actually rose in the first quarter by 3.1%, fell dramatically in the second quarter by 9.9%, and then revived in the third quarter by 2.4% and again in the fourth quarter by 3.8%. (See Table 5.4.) While officially classified as a recession by the National Bureau of Economic Research, there is ample reason to question whether it should have been so designated. The most common rule for designating a recession is that real GNP should fall for at least two quarters; in this recession, it fell for only one quarter. The declaration of a recession, and the identification of the initial and ending periods, have always been somewhat arbitrary decisions, but this one seems unduly so.

In any event, real GNP actually declined by 0.2% for the year due to the drastic decline in the second quarter. Genuine or not, the recession was not an auspicious beginning for Carter's re-election bid. The public may not have been excited about the esoteric debates over whether or not

Table 5.4

Selected Economic Series, Calendar Year 1980 (percent change at annual rates except where noted)

	1980				
	Year	I	II	III	IV
GNP (% change)					
current dollars	8.8	12.6	−1.1	11.8	14.9
real (1972 $)	−0.2	3.1	−9.9	2.4	3.8
Investment (nonres.)	−3.4	0.5	−5.4	−0.4	1.0
fed. gov't expend.	6.5	4.4	2.9	−3.4	0.5
consumption	0.2	0.2	−2.6	1.3	1.7
net exports	42.7	18.7	3.2	11.4	−15.8
Price level (% change)					
GNP deflator	9.0	9.3	9.8	9.2	10.7
CPI (seasonally adj.)	13.5	16.4	15.1	8.0	10.9
PPI do	13.2	13.6	11.1	11.6	8.5
Unemployment rate (%)	7.1	6.2	7.3	7.5	7.5
Money Growth (% at annual rates)					
M1-A	5.0	4.6	−4.4	11.5	8.1
target range		3.0–5.6	same	3.0–5.5	same
M1-B	7.3	5.8	−2.6	14.6	10.8
target range		4.0–6.5	same	3.0–5.6	same
M2	9.8	7.3	5.6	16.0	9.1
target range		6.0–9.0	same	5.5–8.5	same
High-employment budget (bill. at annual rate)	−18.3	−17.4	−21.3	−20.7	−14.0
Budget totals (fiscal year in bill.)					
receipts	$ 520.0				
outlays	579.6				
deficit	−59.6				

Note: *Economic Report of the President, 1981* and Federal Reserve Bank of St. Louis, *Review*, August/September 1981.

a recession actually occurred, but they were aware of the manifestations of economic downturns. For example, the unemployment rate stood at 6.3% in January 1980, rose to 7.8% in July, and ended the year in December at 7.3%. There were a million jobs lost from January to July, and only 500,000 were recovered in the last half of the year. At the same time, these employment trends were occurring, inflation, as measured by the CPI, was recording double digit increases. In the first quarter, the CPI increased at a 16.4% annual rate, fell to 15.1% in the second, and to 8.0% in the third (reflecting the recession), and then shot up again in the final quarter to a rate of about 11%. For the year, the CPI rose by 13.5%, and the producer's price index that foreshadows future changes in the consumer index was not far behind at a 13.2% increase.

Clearly, the public had every reason to be confused by these conditions, and economists were not much help in either explaining or correcting them. It was an unusual period of stagflation, and no easy answers were available, but that is of little solace to a suffering nation looking for relief.

All sectors of private demand contributed to the slowdown in economic growth. Household consumption fell slightly, led by decreases in consumer durables. High interest rates and credit controls forced consumers to retrench, particularly in the second quarter when the recession hit. Even nondurables expenditures fell as energy prices forced conservation. Only consumption of services grew modestly in the period. Residential housing also fell over the period, as high mortgage interest rates pushed housing costs beyond the reach of many households.

Real business investment also fell in 1980, and the causes are not difficult to locate. High interest costs discouraged investment, and the recession and talks of recession prompted firms to withdraw any plans for expansion. Why invest when the existing capacity is not being utilized; manufacturers used about six percentage points less of their capacity (down to 79%) as measured by the Federal Reserve.

Only net exports contributed to the economic growth of the period. Exports fell, but imports fell even more, giving a real increase in net exports of $13 billion. The worldwide slowdown in economic activity accounted for the decline in exports, while the fall in imports of oil and the recession accounted for the decline in imports. The CEA was cheered by these trade developments and encouraged by the ability of the United States to compete in world markets, but its optimism turned out to be premature.

Once again, inflation outpaced compensation per hour (9.9%), and real wages fell by about 2.5%. Meanwhile, the growth of labor productivity was again slightly negative, and labor cost per hour was rising over 10%. The wage standards were bound to be ineffective in such a period, although the administration continued to claim that wages were restrained somewhat by their existence. Yet the CEA pointed out the increase in the "underlying" inflation rate—the rate that excludes food, energy and housing costs and thus records the domestic price pressures—from a range of 6 to 7% to a range of 9 to 10% in 1980.[9] Surely there could be trouble ahead if workers tried to catch up with real wages losses. With no growth of productivity and declining real wages, the potential for a disastrous wage-price spiral was very real.

No doubt inflation dominated the economic concerns of the nation in 1980. Energy prices again crept up due to price increases from the oil-producing nations and to the decontrol of domestic oil prices. Finished energy goods were rising at a rate of over 52% in 1980, with large increases in the first half of the year, declining in the middle months, and again increasing at the end of the year. Although these price increases leveled off in the last half of the year, their influence on economic conditions continued to be felt. Both fiscal and monetary restraints were instituted to combat the vexing problem, and a recession was allowed to develop. Unfortunately for budget watchers, their restraints forced a larger budget deficit than was planned. Higher interest costs due to monetary restraints; higher payments for unemployment, Social Security, and other income security items; higher payments for health care; and higher expenditures on national defense pushed the budget deficit to nearly $60 billion. The recession caused the increases in entitlement programs, and the disquieting world situation in Iran and Afghanistan caused the defense increases.

Monetary policy was also designed to provide restraint in 1980, although the Federal Reserve was not able to restrain the growth of monetary aggregates as well as it would have liked. Only the narrowly defined monetary aggregate, M1-A, managed to remain within its target range, while the other aggregates exceeded theirs. (See Table 5.4.) Once again shifts in the demand for money upset the Fed's plans for monetary growth. Even so, monetary policy seemed erratic in 1980. In the first quarter, the demand for money was strong, and interest rates shot up as the prime rate rose four percentage points to 16.5%, the federal funds rate rose 3.4 percentage points to 17.1%, and mortgage rates rose to 12.6%.

The demand for credit was strong, and speculation tendencies became apparent. To curb credit demands and provide additional monetary restraint, Carter decided in March to impose new credit controls by asking the Fed to require reserves against consumer credit card and other unsecured credit lending. The Fed added additional restraints on its own in the effort to restrain lending. The credit controls worked, much more forcefully and quickly than anyone had forecast, and the demand for credit fell dramatically; the growth of monetary aggregates fell in the second quarter, and interest rates plummeted to about half of their first quarter values by June (except for mortgage rates, which lagged considerably behind the fall in other rates and helped forestall the recovery in the housing market). After the controls were lifted in July, the demand for credit resumed and monetary aggregates grew and far exceeded their target ranges. Interest rates resumed their upward climb; at year's end, the prime rate was back up to 16.5%, the federal funds rate up to 18.9%, and the mortgage rate up to 13.2%.

So again, monetary policy had its difficulties in carrying out its plans for monetary restraint in the face of strong demand pressures. Whether inflationary expectations were strong or were abating, the demand for money was not behaving as predicted. When credit controls were imposed, the strong response of households was unanticipated, and the possible patriotic behavior of consumers was ignored. Putting possible explanations aside, it was a challenging period for monetary policy and the Fed's monetarist experiment.

High interest rates found banks scrambling to meet the situation by offering new deposits and introducing variable interest rate mortgages. Still, Regulation Q, which fixed interest payable on deposits, was in sharp conflict with usury laws, despite federal suspension. These and other problems led to the enactment of the Depository Deregulation and Monetary Control Act of 1980, which removed interest rate ceilings over a six-year period and usury ceilings were repealed on other loans. Interest-bearing checking accounts were permitted for all banks, and thrift institutions were allowed to grant consumer and business loans within limits. Still other provisions began to blur the distinction between commercial and thrift institutions.

Some Remarks on Macroeconomic Policy in the Latter Half of the Administration

In the latter half of the administration, price stability was given top priority. Despite the Humphrey-Hawkins initiative and the traditional Democratic party goals, the administration turned to fighting inflation. Fiscal conservatism was evident, as full employment policies took a back seat, and social programs were allowed to flounder and, in some cases, decline. Given Carter's personal philosophy, this turn should not be surprising. The Federal Reserve was equally willing to pursue policies of restraint and became a partner in fighting inflation.

Yet these monetary and fiscal policies of restraint were taking place in a period of stagnation and recession. Furthermore, these *demand-side* policies were applied to problems emanating from the *supply-side*. On the surface, these macroeconomic policies appear inappropriate and, when applied, ineffective. Price and wage controls might have proved effective under these economic conditions, but voluntary ones did not have a chance of success; more direct controls were needed to curb the wage/price spiral. Thus, a cautious administration was unwilling to meet the challenges of inflation head-on, but offered only a poor substitute.

Restraining the growth of federal expenditures and letting inflation increase tax revenues were the methods of attack in this period—a rather passive approach. Increasing national defense expenditures could be blamed on world events—on the Russians in Afghanistan and upheavals in Iran—while cuts in domestic programs could be blamed on the need to curb inflation. Yet inappropriate policies did not (could not) work and pleased no one; they succeeded only in making the administration seem inept, lacking solutions to the problems it had elevated to prominence. Without a forceful approach, it suffered the criticism of inaction and incompetence.

An overall evaluation of the administration's macroeconomic policies must await the following chapters. Here, it is only necessary to indicate the turn in the administration's attention to the main problem of the period in its view (and many others') and its lack of clear policies to deal with it.

THE PROSPECTS FOR 1981

In its *Economic Report of the President, 1980*, the CEA saw no hope for dramatic progress in 1981. It predicted only modest improvement in the unemployment rate, modest real growth in the GNP, about 2¾, and a modest lessening of inflation. The administration continued to view inflation as the most urgent problem and refused to stimulate the economy through a tax cut, resisting the increase of expenditures except for national defense. But 1980 was an election year, and the Democrats were being pressured by the Reagan campaign, which was pushing for a drastic tax reduction.

As a result, Carter relented in August with a tax cut plan that would liberalize depreciation allowances, expand the investment tax credit, reduce payroll taxes, and offer some tax reforms. In addition, he proposed to replace his voluntary incomes policy with a tax-based income policy (TIP), probably one that rewarded employees of firms that adhered to the government-set wage standard. He also proposed a 10-cent-per-gallon tax on gasoline to conserve energy.

These proposals were in a sense forced by the political campaign of 1980 and by the serious challenges coming from the Reagan camp. As the Reagan campaign gained momentum, the Carter administration simply had to respond. The economic issues in the presidential campaign were so important that a separate chapter is needed to review them. Consequently, we postpone detailed discussions of the administration's proposals and programs until chapter 10.

It should be noted here, however, that just before the election in October, the economic forecasts were not encouraging. Averages of nine leading forecasts, including the administration's, showed an increase in real GNP of only 1.4% for the year 1981, an increase in the CPI of 9.8%, and an unemployment rate of 8.1%.[10] To a casual observer, it appeared that the administration's response in August to these dismal predictions was too late and politically motivated.

NOTES

1. *Economic Report of the President, 1980*, 30–31.

2. For more on the institutional changes creating difficulties for the Fed in defining monetary aggregates, see "A Proposal for Redefining the Monetary Aggregates," *Federal Reserve Bulletin*, January 1979, 13–42.

3. *Economic Report of the President, 1980*, 38.

4. Ibid., 61.

5. See the testimony of James T. McIntyre, director, Office of Management and Budget, in U.S. House of Representatives, Committee on the Budget, *Outlook and Budget Levels for Fiscal Years 1979 and 1980*, 96th Congress, 1st session, January 30, 1979, 109–110.

6. See, for instance, the prepared statement of Joseph A. Califano, Jr., secretary, Department of Health, Education, and Welfare, in Ibid., 308–315.

7. See the U.S. House of Representatives, Committee on the Budget, *Monthly Economic Report*, 96th Congress, 2nd session, various months for the data.

8. See *The Economic Report of the President, 1981*, 53.

9. Ibid., 37.

10. U.S. House of Representatives, Committee on the Budget, *Recommendations for the Second Concurrent Resolution of the Fiscal Year 1981 Budget*, 96th Congress, 2d session, November 10, 1980, 30.

Chapter 6

Summary and Critique of the Administration's Macroeconomic Policies

The previous chapters included many comments and criticisms of the Carter administration's macroeconomic policies. Inevitably, many criticisms were made immediately following the actual policies adopted. They were not, however, spelled out or put in any kind of context, and so appear to be *ad hoc* notes on specific policies. Now, we gather up these criticisms and try to make some sense of the administration's attempt to deal with the macroeconomic issues it faced.

The task is easier said than done. Not only must we discuss what the administration planned to do as it took office, but also how it amended these plans either in the face of actual events in the economic world, or in response to political and social pressures. No administration can control these external events, but how it reacts to them reveals a great deal about the existence of and commitment to a basic philosophy.

TWO CARTER ADMINISTRATIONS?

The Carter administration was divided into two terms. One in which it tried to adhere to its basic convictions, and the other when it appeared to abandon them. In terms of its macroeconomic policies, the first one did not last very long, less than half of the term. Buffeted by events it could not control, it vacillated, compromised, and eventually retreated. The administration was then forced to examine its convictions and found them to be fluid, especially when Carter's personal philosophy seemed to re-emerge. In the second half of his tenure, external events seemed to take control, and the administration succumbed to confronting specific issues and abandoning its rudder. It made concessions, overreacted to short-run incidents, and in general sacrificed its objectives as it was swept along by the waves it could not handle. In the process, it became difficult to discern what its goals really were. Finally, the public was not willing to undertake this task of discovery and simply concluded that there were no anchors (to continue the metaphor) in this administration—better to seek answers elsewhere.

The foregoing represents a fair summary of what many people think of when analyzing the macroeconomic policies of the Carter administration. For many purposes, this summary would suffice, but for more searching examinations, it is not satisfactory.

It is clear that Carter, along with his influential advisors Lance and Blumenthal, was a fiscal conservative right from the start; he was eager to draw back from any stimulus policy at the slightest suggestion. In the beginning, he relented to a stimulus program because he had criticized Ford during the campaign and was forced to deliver on his promise to get the economy moving again. But it went against his philosophy: He did not want more government, only a more efficient one. When he was able to agree with a policy that was more in tune with his personal philosophy, he was certainly more comfortable.

Carter's other economic advisors, particularly Schultze, were more liberal, more Keynesian, and they were heeded, if at all, with skepticism. Schultze described Carter as uncomfortable with macroeconomics under any situation, and with macroeconomic theory under most situations. A trained engineer would not likely respond favorably to the economist's menu of choices or trade-offs. He might approve of the economist's obsession with efficiency, but fail to realize the difficulty of achieving it in practice. Thus, Carter set the tone for the administration and set the parameters for policy choices to which others had to confine their advice and counsel.

Furthermore, political considerations played only a minor role in forcing Carter to make policy choices that violated his personal beliefs. He saw no need to compromise when he thought he was right. Why play political games when the answer was clear? Of course, these repudiations of protocol and political snubs cost him politically, but he continued to defy his critics, many of whom were in his own party. Many Democrats felt that Carter had deserted the traditional Democratic supporters of programs generally associated with the party since Franklin Roosevelt. He appeared all too willing to sacrifice these hallowed programs in the name of inflation fighting or efficiency. It was hardly surprising then to find Senator Edward Kennedy among his most strident and vocal critics. Kennedy presumed to speak for the soul of the Democratic party as he led the rebellion against the Carter movement away from past principles. Internal conflicts within the governing party only exacerbated the economic problems that no previous administration had been forced to face.

So the real challenge to the Carter administration, and the source of many of its troubles, was the choice of goals. A struggling economy was forced to combat inflation while still concerned with unemployment, but there were not enough policy tools to do the job of combatting both. If unemployment were elevated to the most urgent problem, one set of stimulus policies was indicated; if inflation were given priority, another set was appropriate. But in the policy tool kit, there were no policies that would confront these problems simultaneously. The choice of goals, then, was bound to alienate one group or another. As often happens in these circumstances, there was a move to compromise, to split the difference, in order to appease both groups.[1] The usual consequences are that neither group is satisfied, and all feel betrayed. The role of inflation fighters in one year and recession fighters in another left observers wondering what the administration was trying to accomplish, and whether it knew what it was doing. Alternating goals and conflicting policies only brought on the charge of incompetence, when the administration was really trying to avoid extremes and steer a middle course between liberal and conservative views, whether they were enunciated by members of his own party or the opposition. In addition, his fiscal conservatism and Southern populism created conflicts not only for himself but within the administration as well.

Moreover, the administration tried to fight supply-side problems with demand-side solutions. Economic theory had provided no policies for the problems of the late 1970s, at least not the type of policy that would be politically or socially acceptable at the time. So, before passing judgment on the macroeconomic policies of the Carter years, it is essential to keep in mind the paucity of answers to the problems the administration faced. The Carter administration neither created the problems nor did it have the solutions to them, but neither did anyone else.

SOME SPECIFICS

The conflicts within the administration were evident from the beginning. The initial stimulus package of 1977 was a hodgepodge of ill-designed policies. It is not so much that compromises and concessions to more acceptable policies were made—they always are in any administration—it is that the administration settled for less than it needed to. Philosophical disarray was manifest among administration officials at the outset, which again is not unusual for the first term of the presidency, but is magnified when the chief executive appears to be at odds with those entrusted to serve him.

For example, in its initial foray into policy-making, the administration proposed a stimulus package that was too small for the job and unnecessarily restrictive. With unemployment hovering around 8%, prices moderating, and capacity usage down around 80%, more emphasis was needed on short-run expansionary policies that would stimulate the economy quickly.

Why did not the administration push for tax cuts for individuals, particularly the working poor, instead of a (temporary) rebate that nearly everyone opposed? Instead of the investment tax credit in the face of such excess capacity, why did not the administration cut the corporation income tax? Retained earnings financed most of the investment in the past, and reduced corporate taxes would have stimulated investment as much or more than cutting the cost of capital goods. These policies were backward looking, tried in the past with unspectacular success. The administration lost an opportunity to propose something new and at the same time gain the support of two significant groups—traditional Democrats and skeptical businessmen.

Of course, the reason for the conservatism was the fear of inflation. But such timidity at the start of the administration only serves to demonstrate a reluctance to accept the very concept of economic stimulus. Had Carter not made a campaign pledge there may not have been any expansionary policy at all. Having run on a campaign that stressed trust and honesty, Carter had no real option but to propose some economic stimulus to get the economy moving again; his more liberal economic advisors no doubt helped to convince him that some stimulus was also necessary and relatively costless in a period of slack. The point is that the administration squandered the opportunity to change the course of economic policy-making by introducing some bolder initiatives that did not repeat the policies of earlier administrations.

For example, Carter needed to secure the support of organized labor—a significant source of traditional Democratic support. A tax rebate accomplishes nothing with this group. A payroll tax reduction would reduce the cost of labor and could increase employment, possibly increase wages, and if neither of these results followed, a moderation of inflation would still be possible. For any of these, the administration could have demonstrated a concern for labor that was not otherwise evident. True, there was the increase in public service jobs, but while these were welcome as employment-creating, organized labor would not get the credit nor would it get additional members from the program.

Even more direct, a reduction in income taxes targeted at the working poor would have benefited those most damaged by rising prices (particularly in food and energy), while at the same time earning the cooperation of organized labor. Once these or similar policies were put into effect, an incomes policy to restrict prices and wages might have been more acceptable to organized labor (a traditional foe of them). Instead, it offered the more objectionable investment tax credit that labor characterized as a gift and not an incentive. Again, Carter was not interested in mending relations with organized labor nor with other traditional Democratic groups.

Other economic stimulus solutions or inflation-fighting proposals might have been considered that would not have antagonized supporters. An administration so concerned with inflation could have cut excise taxes (running about $10 billion per year) or used grants to subsidize states that reduced their sales taxes. In both cases, inflation would be moderated. The administration could have helped the cities cope with financial difficulties; it could have used revenue-sharing schemes to share the welfare expenses of states, institute medical insurance for the poor, increase public housing funds, rebuild the infrastructure, and so on. These policies would have provided economic stimulus while simultaneously mollifying the traditional Democrats and gaining needed political support. These ideas were debated at the time, and are not inserted here as a piece of retrospective advice.

Instead, the administration chose the safe path by selecting familiar policy options of the past that pleased no one and alienated many. In this sense, it displayed at the outset a fiscal conservatism that was not only out of touch with traditional Democratic values, but also failed to convince its opponents of its conservative credentials.

To make matters worse and compound the confusion over direction, the stimulus package was cut at the first signs of inflation. The blip in inflation quickly revealed—if there was any doubt—that the real concern of this administration would be price stability, not the full employment goal of past Democratic regimes. The first Democratic president since Johnson, with an opportunity to reinvigorate the Great Society, quickly succumbed instead to the conservative *bête noire*—inflation. Since most studies conclude that unemployment does more harm to the poor and disadvantaged than inflation, the hurried switch to controlling inflation was a clear signal that the administration was not overly concerned with major groups that made up the Democratic coalition. Such indifference would later come back to haunt Carter when Reagan learned to exploit the resulting disillusionment in the 1980 campaign.

Of course, the repackaging of the stimulus program cost the administration confidence in its ability to manage the economy, but even more damaging was the erosion of support among Democrats. Never particularly popular among Democratic leaders, Carter seemed in the beginning not even to care that he was alienating many of them and losing favor.

Perhaps the rest of the country was confused as well, for even as the administration was withdrawing some of the stimulus package, it was forecasting a decline in the rate of growth of GNP, with rising unemployment and rising prices. Having failed to arrest the spread of energy and food prices to a wage-price spiral, perhaps through an incomes policy of some kind, inflation became the overriding concern. Under these circumstances what is to be made of another stimulus package proposed for 1978?

The administration apparently became worried over the long-run course of the economy. Inflation and scheduled higher payroll taxes and reduced government spending might have created enough drag on the economy in 1979 to warrant action then. So, more cuts were proposed in income taxes but also in excise taxes and in payroll taxes for unemployment insurance. Tax reforms, such as the elimination of the deduction for state and local taxes and limitations on other deductions (capital gains, medical), were also included in the request (which asked for quick action). In general, the reforms were liberal in character, which is not inconsistent with Carter's views on the tax code, but which was confusing for those attempting to characterize the administration as a whole. Still, the administration did propose some new ideas, such as the reduction in payroll taxes, and some reform measures. By doing so, it showed the willingness to experiment with new concepts and challenge established special interest groups with its tax proposals.

Yet, another stimulus package following so close after the earlier retrenchment would be sufficient to puzzle any observer. The administration was giving off mixed, if not confusing, signals, and when it introduced an incomes policy later in the year, no one could be blamed for questioning the administration's overall direction or its goals. Furthermore, the administration had pledged to reduce government spending, to reduce the number of federal employees, and to reduce or streamline regulations to avoid unnecessary costs and burdens. So on the one hand there was the stimulus package to avoid recession, but there were also proposals to limit government spending, and on the other hand, there was the worry about inflation, which was serious enough to elicit an incomes policy proposal. It is little wonder that the policies were greeted with considerable skepticism.

It is apparent now, and it was then to some people, that there were not enough tools to combat the problems facing the nation in this period.

Moreover, the solutions were demand-sided despite the evidence that some of the problems were emanating from the supply-side. These "Keynesian" solutions had become acceptable and familiar to many and were easily prescribed as a result. To others, they were all we knew how to do.

Still, monetary policy was restrictive, so that the fiscal stimulus that was provided by the administration faced an obstacle anyway. Monetary and fiscal policies seemed to be working at cross purposes as policymakers attempted to fight inflation and stagnation simultaneously. If that were not confusing enough, consider the uncertainty created when the administration once again reduced the tax cuts by $5 billion and postponed their starting date to January 1, 1979. Since government spending was also experiencing another shortfall, fiscal restraint was evident even as the administration was fearing another recession. It was not a happy time for macroeconomic policymakers.

Past solutions also influenced the type of incomes policy adopted. The voluntary restraints suggested by the administration were similar to those proposed by the Kennedy administration. The Nixon administration destroyed direct controls with sanctions with its experiment in 1971–73; the public was hardly willing to undergo another round of controls following that unfortunate episode. So voluntary restraints were a quick and easy solution that made the administration appear to be doing something without actually incurring any costs. Lacking the popular acceptance of the general public, voluntary controls of this type are no better than jaw-boning, open-mouth policies; lacking sanctions, the controls are mere suggestions, and appealing to economic entities to consider the national interest is not likely to produce the desired results, particularly in a period such as the late 1970s. In the end, such voluntary controls are likely to be viewed as a desperate attempt to establish some type of response to perplexing economic problems for political rather than economic ends.

SUMMARY OF THE FIRST TWO YEARS OF POLICY-MAKING

Clearly, after its first two years, the Carter administration was viewed as vacillating and hesitant, using old solutions to combat changing problems. This judgment may seem unfair, but fighting stagflation with traditional means did nothing to allay suspicion that the administration was incapable of managing the economy.

To those making the judgments, it did not matter that it was not the administration's fault. The administration did not create the problems nor did it have the means available to solve them. The real questions are, How did it react to the problems that clearly upset its plans for the economy? What kind of advice was it being given by those who were its most ardent critics?

The administration did not react very well to problems that upset its economic plans. Through its policies it created a great deal of uncertainty about government's role in the economy. In attempting to be flexible, it engendered the accusation of incompetence; in switching goals, it revealed the absence of a guiding philosophy. Thus, it never seemed in command of the situation and appeared inept, even as it tried to explain its actions.

The administration also received conflicting advice based on completely different analyses of the economy. Keynesians were upset at the withdrawal of stimulus packages and the attention paid to inflation. Monetarists were clamoring that the money supply was the crucial variable in the economic system and should be the main focus for any policy, while fiscal policy was essentially useless. At the same time, rational expectations adherents were claiming the futility of both fiscal and monetary policy. Political economists of various stripes were asserting that the wrong model of the economy was being used, which caused the wrong solutions. Marxists rejected both the model of the economy and the solutions. With such disagreements among economists both as to the model of the economy and to the solutions to the problems it faced, it is understandable that the administration could please few economists no matter what it did. Furthermore, the disparate advice indicated that clear solutions were not to be found and reveals the disarray among economists. The administration could hardly be blamed if it resorted to past solutions and appeared hesitant when confronted with seemingly intractable problems.

So in the end, economists must bear part of the blame for the macroeconomic policy failures that occurred in this period. They had not designed policies (that received general agreement) to deal with the kinds of problems that surfaced in the late 1970s. However, before passing any final judgments, it would be wise to review the economic policies during the second half of the administration.

ECONOMIC POLICY DURING THE SECOND HALF OF THE ADMINISTRATION

During the last two years of the administration, it was clear that inflation had become top priority. There were no longer attempts to reduce taxes or propose new spending programs. In short, the apparent vacillation between stimulus and restraint disappeared in favor of restraint. Monetary policy was also restrictive as the Fed was even more eager to promote price stability. In spite of the Humphrey-Hawkins initiative (formally the Full Employment and Balanced Growth Act of 1978), which required the reverse priorities, the administration, and every succeeding one, was willing to allow unemployment to rise in the battle against inflation.

The concern over inflation can be seen in many different ways. Fighting inflation with recession is the time-honored method used in this and other administrations. Letting the unemployment rate rise is a signal that measures to fight inflation are being enacted. Cutting government social programs is another sign. In either case, it is likely to be those with the least power who are made unconsenting volunteers in the effort to reach price stability. (Of course, there are other signals: raising taxes, but political considerations often prohibit this option; restrictive monetary policy is more politically acceptable and hence more often used; reducing cost-enhancing regulations is another among the array of options. Some of these will be discussed later.)

During Carter's second two years, the unemployment rate remained remarkably stable, as previously observed, but was allowed to creep up in the latter half of 1980 (an election year), when it hovered around 7.5%. Electoral politics aside, numerous studies have demonstrated that the poor suffer more from unemployment than inflation.[2] So it is not unwarranted to suggest that those at the bottom of the income scale were enlisted in the fight against inflation and were made to pay for the policy blunders and miscalculations of others. It is more than coincidental to note that the poverty rate rose from 11.4% in 1978 to 11.6% in 1979 and to 13.0% in 1980. The increases in poverty were widespread among population groups but more noticeable among minorities (from 1970 to 1980, a 3.9% increase for Spanish-speaking groups, 1.5% for blacks), farm families (4.2%), female-headed households (2.3%), and children (1.9%).[3] It is not possible to prove from these summary data that the increases in poverty were the direct result of the administration's policies; only a correlation can be inferred. The same correlation, however, is observed for every recession whatever the cause, whether deliberately engineered or not.

One interesting way to view the change in government spending on social programs is to examine the payments to individuals. These are payments that are controllable, not those that are mandated by law. Since the amounts in these programs and changes in them are relatively small, percentage changes are not very helpful and may be misleading. (See Table 6.1.) The total payments to individuals, corrected for inflation, are as follows: from fiscal year 1976 to 1977, the increase was 1.2%; from 1977

Table 6.1
Controllable Federal Government Spending to Individuals (percent change in real 1972 dollars)

Function	1977	1978	1979	1980
Social Security and Retirement	−5.5	−6.8	15.4	− 8.2
Medical Insurance	2.8	4.3	−1.0	5.9
Assistance to Students	7.7	−9.1	5.2	17.7
Housing Assistance	13.5	14.2	7.4	17.5
Food and Nutrition	−10.7	0.6	14.6	23.9
Public Assistance	22,844.9	445.1	−76.2	472.9
All Other Payments	18.6	−22.9	−9.6	140.1
Total Payments to Individuals	1.2	6.6	2.4	21.1
Addendum: National Defense	2.4	0.8	2.5	8.7

Note: Payments to individuals in fiscal years; national defense in calendar years.

Source: Office of Management and Budget, *Historical Tables: Budget of the United States Government* and *Economic Report of the President*, various years.

to 1978, +6.6%; from 1978 to 1979, 2.4%; and from 1979 to 1980, 21.1%. The decrease from 1978 to 1979 indicates a response to inflation and the call to reduce government expenditures. The increase from 1979 to 1980 indicates the slowdown in the economy that called for more spending. It is clear that the Carter administration tried to maintain spending on these programs as long as possible and to limit increases only where absolutely necessary. It was not as cautious when it came to spending on national defense. For the same periods, real national defense spending increased 2.4% in 1977, 0.8% in 1978, 2.5% in 1979, and 8.7% in 1980. Without pursuing the matter, it is evident that national defense spending was subject to the same vacillation found in other areas of the administration. Reductions in 1978 were followed by rapid increases in the following years. International events "forced" the administration to some extent, of course, but it was also responding to the charge that the fall in spending was hurting the defense posture of the United States.

On Monetarism

The experiment with monetarist principles demonstrated the power of monetary policy, but did little to solve the underlying problems in the economy. What the episode of 1979–80 showed was that demand-side solutions to supply-side problems are likely to be ineffectual. This would appear self-evident in retrospect, but at the time the menu of policy choices left few options.

With the determination to fight inflation so strong, any means that promised to do so appeared acceptable. Yet it should have been more obvious that pursuing a tight monetary policy and pushing up interest rates to extreme levels would do little to combat the major sources of inflation. To see this, Table 6.2, adapted from the *Economic Report of the President, 1981*, clearly shows the trends in the components of inflation and indicates that the administration was well aware of these factors. (The data are reproduced here to show the administration's recognition of the real sources of inflation, even though the data for 1980 were preliminary.)

Food prices, as indicated by the *farm value* of food, were volatile but still warning of future price changes in this category. Farm prices at the consumer level began to moderate in the later years of the administration, but the 14.5% increase in 1980 showed cause for concern. The real problem

Table 6.2
Measures of Price Changes, 1976–80 (percent change, fourth quarter to fourth quarter)

	1976	1977	1978	1979	1980
Consumer Prices					
All Items	5.0	6.6	9.0	12.7	12.6
Farm value of food	−12.9	6.4	17.5	7.4	14.5
Energy	6.2	8.2	7.5	36.5	18.9
Home purchases and finance	3.8	8.9	13.4	19.8	17.7
All other items	6.3	6.1	7.3	7.9	9.8
Producer Prices of Finished Goods					
All Items	2.7	6.9	8.7	12.6	12.0
Food	−4.4	7.4	11.6	7.8	7.4
Energy	5.0	9.2	6.4	62.0	28.4
All other items	5.6	6.4	7.9	9.3	11.1
Addendum: Interest rates					
3-mo. treas. bills	4.9	5.3	7.2	10.0	11.5
prime rate	5.3	5.6	8.0	10.9	12.3
mortgage rate	9.0	9.0	9.5	10.8	12.7

Note: Consumer energy prices for households only; home costs include purchasing and financing, taxes, and insurance.

Source: Economic Report of the President, 1981, 148, 308.

of inflation in the latter half of the administration can be explained largely by rising energy prices and the costs of home ownership. Table 6.2 (see also Table 4.3) reveals the real sources of trouble in this period. In fact, nearly 90% of the change in the CPI from 1977–80 can be accounted for by energy and housing items.[4] (It should be noted that the definition of housing costs has changed since this period. Here interest costs were included in the definition; now a type of rental value is used instead.)

Without dwelling on the issue, it is evident that monetary policy would not be effective against these sources of inflation; in fact, a tight monetary policy that drove interest rates up to such high levels would be partly responsible for the inflation that ensued. Supply-side shocks, relatively new in the 1970s, cannot be treated by resorting to policies of the past, but the options were few and the will to use them lacking. Along with the falling or stagnant growth of the productivity of labor, demand-side policies can offer little except political cover in the fight against inflation emanating from other than demand pressures.

Yet rising interest rates and recessionary tactics to combat inflation had repercussions that went beyond the usual identifiable ones normally associated with such policies. In the next chapter, some of these will be discussed.

NOTES

1. See the assessment of Erwin C. Hargrove, *Jimmy Carter as President* (Baton Rouge, La.: Louisiana State University Press, 1988), 81, where he characterizes Carter's response to conflicting advice as "balancing the opposites."

2. See the discussion in Douglas A. Hibbs, *The American Political Economy: Macroeconomics and Electoral Politics* (Cambridge, Mass.: Harvard University Press, 1979), 77–89.

3. U.S. Department of Commerce, Bureau of the Census, *Money Income and Poverty Status of Families and Persons in the United States*, 1980, 1985. Series P-60.

4. See the more complete analysis of inflation in this period in Alan S. Blinder, "The Anatomy of Double-Digit Inflation in the 1970s," in *Inflation: Causes and Effects*, edited by Robert E. Hall (Chicago: The University of Chicago Press, 1982), 261–282.

Part II

Other Initiatives
and Reforms in the
Carter Years

Chapter 7

Trade and Energy Matters

So far, the review of the Carter administration's macroeconomic policies has concentrated on the domestic economy. In any evaluation of the Carter years, the domestic repercussions take priority, especially when political consequences are factored into the analysis. While the general public may weigh domestic outcomes heavily, often international considerations may be more important in the end.

It is appropriate to examine the Carter record of international trade and relations. Foreign relations are beyond the focus of this book and references to them are only mentioned in passing. Economic elements, however, are nearly always present in international relations and cannot be ignored.

The subject of international trade and relations are rich and complex topics, so this discussion will be limited to summaries and overviews, leaving the details to other works. This chapter presents the data on trade during the Carter years and discusses the immediate results. Once the data have been reviewed, we will examine the effects of domestic macroeconomic policies on international matters.

It may seem odd to include trade and energy matters in one chapter. These two subjects, however, were so entwined in this period that their combination is justifiable. So as the discussion of trade issues proceeds, energy problems emerge as a major factor in trade developments; since energy problems cannot be ignored in the examination of inflation, they cannot be ignored in the analysis of trade balances. In addition to affecting trade balances, energy problems also played havoc with the domestic economy. So in conjunction with the problems raised in the international sphere, we will discuss what the administration did about the energy crisis in order to solve the problems in both the domestic and international economies.

THE EVIDENCE

Looking first at the data for international transactions, Table 7.1 provides some necessary statistics. The table reveals some startling developments in the late 1970s. First, the merchandise trade balance jumped from $–9.3 billion in 1976 to $–25.3 billion in 1980, a 172% increase over the period. The major surge took place in 1977 and moderated thereafter. It is not that exports were stagnant over the period; in fact, they increased by 48%, but imports rose even more, by 103%.

We would expect to find that one of the major reasons for the deteriorating trade balance was the supply-side oil shocks, and indeed, the data support that supposition. Imports of petroleum products more than doubled (145%) from 1976 to 1980, with significant increases occurring in 1979. In value terms, petroleum products alone accounted for 32% of imports, up from 27% in 1976. Yet petroleum products were not the only source of difficulty in the adverse trade balance. Some other import categories that increased were (in 1980 value terms): food and beverages, 57%; supplies associated with durable goods output (steel, metals, raw materials), 93%; capital goods, 172%; autos, 67%; and consumer goods, 87%. However, in value terms, these items accounted for about 56% of imports as compared to 32% for petroleum imports. So there is no question that energy played a major role in the trade difficulties of this period, although it is wise to remember that other imports also contributed to the deterioration.

It is interesting to note that there were considerable fluctuations in imports over the period. For example, the rate of change of imports fell in percentage terms in 1978 (to 15.9%), only to resume their upward trend in 1979 (to 20.5%) before falling again in 1980. Part of the answer to these trends can be found in the changing value of the dollar as shown in the last column of Table 7.1. Despite efforts to prop up the dollar in 1978, the trade-weighted value of the dollar fell to 84.2 from 97.3 in 1976. Imports continued to be attractive under these conditions, while exports were discouraged.[1]

In terms of commodities, petroleum products imports actually fell by 6% in 1978, while imports of consumer goods and autos rose by about 29% each. The only other import to experience a decline (in value terms) was food and beverages, increasing by only 10% from 21% in 1977. Yet in 1979, these trends were reversed, with petroleum products surging to a 52% increase, while autos and consumer goods fell to a 5% increase. Some of these fluctuations can be explained, of course, but they are noted here to illustrate some erratic conditions in the trade area.

Table 7.1
U.S. International Transactions, 1976–80 (in billions of dollars)

Exports	Imports	Net	Imports of Petroleum Products	Investment Income Balance	Balance: Current Account	U.S. Assets Abroad (Net)	Foreign Assets in U.S. (Net)	Trade-Wgt. Value of $ (Real) (Mar. 1973=100)
114.7	-124.1	-9.3	34.6	16.0	4.4	-51.3	36.5	97.3
120.8	-151.7	-30.9	45.0	18.0	-14.1	-34.8	51.3	93.1
142.1	-175.8	-33.8	42.3	20.6	-14.8	-61.1	64.0	84.2
184.5	-211.8	-27.3	60.5	31.2	-0.5	-64.3	38.4	83.2
224.2	-249.6	-25.3	79.4	29.9	1.5	-86.0	54.5	84.8
PERCENT CHANGE								
5.3	22.2	232.3	30.1	12.5	-420.5	-32.2	40.5	-4.3
17.6	15.9	9.4	-6.0	14.4	5.0	75.6	24.8	-9.6
29.8	20.5	-19.2	43.0	51.5	-96.6	5.2	-40.0	-1.2
21.5	17.8	-7.3	31.2	-4.2	-400.0	33.7	41.9	1.9

Source: Economic Report of the President, 1983.

Exports rose rather steadily over the period 1976–80 (by 92%), but again showed considerable variability by category. Agricultural products, for example, shot up in 1978 by 370% over 1977, but then collapsed in 1979, falling by 69%. Auto exports rose in 1978 and then fell off in 1979 and turned negative in 1980. A similar fluctuation can be found in the exports of industrial supplies; a steady increase (in chemicals and metals) until 1980, when they began to fall off.

This brief sketch of trade statistics will suffice for the time being, but more discussion will be necessary as the review proceeds. It is apparent from the data that energy problems can explain much of the trade balances in this period; it is also apparent that trade by commodities varied considerably, and these fluctuations can also be tied to energy matters.

Investment income remained positive in the latter part of the 1970s and helped to offset the deficits in merchandise trade. In 1980, investment income actually resulted in a small positive balance on current account. The existence of a positive balance for investment income remained until the mid-1980s, when it too turned negative. U.S. assets invested abroad continued to grow steadily in this period, while foreign assets in the United States fluctuated considerably. Clearly, trade relations exhibited considerable fluctuations in the latter half of the 1970s. At this point, a more searching analysis is necessary of the variations and seemingly contradictory observations (note, for example, that as the trade-weighted value of the dollar declined, foreign assets in the United States declined as well, while U.S. assets abroad rose). These and other trends will be examined more closely, along with the administration's response to them.

INTERNATIONAL TRADE PROBLEMS

The administration acknowledged the huge increase in the current account balance in 1977, but called attention to the fact that many countries were experiencing deficits as well.[2] It blamed the world's trade problems on slow growth, where potential output fell below actual output, resulting in high levels of unemployment along with high inflation. Apparently the oil price shocks and the recession during the 1972–75 period were still affecting the macroeconomic policies of many countries. Nations, particularly in Western Europe, that experienced severe disruptions in this period were still pursuing policies of fiscal and monetary restraint in order to avoid fighting a wage-price spiral. Policies of restraint, of course, mean that U.S. exports were hampered, and the fact that the United States was recovering faster than its trading partners only added to our inability to sell abroad. In addition to these problems, the importation of petroleum products prevented any real improvement in trade balances, since they accounted for about half of the deficit, with no improvement in sight.

Still, anti-inflationary policies seemed to be working in several countries, and current account surpluses continued for Japan and Germany, despite the problems of other nations. The administration continued to maintain, however, that the performance of U.S. exports was not a result of excessive inflation in the United States. The rest of the world was not so certain, for the dollar started to depreciate in 1977, despite the huge increase in interest rates in the United States. Short-term interest rates rose 350 basis points relative to major European nations, and the administration acknowledged that this should have attracted an inflow of funds that would have reduced the current account deficit. It seems as if the rest of the world expected inflation to continue in the United States, reducing the rate of return on investments, and thus were not investing in the United States.[3] In fact, many central banks purchased dollars to avoid appreciations of their own currencies, further depressing the dollar. Now the increase in foreign assets in the United States in 1977 can be understood: Official dollar holdings increased sharply in 1977 as central banks purchased dollars to prevent appreciation, but also to rebuild reserves. Also, the decrease in U.S. assets abroad in the face of the dollar depreciation can be explained by the decline in claims on foreigners by U.S. banks, accounting for half of the observed decline. U.S. banks were responding to the economic recovery in the United States; increases in interest rates in the United States made banks more cautious of lending abroad.

The interpretations of these developments are varied. The administration was reluctant to criticize other nations for their actions, preferring to stress the need for international cooperation in economic policies. With inflationary tendencies lessening in several major countries, there was the hope that more expansionary policies would be pursued. There was also the need to maintain and strengthen international organizations, such as GATT, and to continue to work toward free trade policies. The administration also stressed its adherence to free markets and to floating exchange rates, but warned that it advocated the need for market intervention whenever exchange markets became "disorderly." In brief, the administration did not appear overly concerned about the trade problems in 1977, but hints of apprehension were unmistakable.

Developments in 1978

In the second year of the administration, the move toward fiscal and monetary restraint in order to combat inflation was the central aim of macroeconomic policy. We have already seen the rationale for the shift in policy for the domestic economy, but there were also the requirements of the international economy to satisfy.

As previously noted, the dollar declined sharply in the latter half of 1978, partly in response to the perception from abroad that inflation in the United States was out of control, and from the lack of faith in the administration's policies designed to correct the problem. The dollar was indeed propped up by a support package of $30 billion and by increased interest rates in the United States. In return, the United States had to promise to reduce its inflation rates and trade deficits in multilateral trade negotiations in Geneva and Tokyo and in the economic summit in Bonn in July. Clearly, international trade considerations were reinforcing the administration's domestic agenda of pursuing policies of restraint. These international trade meetings were also designed to remove existing trade barriers and provide for methods to resolve conflicts. Equally important to the Carter administration was the need for more coordination of international economic policies. This was a continuing theme of the administration, but was met with considerable lack of enthusiasm, and actual results were minimal.[4]

Looking at the trade statistics, it is easy to see why the administration was pleased with the results and with the prospects for the future. While the merchandise trade deficit did increase slightly, the rate of increase diminished sharply, and quarterly data reveal the steady improvement over the course of the year. Furthermore, both agricultural and nonagricultural exports increased strongly over the year, from a 5.3% increase in 1977 to nearly an 18% increase in 1978; meanwhile, imports were increasing at only 9% over 1977. The improvements in trade balances can be traced to the economic recovery in Europe, where growth rates increased, and to the lagged effect of the depreciation of the dollar, which increased the competitiveness of U.S. firms while moderating the demand for imports. In addition, imports of petroleum products lessened now that oil from Alaska was available and withdrawals from excessive inventories were undertaken. Still, the administration pledged to support export-related measures in its September "National Export Policy." In this document, the administration committed itself to increase the attention paid to exports, especially by small- and medium-sized firms. The size of the Export-Import Bank activities was to be increased; the Small Business Administration (SBA) was to guarantee small business export activities by $100 million, with $20 million going into marketing areas. Agricultural export credits were increased by $1 billion. The emphasis on exports reflects the view that this area had been neglected in the past.

In general, then, the administration forecasted continued improvement in trade conditions, expecting the trends surfacing in 1978 to continue: the European economic recovery, the reduction in inflation in the United States (and elsewhere), the improvement in the competitiveness of U.S. firms, and the spirit of cooperation that was evidenced in the multinational trade negotiations.

In capital flows, both U.S. assets abroad and foreign assets in the United States rose strongly in 1978. The record for U.S. assets abroad is mixed, with factors that ordinarily reduce the flow—such as increasing domestic demand for funds and the narrowing of interest rate spreads—being offset by the demand for dollars by foreigners who borrowed dollars (that had depreciated) in order to buy other currencies. Also, direct foreign investment increased in this period. The U.S. direct foreign investment was matched by direct foreign investment in the United States, since foreign firms found it advantageous to avoid currency fluctuations by investing in the United States. Still a good deal of the increase in foreign assets in the United States can be accounted for by the dollar-propping purchases of Germany, Japan, and Switzerland.

In sum, the administration believed that international trade conditions were improving and likely to continue. Aside from its macroeconomic policy restraints, it did not see the need for more drastic actions in the trade area. The direct action it did take—the export promotion—was modest indeed, as it relied on economic conditions in the United States and abroad to provide the necessary impetus for bringing international trade balances into line.

Trade Issues in the Latter Half of the Administration

As mentioned before, the Carter administration seemed to change course going into the last half of its term. For macroeconomic policies this meant a shift toward more restraint as the administration began to fear inflation. Did this switch in policy direction affect international trade conditions?

Table 7.1 reveals some interesting changes from 1978 to 1979. The merchandising trade balance improved, despite a substantial jump in imports of petroleum products. Moreover, the deficit in the current account balance was reduced to near zero, helped by a significant increase in investment income. Some of the reasons for the turnaround are quite familiar, while others are somewhat less so.

As for merchandise trade, the growth in the economies of major trading partners exceeded that of the United States, helping to increase exports while limiting imports. Again, the lagged effect of the dollar's depreciation helped as well. Both agricultural and manufacturing exports increased over the year; agricultural exports rose by 18% over 1978, led by sales to the Soviet Union, and nonagricultural exports increased by 31%, led by capital goods and chemicals.

The dramatic rise in import prices of petroleum came as a result of the political crisis in Iran and the cutoff of oil by that nation. While the volume of imports remained the same, the price of oil rose from $13.36 per barrel in December 1978 to $25 per barrel in December 1979. Unlike the situation in 1974–75, other OPEC nations, specifically Saudi Arabia, did not adjust production to maintain the cartel price. Letting the price float resulted not only in higher prices, but also in the scramble of nations to secure the oil they needed to stockpile reserves, even though no real shortage existed.

The Carter administration not only worried about how such price increases would affect the U.S. economy, but also how the increases would affect other economies, including those less developed that, in order to purchase oil, were borrowing funds from U.S. banks that were recycling surplus funds from oil-producing countries. This problem became known as the Third World debt problem, which would require a book of its own to explain. During this period, the Third World debt problem was just surfacing and created no apparent crisis.

The administration recognized that another recession, such as the one in 1974–75, was possible as consumers reallocated funds from other items to energy. It was also concerned that another wage-price spiral was possible, as wage earners attempted to recapture their real earnings. In responding to a recession, it reasoned, a stimulative fiscal and monetary policy would provoke more inflation, while restrictive policies would diminish output and employment. It chose, as we know, the restrictive route, particularly in monetary policy, when it switched to the monetarist prescription that reduced the growth in the money supply, and more important, let interest rates rise.

The dollar declined again in August, as the market was concerned about rising inflation in the United States and the rising price of gold and silver. The dollar recovered somewhat following the monetary policy switch in October, but many other nations were concerned as well and began to protect themselves by raising interest rates in their economies. Still, investment income soared in 1979, by over 51%, as profits from petroleum sectors rose. The rise in investment income was sufficient to bring the current account nearly into balance.

The other important change in trade statistics is the fall of foreign assets in the United States. The decline of 40% was mainly due to the sales of dollars by countries trying to limit the depreciation of their currencies over the course of the year. Foreign direct investment in the United States increased by $1.4 billion, but it was mainly reinvested earnings rather than new areas of investment.

In summary, the administration viewed the international situation as basically favorable and was more concerned about what the huge oil price increase would do to the domestic economy.[5] The policy dilemmas were resolved in favor of restraint, which was considered appropriate not only for the domestic economy but for trade purposes as well. The strains of the oil price shocks were felt throughout the world so that 1980 posed its share of problems for the world community, since all nations had to grapple with the strong possibility of recession. The need for further international cooperation, as evidenced by the 1974 Emergency Allocation Agreement within the International Energy Agency, was even more evident.

In September 1979, Carter reorganized the bureaucracy involved in trade matters. He replaced the special trade representative with a new office of the United States trade representative. The office was designed to deal with trade policy issues, particularly in the implementation of multilateral trade agreements. Since Congress had just passed the Trade Agreements Act of 1979, which resulted from the Tokyo round of negotiations, the administration was anxious to put into place an administrative framework to oversee the series of codes regulating nontariff barriers to trade. To deal with more operational matters, the Department of Commerce was given the responsibility for overseeing industry matters, such as anti-dumping, since it had the expertise in these areas. The overall aim of these reorganizational issues was, of course, to increase exports while ensuring fair trading practices.

Again in 1980, the current account was nearly in balance, as exports remained strong while imports diminished somewhat; the near balance was brought about again by investment income balance as in 1979. Exports increased by nearly 22%, led by capital goods (machinery and equipment, electronic equipment), but agricultural exports increased as well (by 18%), despite the embargo placed on the USSR by the administration following its invasion of Afghanistan. The loss of exports to the Soviet Union was made up by sales to Asia, Africa, Latin America, and to Western Europe, which had been experiencing poor harvests. The value of the dollar fluctuated widely during the year, appreciating in the first quarter, falling in the second when the United States was in a brief recession, and then rising in the latter half of the year. Exports may not have been aided by the dollar's value as they had in previous years, but it was more inclined to follow the kinds of goods sold—those needed by our trading partners and in which the United States had a clear advantage in producing.

Imports were again dominated by petroleum products, but the volume of imports actually declined; price increases accounted for the increase in the value of petroleum imports. In fact, imports declined steadily from 1978, starting at 9.27 barrels per day in 1977 to 7.09 barrels per day in 1980; but the price rose in the same periods from over $13 per barrel to over $30 per barrel. The increase in prices was aggravated by the start of the Iran/Iraq war in September, which initiated fears of oil shortages and pushed up spot prices quickly.

Leaving aside energy matters temporarily, other imports diminished in 1980 as the recession in the United States slowed the demand for capital goods and industrial supplies. Imports of consumer goods continued to increase, particularly automobiles.

Weaker economic activity abroad is credited with causing the decrease in investment income, which might have been worse except for the higher interest rates that accompanied the slowdown. Special one-time factors also contributed to the decline: The sale of a U.S.-owned petroleum company resulted in a capital loss, and also the sale by a Canadian-owned company of its holdings in a U.S. company resulted in a capital gain. U.S. assets abroad increased again as higher oil bills forced other nations to borrow in the United States, despite rising interest rates. Also, U.S. banks shifted loans to offshore banks in the Caribbean (which then made loans in the Eurocurrency market) in response to the increase in reserve requirements imposed by the Fed in March. The U.S. recession in the middle of the year, when few loans were made domestically, also contributed to the shifting of funds. Meanwhile, foreign assets in the United States increased substantially as foreigners purchased large amounts of corporate securities, and OPEC members used their petroleum-generated dollars to invest in the United States.

Tracing these capital flows is difficult enough in normal times, but these were not normal times. For example, the statistical discrepancy amounted to an astounding $35 billion. This discrepancy is usually regarded as unrecorded private capital flows, but what is to be made of a discrepancy this large? Where is the flow coming from, and what is it being used for? The answers are left to others, but it should be noted that the explanations of capital flows are seriously deficient if discrepancies of this size go unanalyzed.

This very brief summary of this and other years of the Carter administration was included here not to portray the intricacies of international trade, for that is beyond this book, but to indicate some trends to which the administration might have been reacting. As in earlier years, the Carter administration took no significant actions in response to trade conditions. Its decision to increase reserve requirements in March resulted in a shift to offshore banking; its decision to allow interest rates to increase may have increased the flow of funds to the United States, but other nations reacted to higher interest rates in the United States by increasing theirs as well.

For this study, the issue here is whether the administration planned to address trade problems with direct actions. The answer is, it did not. It simply worried over how the new oil price shocks would be handled by our trading partners, how future energy needs would be met, how best to meet supply shocks in terms of wage demands and earnings available for investment, and so on. While these admonitions and lessons may have been instructive to all, they did not constitute an active policy nor could they be so construed. In summary, the administration relied more on market forces to guide international trade than interference with direct policies. The same philosophy governed its views on the matter of free trade.[6] Once again, it attempted to rally opinion on the need for international cooperation through existing international agencies or prepare the ground for new ones should the need arise.

Thus, in international trade matters, the administration revealed its more conservative approach to these areas. It simply preferred to leave trade matters to the marketplace and intervened only when necessary, and then only minimally. For its nonactions, it probably received the plaudits of those engaged in trade transactions, as well as from those who generally advocated a laissez-faire philosophy. In any case, it is now time to step back from the statistics and intricacies of international trade and take a look at some of the repercussions of the decisions, or lack of them, made by the United States that are not so readily discernible, but no less important.

ASSESSING THE CARTER ADMINISTRATION AND INTERNATIONAL TRADE

Before analyzing the Carter administration's responses to the international conditions it inherited and later faced, a brief historical perspective is required. The Bretton Woods agreement in 1944 established the fixed exchange rate system that basically made the U.S. dollar the reserve currency. That is, at U.S. insistence, the dollar was tied to gold and became the principal reserve currency. In this "gold exchange standard," other nations were encouraged to hold dollars, and if necessary, these dollars could be exchanged for gold at a rate of $35 per ounce. Gold, however, earns no return, so most nations were happy to hold U.S. assets that did yield a return.

In the post–World War II period, the system worked to supply the necessary liquidity for the resurrection of international trade; the dollar served as the reserve currency and was used frequently as the major currency in the direct conduct of trade. As a result, dollars flowed out of the United States and began to accumulate in foreign banks. When trade deficits began to become chronic for the United States, there was justifiable concern that the United States did not have sufficient gold to satisfy claims, should foreigners present their dollars for redemption.

Contributing to the outflow of dollars were the foreign policy objectives of the United States. Striving for a *Pax Americana*, the United States engineered the Marshall Plan, NATO, aid to less developed countries, and many other foreign adventures. In addition, there were periods when huge outflows of dollars by U.S. corporations, which were investing heavily abroad, added to the problem. In the 1960s, many nations began to object to the free hand given to the United States to pursue its goals, protected in a sense by the trade arrangements agreed to in an earlier and far different period. As the situation stood then, other nations were forced to support U.S. foreign policy whether or not they agreed with it. (The European Economic Community (EEC) was formed partially in response, but was in its infancy.)

Some foreign leaders, such as General Charles de Gaulle of France, objected openly, while others were more diplomatic. For not only were they indirectly supporting U.S. foreign policy, they had become America's creditors, while accumulating dollars and watching their currencies appreciate against the dollar. If they acted to offset the inflow by selling dollars, their currencies appreciated; if they did nothing, they risked inflation, which imposed costs on their exporting industries. The United States, in effect, could export its foreign policy and its inflationary tendencies. The rest of the world was relatively powerless and had to accept the system or work to change it; neither option was appealing.

In the 1960s, Keynesian economists took over the reins of economic policy-making in the United States. Emphasizing economic growth, they regarded international trade as subsidiary to prescribing for the domestic economy. Trade conditions would complement the developments in the domestic economy. Indeed, they advocated interventionist policies for the domestic economy and free trade for the international economy; they did not acknowledge the possible contradiction between the two approaches.[7]

The model was believed to work as follows: In stimulating the domestic economy through aggregate demand policies, output and employment would grow, and private investment would soon increase as well. Meanwhile, free trade would result in domestic firms increasing their exports, increasing employment, and eventually increasing investment in the United States. Thus, even more economic growth would be stimulated by free trade principles; domestic stimulation would be compatible with trade growth and one would complement the other. Perhaps, suggests David Calleo, Professor of European Studies at Johns Hopkins University, the United States was counting on increased agricultural exports, for while the United States preached free trade, its tariffs were higher than European ones. But there was a great deal of resistance from European farmers to U.S. imports, so that the hoped-for increases in agricultural commodities exports were much less than anticipated.

This was how things were supposed to work out, and there was a general consensus that they would work out as predicted. The real world did not cooperate with the model. Inflation in the United States in the 1960s, aggravated by the Vietnam war, served to make the flawed system worse. The economy was overstimulated, and domestic firms invested heavily abroad instead of in the United States. When other nations complained about the exportation of inflation, they were told, with some truth, that the United States was supplying them with defense that they did not pay for. Instead of fighting inflation at home, the United States was berating other nations for not inflating (growing) along with it. Prevented from devaluing the dollar by the rules of the game, the United States searched for ways to free itself from the restraints. The United States blamed its trade difficulties on the discriminating trade practices of Europe and Japan, the fixed exchange rate system, and its role in preserving world peace. It wanted floating exchange rates, but was unable to persuade the Europeans to make the switch.

Finally, Nixon solved the problems in his New Economic Policy in 1971 by unilaterally dissolving the Bretton Woods agreement; the United States would simply not play the game anymore and resorted to a mercantilist trade policy of trade barriers. Eventually, floating exchange rates were adopted and the United States was presumably able to pursue its trade policies free of the constraints imposed by fixed exchange rates. Now the free market would determine the exchange rates, and gold and reserve holdings would no longer pose any problems in the conduct of trade. Led by economic conservatives, the promise of freely floating exchange rates would allow the free market to do the job of currency evaluation and, of course, go a long way to resolving trade conflicts.

Again, the real world did not comply with predictions. Now there were even fewer prohibitions to inflation, and the United States failed to solve its trade problems, incurring increasing deficits and again exporting inflation. The dollar fell in value continuously in the 1970s, as oil price shocks were allowed to permeate the domestic economy. The lack of an energy policy and the failure to stop wage/price increases led to stagflation in the United States, while other nations, such as Germany and Japan, were coping much better with the supply-side shocks. In fact, the failure to deal adequately with the price shocks resulted in relatively cheap energy prices that encouraged consumption rather than conservation. Yet again the United States was exporting its inflation abroad; the declining dollar often resulted in the dirty float, as other nations tried to protect their currencies by buying dollars to prevent appreciation, thus promoting their inflation.

While the foregoing is merely a brief review of the developments in the international trade area, it is sufficient to reveal the outlines of that history to the extent necessary to bring it up to the conditions facing the Carter administration as it took office. Perhaps the administration's response to those conditions will be clearer and more understandable as a result.

Throughout the Carter years, we find that the administration was disappointed at the growth rate of our trading partners, especially the economies of Europe. Their failure to grow, or grow fast enough, meant that the U.S. exports were curtailed. Even those countries that were not experiencing a trade surplus were blamed for not stimulating their economies sufficiently. The tendency to blame others for U.S. trade problems continued throughout the Carter years. The fact that the stimulation of the U.S. economy led to inflation, and the inflation led to export losses, did not seem relevant to the analysis. The concern of Europeans about inflation in their economies and about the spread of U.S. inflation did not alter U.S. analyses of the problems or its policies.

The oil price shocks only added to the schism. Without an energy policy in the United States, energy prices were allowed to rise, which as previously mentioned, were low in comparison to other nations and thus did little to discourage consumption. While Carter did call for sacrifice and conservation, his voice and policies were not heeded. The consequences were a declining (or fluctuating) dollar, a rise in imports, and the discouragement of exports. Other nations, particularly Germany and Japan, were better able to manage the oil price shocks and had little sympathy for the failure of the United States to do so. They and others were fighting inflation, while the United States was battling stagflation.

It is clear now why the Carter administration continuously called for more cooperation in economic policy-making by the major trading nations; since the United States was not able to deal with the oil crisis and the subsequent stagflation, why not try to make others act in the same way so as not to injure U.S. trade? Multinational macro policy agreements must necessarily entail some loss of sovereignty of the participants, and it is little wonder that other nations were not so willing to accommodate the United States. That some efforts were made to prop up the dollar by some nations only indicated a desire to avoid appreciation of their currencies, and showed more the power of the United States than the desire for multinational cooperation. Still, some less developed nations were only too eager to get rid of dollars as their value continued to fall.

The policies the administration enacted to fight inflation in the second half of its term were not sufficient to placate other nations. Tax cuts to compensate for inflation were hardly viewed as anti-inflationary, whatever other programs were proposed. It was only when the monetary authorities initiated their monetarist prescription that the anti-inflation rhetoric was consistent with policy actions. As interest rates soared and recession threatened, nearly everyone came to believe in the sincerity of the administration's anti-inflation resolution. Too late, perhaps, to avoid the inflation-ratifying policies of the early years, but not too late to have serious repercussions in both domestic and international areas.

In the domestic area, many firms were seriously hurt by high interest rates, and many did not survive. Most of these firms were relatively small and could not afford to borrow at such high interest rates. The number of bankruptcies rose dramatically from 1977 to 1980. Total bankruptcies increased by over 48% for all firms, with the distribution spread over all sectors, from mining and manufacturing (43%) to retail trade (44%) and construction (61%). Internationally, many investors found the high interest rates in the United States to be very attractive, and foreign investment increased in the latter half of the 1970s.

However, Third World nations found their debt payments mounting and the burden of the debt overwhelming. Forced to borrow even more to service their debt, they faced stringent conditions imposed by lending authorities: cut domestic spending, reduce government involvement in the economy, tighten the money supply, all of which meant austerity at home in order to increase exports to pay their creditors. The burden placed on these countries was severe but was deemed necessary by those who saw little difficulty when they borrowed in the first place.

For the United States, the situation was even more ambiguous. On the one hand, it was U.S. banks who were the main lenders to Third World countries, and they stood to benefit from higher interest rates—if they ever got repaid. On the other hand, exports to Third World countries were curtailed because their economies were in trouble and because the decline in imports was a condition of receiving new loans. Needless to say, the United States was a major exporter to Latin American countries, often those who were hurting most. For the United States, the loss of exports came at a time when exporters were having difficulty anyway, and this was not a welcome development.

CONCLUSIONS

The Carter administration inherited a system of behavior in the international trade area that contained an inherent conflict between goals: the interventionist domestic policy to keep or maintain a high level of economic activity and a commitment to a free trade policy. It is not surprising that it did little to alter these goals because there was little that could be done without a major revision of historic principles. It was certainly not prepared to upset these generally accepted views.

The administration did, however, recognize the need for multinational cooperation in macroeconomic policy-making to rationalize trade relations. While it did not get very far in this direction, there was at least the acknowledgment that the United States could no longer dictate trade matters as willfully as it had done in the past. Other economies, notably Japan and Germany, as well as the growing strength and influence of the EEC, forced a reassessment of the U.S. role in the global economy.

Hence, in international trade matters, the administration was essentially a victim of past policies and of the dependence on foreign supplies of a critical resource—oil. In neither case was it responsible for the conditions it faced, and in the case of energy supplies, it at least made a sincere attempt to meet the challenges encountered. It is also fair to say that except for the oil crisis, the administration was more concerned with domestic matters first, before events in Iran and Afghanistan forced it to be consumed by international relations.

Many observers agree that the administration performed according to expectations, given its economic philosophy, for the times in which it was in office. It would be left to succeeding administrations to determine how the Federal Reserve's strategy for the domestic economy under Paul Volker would be allowed to affect conditions in the international area.

ENERGY PROBLEMS IN THE CARTER ADMINISTRATION

In the 1970s, energy issues were pushed to the forefront of U.S. concerns, and perhaps for the first time, the general public was jolted into reality about energy resources. It was not that energy matters had been entirely neglected in the past. In fact, in the late 1930s there was considerable attention paid to energy resources and the role of government in managing them.[8] The advocacy of government controls over energy resources and the mistrust of the marketplace to manage them was clearly expressed, but this sentiment was soon replaced by the needs of World War II.[9]

Following World War II and after the energy concerns raised during the Korean conflict, the President's Materials Policy Committee (known as the Paley Commission) issued a comprehensive report in 1952 on energy requirements and supplies. It was concerned that energy needs would outstrip output in time and advocated an energy policy that included the need to explore technological means to increase output (e.g., oil from shale), the importation of energy resources to conserve domestic supplies, the stockpiling of supplies, and the avoidance of dependency on Middle East oil.

These warnings went basically unheeded, and this prescient document, as well as others, was ignored by a society eager to participate in the development and use of energy-dependent technology. Thus, up to the Arab oil embargo of 1973, there was a good deal of complacency as far as energy usage was concerned. Cheap energy encouraged consumption, not conservation, and the depletion of known resources, not the exploration of new sources. For example, in October 1973, real oil prices were lower than they were in the 1950s and 1960s. Consequently, homes and factories used more energy over time, much of it without regard to efficiency. People moved to the suburbs, followed by firms and services, requiring lengthy commuting times for city workers and for trucks that serviced the firms. Energy usage rose for all types of transportation: air travel, buses, trucks, and, of course, automobiles. Meanwhile, mass transit was dismissed as inferior and declined steadily. Appliances were purchased for convenience and comfort without regard to energy consumption; air conditioners became common for the summer months, and overheated homes made the winter months more bearable.

Increasingly, oil and natural gas became the major fuel sources, replacing coal with its inconvenience, dirtiness, and later environmental damages. There was no fear of energy shortages and no thought given to energy efficiency. In short, even as U.S. production was falling, the American appetite for oil and gas was growing, necessitating imports to meet the demand. By 1973, nearly half of U.S. energy usage was provided by oil, and over a third of that usage was provided by imports; by 1979, demand was unchanged, but imports had risen to 45% of usage.[10]

The increased usage, however, was running afoul of previous practices and laws governing the operations of oil and gas producers. In the 1930s and 1940s, U.S. oil producers banded together to prevent competition from depressing oil prices. Producers kept production below demand to control prices, and quotas were assigned to members. When oil reserves were found in the Middle East and threatened to upset world oil prices, American, Dutch, and British oil companies split up the oil market to manage supply to match anticipated demand.

As demand for oil grew, so did imports (at lower prices), so that the oil companies complained of competition and depressed prices. President Eisenhower responded by imposing import quotas; each refinery was given a license to import a predetermined quantity of oil. This quota system lasted until April 1973, when Nixon finally abandoned it in favor of import fees, despite the fact that domestic oil prices exceeded import prices and were still rising as demand continued to grow. The price increases were halted by Nixon's wage and price controls until a new system was designed by the Cost of Living Council in 1973. Controls were removed from "new oil" tapped since 1973, but retained for "old oil" from existing wells.

Despite the criticisms of the oil companies regarding possible price gouging and windfall profits (and suspected withholding of supplies), attention soon switched to the fair and proper allocation of the scarce supply of oil. Congress passed the Emergency Petroleum Allocation Act (EPAA) in November 1973 that mandated that the president allocate supplies and stabilize prices. Nixon objected to this or any allocation scheme not based on market outcomes, but was forced to accept the unwanted power.

As the year 1973 progressed, the Nixon administration was fighting for survival, and energy concerns were not high on its list of priorities. Still Nixon's "project independence" and later initiatives did comprise a comprehensive list of ways to respond to the energy crisis. Included in the list were the following: authorize the president to impose restrictions on public and private use of energy, impose a 50-mile-per-hour speed limit, permit year-round daylight saving time, order power plants to use coal, ration energy supplies, construct the Alaskan oil pipeline, permit competitive pricing of new natural gas and oil, set up the Department of Energy and Natural Resources, and create an Energy Research and Development

Administration to achieve self-sufficiency by 1980. In 1974, the Nixon administration added more elements to its energy package: an emergency act to relax the requirements of the Clean Air Act; a windfall profits tax to prevent profiteering; and a requirement that fuel producers provide more information on reserves, production, and inventories (formerly energy producers controlled the data on these items).

For a variety of reasons, relations between Congress and the president were strained, and deep divisions over energy matters were apparent within Congress and with the executive branch. Without reviewing these, the Nixon administration left office with only these surviving parts of its energy program: the Alaskan pipeline; mandatory oil allocation and pricing powers; a 55-mile-per-hour speed limit; a reorganization of the energy bureaucracy into the Federal Energy Administration (FEA), responsible for fuel shortage problems; and the Energy Research and Development Administration (ERDA), responsible for consolidating energy research; and funds (minimal) for energy research into nonnuclear energy research and development.

It is clear that the Nixon administration had proposed a variety of weapons to fight the energy crisis of the early 1970s. They are covered here in outline form to illustrate that succeeding administrations built on the schemes and ideas first introduced in this administration. Yet, for all the hoopla, not much was really accomplished. As one observer put it, the Nixon administration was involved in "mainly putting out fires" for it failed to convince the public that the government was partly to blame for energy problems because of its past regulatory policies on oil and gas, creating along the way a powerful special interest group; that it undermined its case for regulation by allowing imports while claiming to support domestic exploration and development; that its proposals ran counter to environmental concerns; and that its actions in response to the oil embargo were not appropriate for the long-run solution to energy problems.[11] Of course, other political problems between Nixon and Congress must also be factored in after the Watergate affair transformed the relationship.

The Ford Program

The Ford administration acted swiftly to produce an energy program to reduce America's energy shortages and dependency. Ford thought the way to achieve this was to increase the price of fuel to encourage domestic production and discourage consumption. Hence, he proposed an import fee on imported oil that was challenged for legality by Congress and finally sanctioned by the Supreme Court. It was later removed when Congress passed the Energy Policy and Conservation Act in 1975, which incorporated many of the proposals that Ford had made in his version of the Energy Independence Bill presented early in 1975. As passed, the Energy Policy and Conservation Act included the following: expansion of FEA powers so it could order the switch to coal and make loan guarantees to encourage development of new mines for less-polluting coal; increased authority to the president to control the use of energy supplies by restricting exports, allocating supplies, and requiring refineries to maintain or distribute inventories; provision for a strategic petroleum reserve; expansion of presidential powers to order conservation and gasoline rationing; mandatory fuel economy standards for autos, requiring an average of 26 miles per gallon by 1985; energy testing and labeling of major appliances; continuation of oil price controls on domestic oil into 1979; and authorization for federal audits of anyone required to submit energy information.

In addition to this major act, Congress provided $5 billion in funds for the new Energy Research and Development Administration for programs in solar, geothermal, and fission research. Of the $5 billion, $4 billion was directed toward nuclear programs. Opponents of the Clinch River, Tennessee, breeder reactor did not succeed in eliminating this contentious project designed to produce electricity and nuclear fuel from plutonium. Moreover, Congress extended for ten years the legal limit on the nuclear industry's liability for an accident. Congress and the president were at odds, however, over higher gasoline taxes or taxes on gas-guzzling cars, as well as a Ford proposal to subsidize private industry to encourage energy development of new or existing energy sources.

Ford's problems with Congress continued into 1976, and not much in the way of energy legislation was passed in that election year. The FEA was extended until the end of 1977, and an act was passed awarding grants and loans to coastal areas where offshore oil was being considered in order to study social and environmental issues and to provide for public facilities or services in regard to coastal activity. Congress also overrode Ford's veto and provided funds for the development of the electric car. But no action was taken on gas taxes, natural gas deregulation, synthetic fuel subsidies, or revising federal rules on outer continental shelf development.

Ford's opponents in Congress simply had a different philosophy on energy matters. For instance, they considered price controls on fuels as necessary since their removal would exacerbate inflation and hurt consumers. To encourage production, they felt that prices were already high enough and fought to limit the windfall profits that would emerge once price controls were removed. They wanted to discourage consumption by imposing new taxes as a stick and encourage conservation by using tax credits as a carrot. They wanted to ban fuel-inefficient cars and appliances, mandate coal usage where possible, and seek alternative sources of energy, while preserving environmental standards. It is clear that this agenda would have clashed with the more conservative approach of the Ford administration. The difficulty is that with such confusion within and without the administration, the focus is likely to be on the short term as policymakers respond to the need for action. Long-term policies are likely to be ignored in the process, leaving technology advances to remedy future problems.[12]

THE CARTER PROGRAM

Space limitations prevent a complete description of the energy situation prior to the Carter administration; however, the foregoing description is sufficient to indicate the responses to the energy crisis in the period 1973–1976. Since Carter made energy matters such a small part of his campaign, it is now time to ascertain why there was a turnaround and how he intended to address the issue in concrete terms.

On his inaugural day, Carter promised to announce his energy plans by April 20, 1977, an unwise promise perhaps, but he managed to meet it. Before analyzing this comprehensive plan, it might be better to review the other energy matters in the administration's first year. The bitter winter of 1977 forced Carter to act before his full energy plan was completed. On January 26, shortly after his inauguration, he asked Congress for emergency powers to transfer natural gas supplies to areas that had depleted their supplies and to permit sales of gas to interstate buyers at unregulated prices. The shortages were so severe that industries and schools were forced to close in some parts of the country. Congress acted swiftly and passed the Emergency Natural Gas Act of 1977, giving the president the powers he requested for one year. Carter signed the bill on the same day and then appeared on national television, in a sweater, to explain the crisis to the American people.

On March 1, Carter proposed (wisely separate from his national energy plan) a cabinet-level Department of Energy that would consolidate the functions of the Federal Energy Administration (FEA), the Federal Power Commission (FPC), and the Energy Research and Development Administration (ERDA) into one unit. This would permit, according to Carter, the treatment of energy problems in a comprehensive way with the responsibility centered in one agency. Congress agreed with one exception: The energy secretary would not be given the power to set prices for natural gas, oil, or electricity as originally proposed. So much power invested in one individual was rejected by Congress as unwise. Still, the establishment of this new department was a victory for Carter, and on August 4, he signed the act into law. The first secretary was James Schlesinger, who had developed the original energy plan of the administration.

In March, Carter asked Congress to stockpile 500 million barrels of crude oil in reserve by the end of 1980 rather than 1982 as proposed by Ford. Congress agreed and appropriated the funds necessary in June. In November, Congress also approved the administration's route for the transmission of oil from Alaska and, in August, eliminated the Joint Atomic Energy Committee, transferring its jurisdiction to other committees. The once-powerful committee had come under increasing criticism as the protector of nuclear energy, which was being questioned as a safe source of energy. The long battle by environmentalists to regulate strip mining was finally won by the passage of the Surface Mining Control and Reclamation Act. Finally, Carter vetoed a bill that would have authorized $6.2 billion for energy research because it contained funds for the Clinch River Breeder Reactor, which was supposed to "show that plutonium fueled and plutonium-producing 'breeder' reactors were a feasible source of electricity and nuclear fuel."[13] Carter was concerned that the use of plutonium would increase the risk of nuclear proliferation, and he requested funds only for the shutdown of operation. (In February 1978, a new bill authorizing funds for energy research minus the funds for the Clinch River Reactor was passed with $3.2 billion for nuclear programs and $1.8 billion for nonnuclear research.)

The National Energy Plan

In a speech to the nation on April 18, Carter unveiled his plan and, as hoped for, received a great deal of publicity. The energy plan was eagerly awaited, not really because of campaign pledges, since energy issues failed to excite the electorate, but because of the cold winter that forced the president to hold a fireside chat, à la Roosevelt, to warn the American people of energy shortages. Whatever excitement that was generated over the energy problem was induced by fear and apprehension.

Also adding to the anticipation was that the administration's plan was being developed in relative seclusion by a team led by Carter's energy tsar, James Schlesinger. The CEA was not kept abreast, for instance, of what was being considered.[14] The administration did request advice from some 450,000 citizens, but the responses, while impressive in number, did not produce much that was new or useful.[15] The lack of participation in the construction of the energy plan was probably a mistake in judgment, which would prove characteristic of the early years of the administration. According to White House observer James Fallows, Schlesinger convinced Carter that total secrecy was necessary, "But the major decisions about energy were political, not technical. . . . Instead, Schlesinger developed his technically plausible energy plan in a political vacuum, submitting it to the scrutiny of Carter's other advisors and the members of Congress only after all the basic choices had been made. To Carter and Schlesinger, solving the energy problem must originally have seemed like solving a cube root. Once they had the right answer, they thought their work would be done."[16] Carter justified the procedure as follows: "Because of the short time allowed [which he set!] for completing the project, creating a plan would require maximum coordination among the many agencies involved and would not permit the extensive consultation with congressional leaders that might insure swifter action once our legislation was sent to Capital Hill. . . . The plan needed to be completed without delay if Congress was to debate the matter during the first year."[17]

The plan was introduced using the hyperbole designed to arouse public awareness and support. "The energy crisis has not overwhelmed us, but it will if we do not act quickly. It is a problem we will not be able to solve in the next few years, and it is likely to get progressively worse through the rest of this century. . . . Our decision about energy will test the character of the American people and the ability of the President and the Congress to govern this nation. This difficult effort will be the 'moral equivalent of war,' except that we will be uniting our efforts to build and not to destroy."[18]

The plan had three energy objectives: (1) to reduce dependence on foreign oil and vulnerability to supply interruptions; (2) to keep U.S. imports sufficiently low as world oil production reaches its capacity; and (3) to develop renewable sources of energy. To reach these goals, the energy plan stressed conservation and production. Specifically, the goals, to be achieved from 1977 to 1985 (the plan's horizon), were to:[19]

- reduce the rate of growth of energy consumption to below 2 percent per year
- reduce gasoline consumption by 10% below the 1976 level
- reduce oil imports to less than 6 million barrels per day
- establish a Strategic Petroleum Reserve of 1 billion barrels
- increase coal production by about two-thirds, to more than 1 billion tons annually
- insulate 90% of American homes and all new buildings; use solar energy in more than 2½ million homes.

For conservation, the plan included these main items:

- a graduated excise tax on new automobiles with fuel efficiencies below the fleet average required now (27.5 mpg by 1985) but moving the date to 1978 for purposes of imposing the excise tax; taxes would rise from 1978 to 1985 and then remain constant. Rebates (graduated) would be given for new cars that exceeded the standard. A similar system was proposed for light-duty trucks.
- a standby gasoline tax to take effect if total national gasoline consumption exceeded stated annual targets. The tax would begin at five cents per gallon and could rise to fifty cents in ten years. Taxes collected would be returned to the public through the income tax or transfer payment programs.
- removal of the federal excise tax preference for motorboats, and a tax increase on general aviation fuels.

The emphasis placed on transportation issues testifies to the importance of this area in the consumption of fuel. Transportation consumed 26% of U.S. energy, with autos accounting for half of that amount, about 5 million barrels per day. The plan then turned to energy issues in the building area. About 20% of the energy was used to heat and cool buildings, much of that wasted. To combat this, the plan proposed the following:

- a tax credit of 25% on the first $800 and 15% of the next $1,400 spent on approved residential conservation measures
- conservation loans for residential measures and rural programs to encourage conservation measures
- increased funding for weatherization programs for low-income households
- grants programs to aid schools and hospitals to insulate their buildings
- fuel efficiency standards for new buildings
- mandatory minimum efficiency standards for major appliances
- an additional 10% tax credit for energy-saving investments for certain industrial conservation measures
- the removal of institutional barriers to cogeneration, the simultaneous production of process steam and electricity
- a host of measures designed for utility reform, such as the removal of programs that offered declining rates as usage increased.

Note that most of these proposals were designed to reduce the demand for energy, but the plan also called for actions on the supply side. For oil, the plan was designed to encourage production, to provide for a more rational distribution pattern, but to prevent windfall profits. It included the following:

- the retention of price controls, but the current price ceilings for previously discovered oil of $5.25 (from wells prior to 1975) and $11.28 for new oil would be adjusted for inflation.

- newly discovered oil (since 1975) would be allowed to rise over a three-year period to the 1977 world price (adjusted for inflation); thereafter the price of oil would remain at that level adjusted for inflation. Oil from stripper wells would be priced at world prices.

- since the new pricing scheme would result in more revenues for oil producers, this "windfall" would be subject to taxation. All domestic oil would become subject in three stages to a crude oil equalization tax equal to the difference between its controlled price and the world oil price. The revenues from the tax would be returned to consumers through the income tax system or transfer payment programs. Once the tax was in effect, there would be a more realistic price structure (that would encourage conservation), and all oil would have the same price. Some regulatory programs would also be eliminated.

The administration's plan for natural gas recognized that the demand for natural gas had changed significantly over time and now was under-priced and subject to excess demand. It was no longer a by-product of oil production, but was becoming the fuel of choice. Past regulations established when gas was in surplus and cheap were no longer sensible; supply would have to be brought closer to demand. This might entail deregulation in the long run, but for now the plan was to bring about balance gradually before full market pricing would be feasible. Accordingly, the administration asked for price controls on natural gas from old wells, while removing them for new discoveries. This meant that gas would be priced at $1.75 per thousand cubic feet (mcf) in 1978 and be allowed to increase with inflation; new gas was expected to rise to $3 per mcf.

This rather complicated scheme for natural gas was supplemented by several additional elements, which concerned regulations of outer continental shelf leasing programs, liberalization of the importation of liquified natural gas, and the expansion of strategic oil reserves.

In order to bring about balance in the oil and gas markets, the administration placed heavy reliance on coal to bridge the gap. Coal, of course, has environmental impacts that cannot be ignored. Hence, the administration advocated various research programs to make coal usage compatible with pollution standards. Still, coal usage was encouraged for utilities and industries, and that encouragement was in the form of taxes on the use of oil and natural gas. The tax on industrial users of natural gas would be the difference between their average cost of natural gas and the target price of distillate oil. Since the price of oil was expected to rise into the 1980s, the price of natural gas would rise also, bringing in tax revenues to the government. Thus, on the one hand there were sticks, taxes and regulations, to encourage the use of abundant coal, and carrots in the form of an additional investment tax credit for those converting to coal and promises of technological advances that would make coal more attractive.

The national energy plan had little to say regarding nuclear energy or hydroelectric power. Instead, it hoped to stimulate alternative sources of energy. It proposed a tax credit for solar energy, and an extension of the tax deduction for intangible drilling costs to geothermal drilling. In addition, the plan called for federal support of many research and development programs and an information system to collect data on fuel sources. Finally, a program for emergency fuel assistance to low-income persons was being developed for congressional approval.

The administration claimed that the macroeconomic effects of this energy plan would be quite small. Admitting to some imprecision of the estimates, it claimed that the overall effects could be slightly stimulative, with employment and capital investment rising along with GNP. Inflation, however, could rise on the order of one-quarter to one-half percent per year over the next four years. The price of fuels would rise in any case, with or without the plan, but the trade-off between inflation and energy plans had to be faced. Independent agencies generally agreed with the general assessment of the administration as to the nature of the energy problem facing the nation. Both the Congressional Budget Office (CBO) and the Office of Technology Assessment (OTA) analyzed the plan as submitted, and while both had some reservations as to the amount of energy that would be saved with the plan, they generally favored the approach.[20]

The Fate of the National Energy Plan

Whatever one's views on the efficacy of any portion of this energy plan, it must be admitted that it was a comprehensive and far-ranging plan. Since it touched on so many aspects of the energy problem, it was to be expected that many objections would be raised as it was debated, and so there were, but not from the House. Under the leadership of Speaker Tip O'Neill, who cleverly selected a pro-energy special committee, and who browbeat members of standing committees into completing work before Carter's deadline of October 1, 1977, the House passed the energy plan virtually intact on August 5.

The Senate, however, broke down the energy bill into separate pieces and, on October 31, passed five bills. They differed drastically from the House versions, and extensive conference sessions were inevitable. The major problems revolved around natural gas pricing and energy taxes, both areas controlled by powerful special interests and influential senators from oil-producing states. Finally, a five-part energy bill was completed and signed into law on October 15, 1978, eighteen months after it was proposed. As passed, the act was a watered-down version of the one presented by Carter in April 1977. Gone were some of the key elements of the original plan: the standby gasoline tax was dropped early; the tax on domestic crude oil to raise prices to world levels was gone; and the tax on industrial users of oil and natural gas was eliminated. The original plan estimated an oil savings of 4.5 million barrels a day by 1985, but with the elimination of key provisions, the savings was reduced by half.

What remained in the National Energy Act of 1978 might well be considered a victory of sorts, since it advanced the cause of conservation that Carter had stressed. (The energy plan originally proposed did not contain much that was new, in the sense that previous administrations and observers had made similar suggestions in the energy field. Still, here was something tangible that Carter had managed to secure over the suspicion of the public that no energy problem existed.) The act did retain many of the conservation programs that the administration wanted: weatherization grants, conservation loans, solar energy programs, prohibition of the use of oil or gas in new plants or utilities, prohibition of declining utility rates as consumption increases, and a host of new taxes and tax credits.

After all the bitter struggles over the energy plan in 1977 and 1978, after all the maneuvering by special interest groups and members of Congress, and after all the resistance by the public to arguments that an energy crisis was at hand, the watered-down plan was passed, but it was evident that major problems remained. The pricing policies of oil and natural gas had caused many conflicts and opened many wounds. More work in this contentious area remained as Carter acknowledged even as he celebrated his victory.[21]

ENERGY MATTERS IN THE LAST HALF OF THE ADMINISTRATION

The administration did not expect to devote much of its time to energy concerns in the remainder of its tenure. Having proposed a comprehensive energy plan in its first year, there seemed little else to do. In fact, the CEA did not even consider energy matters after its annual report of 1978. The world, however, did not cooperate, and the administration was soon forced to respond to events it could not control. The reduction of oil from Iran followed by Carter's cut-off in November of oil imports from Iran after the U.S. embassy was seized was not foreseen by anyone. Everyone remembered, however, the gasoline shortage in the spring of 1979 and the long lines of automobiles at filling stations. Then the accident at the nuclear power plant on Three-Mile Island, Pennsylvania, cast a long shadow on the future of nuclear power. Added to the question of safety was the growing concern over the disposal of nuclear waste. The inevitable result was the disenchantment with a source of energy favored by the administration.

In response to the gasoline shortage, Carter asked for a stand-by plan to ration supplies via coupons as in World War II. Congress balked at the allocation schemes, and Carter responded with shock at Congress' actions. Eventually, Congress authorized the president to produce a rationing plan, but it reserved the right to veto it.

In April 1979, Carter again appeared before the nation with another energy speech that contained myriads of proposals, some carrots and some sticks, some pleas for conservation and some warnings. The main element was the decontrol of oil prices beginning June 1, and the ending of all controls by October 1, 1981. A windfall profits tax of 50% of already-flowing oil was proposed, while new oil would not be taxed. The proceeds of the tax would be returned for general use and to support the development of synthetic fuels. In addition, an "OPEC tax" of 50% would apply indefinitely to oil profits gained whenever OPEC raised the price of world oil. The proceeds would be used to help low-income households pay their energy bills, to improve mass transit, and to develop alternative sources of energy. Carter proposed an energy trust fund to disperse these revenues from oil taxes.

Both houses of Congress passed somewhat watered-down versions of the windfall profits tax, with the Senate vetoing all proposals to use revenues for alternative energy development. At year's end, conferees were still debating the issue and arguing over the amount of revenue that would be raised. Finally in April 1980, Congress passed The Crude Oil Windfall Profits Tax Act that differed from Carter's proposal. The tax would not be indefinite but end when the revenue raised reached $227.3 billion, or in October 1993. Congress rejected the idea of an energy trust fund and the development of alternative energy sources in favor of the revenue flowing into the general fund. Finally, Congress rejected the flat

50% rate in favor of a sliding scale, depending on the type of oil, when it was first tapped, the method of production, and the producer.

In July 1979 after returning from an international conference in Tokyo that imposed oil imports limits, Carter found the mood of the nation worrisome. He retreated to Camp David where he sought the advice of over 100 leading citizens and then abruptly requested the resignations of his cabinet. He accepted those of his energy chiefs (and others), and replaced them quickly. After postponing a speech on energy on July 5 in order to seek advice, he finally delivered another energy speech on July 15. He told the nation that he had learned that the United States was suffering from "a crisis of confidence," and called for "a rebirth of the American spirit" to combat the energy crisis.

Out of the apparent chaos of the administration, the July speech did question the values of the American public, but also made some new energy proposals. Carter wanted to create an Energy Security Corporation that would direct the development of synthetic fuels. Moreover, he proposed an Energy Mobilization Board that would expedite construction of critical energy facilities. The final major element was the imposition of a ceiling on oil imports, probably in response to foreign criticisms of U.S. oil consumption. At the end of 1979, these proposals were in conference sessions, and the only major energy legislation passed was the gasoline rationing authorization.

On June 30, 1980, Carter signed into law the Energy Security Act that authorized the creation of the United States Synthetic Fuels Corporation. The act provided the seven-member corporation board $20 billion to utilize in joint ventures with private firms to construct synthetic fuel plants or to help finance coal mines or transportation facilities. Also, the act promoted the use of alcohol fuels, solar energy, and the production of fuel from urban waste. Passage of the act represented a victory for Carter, since he had stressed the need for alternative fuels from the beginning of his administration.

Congress, however, rejected the president's Energy Mobilization Board proposal. The House passed a bill creating a board resembling the one proposed by the president, but the Senate bill created a board with different powers. The Carter proposal envisioned a board that could cut through the red tape usually found in bureaucracy. The board could establish binding schedules for designated projects and could act in place of the unit, be it federal, state, or local, if deadlines were not kept. The Senate objected to the intrusion into states' rights and worried that environmental standards could be violated. The House voted for an even stronger board, and when the conferees met, they compromised by requiring the board to justify its actions before Congress. The House voted down the bill, largely because of the pending presidential election.

As part of the windfall profits bill, Congress included a provision limiting the president from unilaterally imposing oil import quotas. The president could be blocked from imposing quotas if both houses approved identical resolutions opposing his action. The only other piece of legislation was the passage of the low-level nuclear waste disposal bill that made the disposal of nuclear waste a state responsibility. Unable to fashion a bill that seriously dealt with nuclear waste disposal, Congress finally agreed after much turmoil to this mild version that did very little in this critical area.

CONCLUSIONS

This then is the outline of the record of the Carter administration on energy matters. It would have been a difficult time for any administration, for many of the energy problems were beyond immediate control. Although Carter proposed nothing that was radically different from previous administrations, he did attempt to dramatize the serious nature of energy problems. Perhaps his emphasis on conservation and demand-side problems were his major contributions to the debate on energy usage and availability. Still, he had to overcome the skepticism of the public, the power of special interest groups, and a contentious Congress. No one could debate the fervor with which he presented his assessments of the energy situation facing the United States. Despite his failure to overcome some of these obstacles to needed legislation, the sincerity of his message should not be doubted. In his own assessment, he wrote, "In looking back on the 'moral equivalent of war' against energy waste and excessive vulnerability from oil imports, I see nothing exhilarating or pleasant. It was a bruising fight, and no final clear-cut victory could be photographed and hung on the wall for our grandchildren to admire."[22]

With the benefit of hindsight, and far removed from the "bruising fight" and passions of the times, it is fair to ask how the Carter administration performed in the battle. While it is certainly true that the problems in the energy field were not of its own making, the reactions and responses to them are legitimately subject to review.

Assessment

Clearly, the energy plan proposed in 1977 was the major initiative of the Carter administration; other proposals were necessitated by events to which the administration responded. The administration must be given high marks for its comprehensive plan and for its attempt to confront energy issues with the due warnings about energy problems generally. It was a sincere effort to rally the American people to recognize the problem and offer a solution—conservation—that was necessary, if not sufficient.

Yet, this energy program was flawed, not so much in the technical sense (although experts do suggest some technical flaws), but in its development and presentation. First, it was developed in secret, without input from others knowledgeable in energy matters.[23] There was no consultation within or without the administration. As previously indicated, there were many political issues involved with these energy problems and solutions, yet Congress was not consulted. It was as if politics did not matter—the technical solution was paramount, and once the program was unveiled, acceptance was sure to follow. Congress and others were alienated at the beginning, and some resistance to the plan was bound to result. Carter, after all, did not have a mandate to propose such a sweeping change.

Second, the plan was too complicated for easy understanding. Carter wrote to Schlesinger, "I am not satisfied with your approach. It is extremely complicated (I can't understand it)."[24] Perhaps the plan was too ambitious for everyone, including Congress, that had to wrestle with it. It might have been preferable to concentrate on a few major issues and gradually add new ones when the others were disposed of.

Third, there was that artificial deadline for passage of the bill. Granted, the administration wanted to create an atmosphere of crisis, but to force a deadline on such a comprehensive plan was to push Congress unnecessarily.

Fourth, as already indicated, there were powerful special interest groups affected by the plan, and powerful congressmen ready to object to constraints put on their constituents and benefactors. Fifth, the plan was poorly sold to Congress—typical of the early years of the administration—and engendered unnecessary resistance.

Finally, the plan lacked a real constituency. The public was skeptical of all energy problems. It was convinced that a giant conspiracy was responsible for fuel shortages, and reports to the effect that oil shortages were not genuine did not help. The plan and subsequent energy proposals called for sacrifices from the public, but these could not be secured when the data were suspect and rumors were rife. In Carter's own words, "I was concerned about the difficulty of arousing public support for so complicated a program. . . . The skepticism about oil and gas companies was pervasive, leading many people to doubt the need for any sacrifice or new legislation.

This doubt would continue to plague our efforts during the months ahead."[25]

The initial energy plan had a rather short horizon—from 1977 to 1985. Little was indicated about plans for the long term. Later, the emphasis on alternative energy sources would remedy some of this omission. Still, the overall macroeconomic effects of the energy plan were not calculated beyond the short-term horizon, nor were macroeconomic policies discussed to cope with tax and expenditure changes that might occur. The short-run macroeconomic effects were calculated to be rather small, but over time, the redistribution of income from households to energy producers and government could have been large and disrupting. Rebates on energy taxes would address some of the problem, but they could not be counted on, since Congress could and did balk at them. In general, the macroeconomic effects of the energy plans were not given the consideration they deserved.

Subsequent efforts at developing an energy program would not suffer from the same defects but, instead, ran into others. The calls for sacrifices and changes in values continued to fall on many deaf ears, although conservation efforts did have some success. Long gas lines were convincing where appeals were not. Eventually, the public did respond, and many conservation measures were put in place. Alternative sources of energy were seriously considered, and funds were secured for their development. Yet, whatever success the administration had, it was still blamed for the energy crisis, and the closer the presidential election of 1980 came, the more it was blamed, and the more Congress played political games.

In brief, the Carter administration deserves considerable credit for arousing the nation to the energy problem and for proposing viable solutions to meet it. It stumbled in its presentation of the solutions to energy matters and suffered the consequences of long delays in implementation, leading to the charge of incompetence when it should have received credit for its thoughtful program. Carter did not shy away from the energy problem, nor did he seek any particular political advantage from it. In energy matters, then, the Carter administration deserves recognition for its efforts to lead the nation at a time of genuine stress.

NOTES

1. Another interesting facet of these trade data that will not be pursued here is that if the nominal values are corrected for price changes using aggregate import and export price indexes, the merchandise trade turns from deficits to surpluses. For 1977, the

positive balance would be $6.9 billion; for 1978, $1.3 billion; for 1979, $2.9 billion; and for 1980, $11.2 billion. However, these price indexes are too aggregative for accurate results and not always comparable in definitions with the rest of the world categories in this time period. They are inserted here as a reminder that trade data are usually presented in nominal terms without regard for relative price changes. Instead, the trade-weighted value of the dollar often serves as a necessary substitute.

2. The administration's view of trade problems is taken from its *Economic Report of the President, 1978.*

3. This experience of trade in this period is surely a fascinating one but cannot be treated in a book of this kind. For more, see Jacob A. Frankel, "United States Inflation and the Dollar," in *Inflation,* edited by Robert E. Hall (Chicago: University of Chicago Press, 1982), 189–209.

4. Again, most of the information pertaining to administration views comes from the *Economic Report of the President, 1979.* Also see U.S. Department of Commerce, *Survey of Current Business* (March 1979), 38–62, for trade data and analysis. For the views of the Federal Reserve System, see *Federal Reserve Bulletin* (April 1979), 299–304.

5. Administration views can be found in the *Economic Report of the President, 1980,* and more detail on trade data can be found in U.S. Department of Commerce, *Survey of Current Business* (March 1980), 44–72.

6. See the *Economic Report of the President, 1981,* 182–213. For the data on trade, see U.S. Department of Commerce, *Survey of Current Business* (March 1981), 40–67, and the *Federal Reserve Bulletin* (April 1981), 269–276.

7. The analysis here owes much to David P. Calleo, *The Imperious Economy* (Cambridge, Mass.: Harvard University Press, 1982).

8. See the report of the Energy Resources Committee to the National Resources Committee, *Energy Resources and National Policy* (Washington, D.C.: Government Printing Office, 1939).

9. For a very comprehensive review of energy policy over the years, see Craufurd D. Goodwin (ed.), *Energy Policy in Perspective: Today's Problems, Yesterday's Solutions* (Washington, D.C.: The Brookings Institution, 1981). The analysis in the text owes much to this valuable work.

10. For additional details and for a thorough compilation of energy legislation, see Congressional Quarterly, *Energy Policy* (Washington, D.C.: Congressional Quarterly, 1981). For the proportions cited in the text, see page 8.

11. Neil de Marchi, "Energy Policy under Nixon: Mainly Putting Out Fires," in Goodwin, *Energy Policy in Perspective,* 395–397.

12. For a detailed analysis of the Ford administration's response and problems in the energy area, see Neil de Marchi, "The Ford Administration: Energy as a Political Good," in Goodwin, *Energy Policy in Perspective,* 475–545.

13. Congressional Quarterly, *Energy Policy,* 185. This is a useful source for energy analysis and legislation and was relied upon for much of the discussion in the text.

14. For a discussion of the development of the energy plan as well as a detailed description of Carter's energy policy, see James L. Cochrane, "Carter Energy Policy and the Ninety-fifth Congress," in Goodwin, *Energy Policy in Perspective,* 547–600. See also Joseph A. Yager, "Energy Battles of 1979," in Goodwin, *Energy Policy in Perspective,* 601–636.

15. For those interested in the suggestions, see Executive Office of the President, *Energy Policy and Planning the National Energy Plan: Summary of Public Participation* (Washington, D.C.: Government Printing Office, no date).

16. James Fallows, "The Passionless Presidency," *The Atlantic Monthly* (May 1979), 40–41.

17. Jimmy Carter, *Keeping Faith* (New York: Bantam Books, 1982), 93.

18. Address to the Nation, April 18, 1977.

19. Executive Office of the President, Office of Energy Policy and Planning, *The National Energy Plan* (Washington, D.C.: Government Printing Office, April 29, 1977), 83–84.

20. See Congressional Budget Office, *President Carter's Energy Proposals: A Perspective*, June 1977; and Office of Technology Assessment, *Analysis of the Proposed National Energy Plan*, August 1977. Both reports are much too detailed to discuss here, but the interested reader can find a more complete assessment of the plan than can be presented here. For those interested, the CBO estimated a reduction in GNP of –0.2% in 1978, –0.5% in 1979, and –0.7% in 1980. Unemployment was estimated to rise by 0.1% in 1979 and 0.2% in 1980. Both consumption and investment expenditures were projected to fall in the period 1978–1980, reaching a high of –0.4% for consumption and –1.8% for investment in 1980. The CBO cautioned that these estimates might be on the high side. CBO, *President Carter's Energy Proposals*, 113.

21. See his assessment of the energy act and his plans to continue the fight for a more rational oil pricing scheme in Carter, *Keeping Faith*, 107–108.

22. Ibid., 123–124.

23. For some of these criticisms see the Congressional Quarterly, *Energy Policy*, 191.

24. Carter, *Keeping Faith*, 96.

25. Ibid., 93.

Chapter 8

Reforms in the Carter Years

No analysis of the Carter administration would be complete without some reference to the other pledges Carter made during and after the campaign. Some of the economic elements have already been examined—the economic stimulus package, an energy plan, and the plan to balance the budget by 1981. But recall that Carter also pledged to make government run more efficiently largely through reorganization, to revamp the budget-making process of the federal government by employing a zero-budgeting technique, to reform the welfare mess, and to reduce government intrusion in the economy by eliminating unnecessary regulations. Before summarizing the economic accomplishments of the Carter administration, we will examine its performance in these areas as well.

GOVERNMENT REORGANIZATION

Of course, every administration takes office promising to reform government operations, reduce the size of the bureaucracy, and in general make the government run more efficiently. The results of such promises have not inspired confidence in such intentions, and more often than not, government operations carry on as before, and the bureaucracy expands. Therefore, Carter's pledges would normally invite cynicism and be dismissed as just another example of political hyperbole. Yet, Carter was different in the sense that he ran as a Washington outsider with a very definite promise to clean up the mess there as he had done in Georgia. Appealing to his past record in these matters offered him some allowances that others would not have received. In a speech at the National Governors Conference in 1974, he maintained that Georgia had "reduced the number of state agencies from about 300 to 22 major operating agencies and combined functions to eliminate duplication and overlapping of services."[1]

Carter's commitment to restoring confidence in government can be seen early in his administration, when he requested the authority to reorganize the federal government. The Reorganization Act of 1949, enabling a president to examine all agencies and determine what changes are necessary, had expired in April 1973. After Nixon, Congress was reluctant to grant any president such sweeping powers to reform government. Therefore, Carter had to request the renewal of authority, but his plan to do so ran into some strong opposition, largely on constitutional grounds. (The plan set some stringent time limits for Congress to act upon reorganization plans, and they would take effect after 60 days unless either house passed a resolution of disapproval during that time period. This rejection would constitute a legislative veto, which raised a difficult constitutional issue.)[2]

The authority was granted in March 1977, and Carter proceeded to send to Congress numerous reorganization plans. It is instructive to note that the responsibility for reorganization plans was given to OMB, indicating the importance attached to them by Carter. The plans covered the following areas:

1. *Executive office of the president*—streamlined the office and reduced the staff.

2. *International public diplomacy*—merged the U.S. Information Agency and State Department's Bureau of Educational and Cultural Affairs.

3. *Equal Employment Opportunity transfers*—consolidated all equal opportunity enforcement activities.

4. *Civil Service Commission transfers*—divided the Civil Service into the Office of Personal Management and the independent Merit System Protection Board.

5. *Federal Emergency Management Agency*—consolidated federal programs dealing with domestic disasters.

6. *Employee retirement income security*—clarified responsibilities for the Employment Retirement Income and Security Act (ERISA).

7. *Federal Inspector for Alaska Natural Gas Pipeline*—consolidated enforcement functions under a single inspector.

8. *International Development Cooperation Agency*—combined assistance programs under this agency.

9. *International trade functions*—centralized authority to ensure trade agreements are fully realized.

10. *Nuclear Regulatory Commission*—reforms concerning nuclear power plant safety (no action on waste disposal).

These were the main reorganization plans approved by Congress. In addition, there were attempts to reduce the amount of paperwork involved in many agencies. When asked about the cost savings these plans would produce, Harrison Wellford, executive associate director for Reorganization and Management of OMB, replied that many of the reorganization plans were not designed to reduce costs but increase efficiency, and the numbers he did supply were simply guesses.[3] In many cases, cost savings would be difficult to estimate, and in other cases, the cost savings would accrue to the public, not necessarily to the treasury. Nevertheless, the absence of better cost reduction estimates represented a shortcoming if the aim was to convince people of the benefits of reorganization.

Carter was pleased with his legislative success overall but regretted his failure "to abolish many of the small and unnecessary agencies, commissions, and boards in the federal bureaucracy. Only a positive action by Congress—rather than the special reorganization act—could have eliminated them."[4]

He could boast that he had accomplished some of his goals: Cabinet-level departments were created for education and energy. The creation of these departments represented a victory for Carter, who saw the need to consolidate (and elevate) the functions of these areas to make them more effective. He was also proud of his success in revamping the civil service. The civil service had long been criticized as a haven for the "play-it-safe" type of person who exerted no initiative, took no chances, and simply sought security. According to knowledgeable observers, this resulted from an organizational fault, in which the top positions of the civil service are filled by political appointees brought in by each new administration. There was no incentive to perform to the best of one's ability if recognition and promotions were blocked by positions of power held by appointees. What was needed was a number of positions at the top for professional civil servants whose careers would survive the changing of administrations or would be subject to removal because of ideological differences.

Furthermore, the civil service had always been criticized for its inability to award merit or punish poor job performance. The bureaucracy was simply rigid and inflexible. With these general criticisms in mind, the Civil Service Reform Act of 1978 promised to address these issues. Carter certainly deserves credit for attacking the central problems of the civil service bureaucracy, even though he presented the bill to do so with the usual "bureaucratic bashing" rhetoric normally associated with less thoughtful critics and that speaks more of housecleaning than reform.[5]

Conclusions on Reorganization

Carter took office with the promise to use a new broom to sweep clean the mess in Washington. As far as reorganization of government is concerned, he left with a mixed record. His main successes were in the establishment of the departments of energy and education and in the reform of the civil service. He could justly be proud of his efforts in these areas and fulfilled a promise to make government more efficient. Furthermore, his reorganization of the agencies mentioned above resulted in needed consolidation and reforms that were not glamorous but probably made government more efficient.

Yet, he did not accomplish all that he had pledged in restructuring government. Perhaps four years is insufficient to do the job; perhaps he mismanaged the attempt. In the words of one observer, "Jimmy Carter did not so much fail in accomplishing the objectives of reorganization and management reform in the Federal government as much as he did not fully appreciate the structural, political and personal constraints to success."[6] To this could be added that it was a period of fiscal constraint, and one dominated in the end by foreign policy events. Still, according to one observer, the lessons that follow Carter's experience could be instructive to reorganizers of the future. Carter had too many reorganization plans; he did not secure the cooperation of the business community; he failed to get congressional support; he did not seek the cooperation of the agencies being reorganized; he was too involved personally in overseeing the efforts; and he did not recruit managers who were experienced in reorganizational efforts.

Similar criticisms seem to permeate the Carter administration in whatever task it undertook. What lessons it did learn from the early years came too late to remedy. The charge of incompetence, warranted or not, was too difficult to overcome. Still, Carter recognized the need for governmental reform and eagerly set about to realize it. His partial success should not detract from the vision.

ZERO-BASE BUDGETING

As part of his overall plan to reorganize government, Carter was eager to introduce zero-base budgeting to the federal government. He had adopted this budgeting technique in Georgia and was certain that the experiment was successful there and worthwhile adopting at the federal level. As governor of Georgia (but already eyeing the presidency), he boasted of his new approach in a speech at the National Governors Conference in 1974:

In budgeting, we initiated a new concept called zero-base budgeting to help us monitor state problems better and attain increased efficiency. In the area of planning, we merged the roles of planning and budgeting—which had previously operated completely independent of each other—so that they could work together in promoting more economy in government. . . . Under this novel concept, every dollar requested for expenditure during the next budget period must be justified, including current expenditures that are to continue. It also provides for examining the effectiveness of each activity at various funding levels.

It is easy to see why such budgetary techniques would appeal to the engineer's mind, for it brings rationality to an otherwise messy process. For one consumed with efficiency in government, zero-base budgeting must have seemed like a godsend. Any system that promised to eliminate waste and bureaucratic obstruction, while improving the effectiveness of government, would be attractive to an efficiency-minded executive. Yet the nation had embraced budgetary innovations before with similar promises for efficiency, only to abandon them in favor of the usual incremental technique. What made this budget procedure different?

First and foremost, there was the perceived need to reform the usual budget procedure called "incremental budgeting." Most budgets are of this type, whereby each budgetary period starts with the current operating budget and proceeds to add to or subtract from this established base. Since only changes to the existing budget are examined, there is no incentive to economize for any part of the organization. Neither is there any attempt to examine alternative ways to accomplish the task at hand, the efficiency of current activities, and the possible elimination or reduction of current activities in favor of new programs. In short, the bureaucracy stumbles on, protecting turfs, resisting change, and preventing rational attempts by managers to improve operations. These criticisms and more have been leveled many times at incremental budgeting, and everyone has witnessed examples of its inefficiency.

How does zero-base budgeting correct these obvious deficiencies? Without delving into the details of budget-making (which will differ with each organization), the following summarizes the general approach to budget preparation by the zero-base technique.[7]

1. Identification of "decision units" for which budgets must be prepared.

2. Analysis of each decision unit in a "decision package." Determine the objectives of each unit and provide justification for its programs or activities.

3. Evaluation and ranking by priority of all decision packages to develop appropriations.

4. Preparation of detailed budgets from reviews of rankings and final decisions of authorities.

Once a decision unit has been identified, it is clear that the second part of the process holds the key to successful budgeting. It is here that the purpose of the unit is discussed, workload measures determined, costs and benefits weighed, alternative ways to accomplish the objective outlined, and various levels of activity for the unit examined. (That may include some minimum level of effort.) Once these reports are concluded, someone must decide how much to spend and where to spend it. By ranking these packages according to the benefit received from each level of expenditure, and considering the consequences of not funding packages that fall below the expenditure level chosen, management constructs its budget. This procedure provides flexibility in that should the expenditure level have to be adjusted, it is an easy matter to refer to the ranking list and adjust the budget to units accordingly.

While this procedure sounds reasonable enough, there would be a considerable amount of work involved to implement it. Most bureaucrats would likely resent having to justify their operation, defend its effectiveness, and prepare the necessary documentation. This is the type of budget that demands a long-term horizon to be successfully implemented; a year-to-year approach simply would not work. Planning would thus be facilitated with such an approach but not necessarily guaranteed.

Given this rational budget system, it is necessary to ask, What went wrong? What looks so obvious and straightforward on paper was not at all so in practice. Throughout every phase of zero-base budgeting (ZBB) there were obstacles to achieving the aims of the process. These problems were gradually acknowledged in the implementation of ZBB and eventually the concept was abandoned, a victim of overpromising results and underestimating impracticalities in design.[8]

In the first place, defining goals and objectives is easier said than done. There are enormous opportunity costs involved in defining goals, for all too often, the goals have not been explicitly stated, may involve multiple goals or conflicting goals, and may even involve unclear goals. As so often happens in the real world, programs that promise efficiency conflict with equity concerns. When this happens, political considerations come into play, and political solutions may supplant the economic ones. Yet each compromise leads away from the ZBB process, and each solution begins to approach the old budget methods. It is here that someone such as Carter would fail to realize the role of politics, compromise, and trade-offs that occur in a bureaucratic framework.

Moreover, listing the objectives of each function or unit may not be possible for many units of the organization and irrelevant for others. Yet, what is to be achieved by each unit is a crucial element in the process. Furthermore, even if the objective can be ascertained, examining alternative ways to achieve them may be hopelessly idealistic. This amounts to a recognition that what was perfectly acceptable in the last budget cycle may not have been correct or justifiable—an admission of inefficiency. Bureaucrats cannot be expected to make such admissions; hence, alternative ways to achieve some goal are bound to be perfunctory paths used mainly to satisfy the requirements of ZBB rather than represent true options.

In the ideal process, the preferred way to accomplish some goal precedes any consideration of the funds needed. This simply cannot work as any budget manager can predict. One has to know the monetary constraints before entertaining how goals can be reached within the confines of funding. If investing in machine X clearly would be the preferred way to increase production, but machine X is far too expensive even to consider, what is the point of constructing a budget based on using machine X?

Still, even if alternatives can be enumerated, how can benefits and costs be assigned to each with some degree of confidence? Estimates of costs and benefits have been notoriously difficult to make, especially for new ways to accomplish some goal. Yet this is the essential requirement with ZBB in order to rank the alternatives for final decision-making. In the end, someone must take all these rankings by benefits and make decisions on which to undertake and in what order. Yet, this person is confronted with comparing apples and oranges because decisions must be made across units that vary widely in their functions; decisions must be taken and judgments made where conflicts exist between equity and efficiency and where some functions are vital and others less so. Allocating scarce resources is a difficult job, and ZBB does not seem to make it easier or more rational. According to actual practice, participants tended to ignore this part of the process, and by doing so subverted one of its main ingredients. One example was found in the Department of Commerce, headed by Juanita Kreps, an economist, who flatly refused to make such judgments.[9] Other departments faced similar problems and complied, if at all, reluctantly.

Finally, ZBB was supposed to aid in the planning process by separating goals and objectives from budgets. Also, the process was supposed to result in the reallocation of resources once all the unit analyses were completed. In practice, very little reallocation took place, and whatever changes in the budget allocation that did occur were the result of changes in new administrations taking office with different budget philosophies and priorities. An example cited refers to the changing of the guard from the Ford to the Carter administrations with consequent shifts in spending priorities, not from the rational shifts due to the operation of ZBB.

Of course, there are many more criticisms of ZBB both in theory and practice, but it would not be productive to extend the discussion to cover them. The highly touted budgetary innovation gradually faded away when actually employed; the Carter aim to rationalize budget-making was given a trial and found wanting, and has since disappeared from view. The real question is, Why did it attain such popularity? The answer is that probably people thought it rational, and they could convince themselves that they were participating in a useful exercise. Some even learned a lot by the initial foray, but the opportunity costs involved in the lengthy procedure began to convince others that not much was really gained. Soon, shortcuts were taken, and in them the return to incremental budgeting with the trappings of ZBB. The rationale for ZBB was subverted in practice by harried budgetmakers impatient with the time-consuming requirements of ZBB.

Both at the state and federal level, the ZBB failed to live up to its promises and gradually budgetary processes began to resemble the incremental budgeting it was designed to replace. The experience in some states was positive even though the difficulties were acknowledged. Even in Georgia, there were serious reservations on its working in practice.[10] In Texas, the evaluation concluded that "zero-base budgeting is not the long-awaited panacea that has been the object of search for so many years by budget examiners."[11] Other examples are more favorable to ZBB, but seldom does one find evidence that it was working according to plan.

While it is difficult to quarrel with the procedures and objectives of ZBB, it simply was too demanding for real-world applications. It might work in some cases, but as a general procedure, it simply required too much effort and time for marginal results.

ZBB fit well into Carter's philosophy and predilections, but it is another example of his inability to recognize the flaws it might contain in operation. He overestimated its success in Georgia, and thus overestimated its usefulness at the federal level. To move an entrenched bureaucracy would have required an enormous amount of time and cooperation in any case, but Carter had neither time nor support for such an overhaul. In pushing a system with inherent flaws, Carter was once again setting himself up for failure; his preoccupation with efficiency led him to ignore other goals and political conflicts. He cannot be blamed for wanting to make government more efficient, but he can be questioned about his methods for making it so.

Other Initiatives

The conflict over goals is easily seen in the shorthan[...]
The dilemma can be expressed as follows:

$$B = Y/r + d$$

where B = break-even income level wh[...]

Y = income floor or guarantee

r = marginal tax rate on earned[...]

d = earnings disregard or s[...]
    reduced.

If Y is to be large e[...]
be low enough to[...]
will bring in[...]
lies) and cl[...]
families[...]
d, ag[...]
of[...]

tests" collided with complaints about inefficient targeting of welfare payments to the middle class. The demand from state and local fiscal relief ran afoul of efforts to reduce federal expenditures. Computerized systems to combat fraud similarly did not square with the demand for more personal, individualized administrative procedures.[12]

Furthermore, there are inherent conflicts with the three main goals of a welfare system: income provision, work incentives, and cost minimization. All three goals are laudable but, unfortunately, mutually exclusive. To protect people from the miseries of poverty, a high income guarantee is desirable; but to encourage the incentive to work, a low marginal tax rate on earned income is necessary; but to keep costs down, limits must be placed on both the other goals as well as on who is eligible for benefits. Obviously, compromises are necessary if all goals are recognized, but the emotional content of the issue often presents an obstacle to rational resolution of the conflicts.

d of mathematics.

ere all benefits cease,

income
me minimum income earned before benefits are

ough to avoid the hardships of poverty, and if r is to
encourage work, then B will rise as the break-even point
more families (working poor and lower-middle-class fami-
early costs will rise, and benefits are extended to more and more
. Allowing families to earn some income before taxation sets in,
in to encourage work, complicates the formula and increases the cost
the program. Clearly, some compromises are required, but they are not
easily obtained in this controversial issue.

If the income disregard, d, is absent (for simplicity), the problem can
be illustrated by the "tough triangle" of Figure 8.1. In Figure 8.1, point Y
is the income guarantee of $4,200; with a 50% tax rate on earnings
exceeding that level, this family of four would lose all benefits when its
income exceeded $8,400 (point b). The dilemma is easily seen when the
income guarantee is raised to increase benefits. The slope of the line YB

Figure 8.1
The Tough Triangle

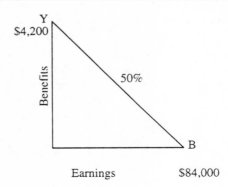

Y
$4,200

Benefits

50%

B

Earnings $84,000

would increase, meaning the marginal tax rate would rise, thus hurting incentives; if the break-even point is raised to keep the tax rate constant, then costs rise and welfare benefits are extended to more families, perhaps including some from the middle class. Again, there is no ready solution to these conflicts, and only compromises can resolve them—but compromises mean political solutions, not Carter's forte.

The Carter administration did not, indeed could not, escape the inherent contradictions of the welfare mess, and the conflicts were to haunt it as they had every previous attempt at reform. But before looking at its proposals, it would be appropriate to look at what constituted welfare and costs to the system in 1977. Welfare encompassed the following means-tested programs (based on family need, as opposed to social insurance programs where contributions were made by recipients, e.g., Social Security): Medicaid ($17.2 billion), Aid to Families with Dependent Children (AFDC) ($10.3), Supplementary Security Income (SSI) ($6.3), Food Stamps ($4.5), Veterans Pensions ($3.1), Housing Assistance ($3.0), Basic Educational Opportunity Grants ($1.8), Earned Income Tax Credit ($1.3), and General Assistance ($1.3). These programs amounted to about $49 billion or about 12% of total expenditures.

The Proposals

The last serious attempt at welfare reform was the Family Assistance Plan (FAP) of the Nixon administration. This plan called for a national guarantee of a minimal level of income instead of the bundle of welfare programs in existence. It was criticized from all sides. Conservatives argued that it was just a dole, and liberals argued that the amounts suggested were totally inadequate. The plan did not survive in this climate and in the maneuvering of the political campaign. Only the SSI feature remained after it was abandoned. Although welfare reform continued to be a standard topic for some time after the fall of FAP, no plan was given serious consideration by Congress. Interest in welfare reform was again sparked by Carter's emphasis on the necessity for revision. As soon as it was known that welfare reform would once again be given importance, some of the old ideas were dusted off and some "new" ones designed.

One old idea was the negative income tax (NIT) identified with Milton Friedman, although liberals such as James Tobin had also endorsed the idea. The concept was illustrated by Figure 8.1, where a *national* income guarantee would be established as a right, available to all. The NIT would not nor could not avoid the dilemmas posed by the conflicts among goals—adequate income, work incentives, and cost control—but it would be simple and uniform across the nation. All other welfare programs would be consolidated into this one program, replacing the case-by-case determination of eligibility. Administrative costs would be reduced and administrative abuse virtually ruled out.[13] The NIT proposal, however, was better suited for those who were trapped in low-income situations, not for those who move in and out of the need for temporary income supplements. Temporary variations in income occur for many families, and their need for help is immediate rather than at year end when income tax forms are prepared and refunds disbursed. NIT would thus solve some welfare problems, but would still run into mutually exclusive goals, and would likely prove more rigid and unresponsive in application. Still, the concept had the backing of welfare reformers at the Department of Health, Education, and Welfare (HEW).

Another attack, which appealed to Carter, favored the creation of public and private jobs by the government through tax policies or direct expenditures as an alternate to existing welfare programs. One such proposal—dubbed the "triple track" proposal developed by Tom Joe, an outside consultant—called for the grouping of families according to their ability to work.[14] In the first group were families not expected to work, for instance, those headed by an aged person, a disabled person, or a single parent with preschool children. In the second group were the heads of families expected to work, and in the third group were the working poor whose income from full-time work still placed them below the poverty level. The income or help that each group would receive depended upon its status. Families not expected to work would receive a basic income guarantee, but any income earned would be taxed by a 100% marginal tax rate. Those families expected to work would receive unemployment compensation for 26–39 weeks with income earned taxed at a 60% marginal rate. If no job was found, the unemployment compensation period could be extended. However, workers would have to accept a job offer or forfeit benefits. CETA would be expanded to ensure the availability of a job. For the third group who were already working, there was only the recourse of the earned income tax credit (EITC) to supplement their incomes. (The earned income tax credit is a refund of income taxes—in effect a form of the negative income tax concept.)

A third approach to addressing welfare problems could be labeled incrementalism. No sweeping changes were needed to the welfare system in this approach, only incremental changes to existing programs would be sufficient to remedy the system's faults. All that was needed in this politically explosive area were reforms here, structural changes there, some expansions or curtailments of programs, or other modifications.

Add to these approaches the possible permutations and combinations of them, and we can gain some appreciation of the many voices being heard on this issue. Finally, there were those who had simply given up on the possibility of welfare reform given the nature of the problems, the political repercussions, the welfare recipient's intransigence, the emotional content that was just beneath the surface, and the long-held biases and prejudices of nearly everyone involved.

Thus, welfare reform meant different things to different people. The administration concentrated its attention on the negative income tax reform (favored by HEW, headed by Joseph Califano) and the triple track proposal (favored by the Department of Labor, headed by Ray Marshall). Califano, in an impulsive remark, suggested a date of May 1, 1977, when a welfare reform measure could be ready.[15] Carter, anxious to win political points, fixed the date, and once again, as with the energy bill, put undue pressure on everyone to meet this rather artificial deadline. Whatever program emerged under this constraint might always be tainted and accused of being hastily conceived to justify the presidential directive. The president, however, remained aloof from the development process, relying on Califano and Marshall to do the preliminary work.[16] As far as Congress was concerned, the administration faced rather uncooperative chairmen of key committees who were extremely wary of welfare reform. Senator Russell Long of the Senate Finance Committee favored pilot programs before wholesale revisions, and congressman Al Ullman, chair of the House Ways and Means Committee opposed any negative income tax scheme. Neither man considered welfare reform to be a priority for their powerful committees.

After many meetings of the various welfare advisory groups, and after many proposals had been tossed on the table, Carter disrupted the entire process by insisting that any welfare reform be costless—it should be designed so as not to require any additional spending—the so-called zero-cost planning approach advocated by Carter. Yet the zero-cost constraint imposed another burden on those committed to welfare reform and placed another obstacle in the quest for one. Many proposals had to be reconsidered due to the new cost constraint.

Nevertheless, the committees working on welfare reform labored to work within the limits imposed by the cost constraint, but all sides of this controversial system were surprised to read Carter's statement of principles on May 2.[17] The deadline was met by a set of principles instead of a definite reform proposal, which was put off until August. The set of principles provided something for every faction, and hence, were unobjectionable in that sense, but they hardly constituted a coherent program, nor did they provide guidance to those working so diligently on the details of a viable welfare system.

THE CARTER PLAN: PROGRAM FOR BETTER JOBS AND INCOME

The proposal, labeled the Program for Better Jobs and Income (PBJI), that finally emerged from months of negotiations contained three main elements: (1) a work-incentive program to encourage low-income families who can work by providing access to jobs; (2) the consolidation of cash assistance programs into a single, simple, and more equitable one for those whose income is inadequate; (3) an expansion of the earned income tax credit integrated with (1) and (2).

The program consolidated the three largest cash assistance programs into one: AFDC, SSI, and food stamps. Eligibility rules were changed to eliminate inequities, while at the same time preventing families from splitting by extending benefits to those previously denied—low-income two-parent families, single persons, and childless couples. In addition, a national benefit floor for AFDC families would be established at $4,200 for a family of four, with reduction rates of 80% on unearned income and 50% on earned income. This floor was 65% of the poverty threshold at the time. States would be encouraged to supplement these payments as they saw fit. The administration estimated that the number of persons eligible for cash assistance would decline from 40 to 36 million persons (1 million AFDC recipients and 3 million food stamps recipients).[18]

For those able to work, the administration claimed it would create 1.4 million jobs. The jobs were low skilled, paying close to the minimum wage, and thus would not upset local wage structures, a worry of organized labor. Examples included jobs for improving recreation facilities; home care for the elderly; paraprofessionals in schools, child care, public safety; and pest control.[19] While these jobs were supposed to be avenues for training as well as income, many of them would have required more skills than was contemplated by the Department of Labor. Critics seized on this fact as they doubted the 1.4 million job estimate. They also pointed out that providing this many jobs was perhaps an overly ambitious goal, particularly when the demand for many such jobs was declining, for example, teacher's aides.

The final piece of the proposal was the expansion of the earned income tax credit. It was designed as follows: a 10% credit on earnings up to

$4,000 (same as the existing law); an additional 5% credit on earnings between $4,000 and the point at which a family ceases to be eligible for welfare benefits. The credit was phased out above this income level at a rate of $1 for each $10 of income.

Costs of the Program

The costs of the PBJI as estimated by the CBO for FY1982 (the first full year of operation) was $50.9 billion for all levels of government, $42.2 federal and $8.6 state and local. However, offsets attributable to discontinuing some programs and including the new rules under PBJI would have brought the net costs down to $13.9 billion, $17.4 billion federal and –$3.4 billion state and local.[20] Thus, the program fulfilled its promise to relieve states and localities from financial burden.

The administration's cost estimates were the source of considerable controversy. The original estimate was $8.8 billion for FY1982. The difference in estimates cannot be reconciled given the available supporting data. In the end, it really does not matter, since the administration insisted on using cost data for 1978 when justifying the program. The estimate given for that year was only $2.8 billion, and even when questioned, administration officials still defended the lower estimate.[21] The administration was using additional offsets to reduce the costs of the program— energy tax revenues from the windfall profits tax and fraud elimination. In any case, the congressional committees were quite upset at the lower estimate, armed as they were with much higher figures from independent sources. It is not surprising that different estimates were made, given the assumptions that had to be made in making them, but what irritated congressmen was the intransigence of the administration and its refusal to acknowledge that higher costs were likely.

By this time, Carter had lost interest in welfare reform. Costs now seemed irrelevant as Carter was apparently unwilling to risk political capital on the issue. Confronted by the conservative tide sweeping the nation, and by tax-limiting proposition 13 in California, Carter retreated from this controversial issue.[22]

Conclusions

The basic elements of PBJI as presented before congressional committees was supplemented by many oral and written testimonies by the general public. The public generally supported the thrust of the proposal but had numerous suggestions for additions and deletions. Special interests of all types appeared before the committee to extol their particular interests. These suggestions might have been worthwhile to examine in detail, but the fact is that the Carter plan never got out of the Senate committee and never reached the House floor for a vote; it simply faded away.

Despite the establishment of a special subcommittee on welfare reform, designed to bring the major players together, Carter's welfare proposal could not and did not overcome some basic objections. Conservatives could be expected to object to some provisions but even those disposed to reform found the proposal too sweeping. For example, Sen. Russell Long objected to the extension of welfare to childless couples and single individuals, insisted on more work effort for women with children above six years of age, and continued to push for pilot programs instead of sweeping changes; Congressman Al Ullman objected to the cash-out of the food stamp program as adding to the welfare rolls and to the payments of benefits according to family size. The specter of huge spending increases rallied conservatives and made liberals hesitant. The administration responded in 1979 with a modified welfare reform plan that was a more modest version of the original one, at a cost of $5.7 billion. It was unsuccessful, and even a scaled-down version that concentrated on the cash assistance part of the proposal (that reduced the $5.7 billion to a cost of $2.7 billion) failed to win approval in the Senate, although it did pass in the House. At the same time, congressmen were producing their own versions of welfare reform so that there were now five bills up for consideration. While they were less ambitious than the original Carter proposal, none of them survived, and welfare reform was dead once again.[23]

In addition to the problems mentioned above, how can the failure be explained? As usual, there are numerous explanations and rationalizations, and all contain some element of truth. Califano blamed the defeat on the conservative movement in the nation, as evidenced by proposition 13. Also, workers simply do not approve of supporting with their tax dollars those who do not work. Moreover, there is no constituency for welfare recipients (who are often their own worst enemy with their demands), and people do not want to be reminded of poverty. Racism, however subtle, may also play a part in resistance to welfare. In the 1970s when fiscal constraints were prominent, there may have been too many competing demands for the limited funds for any welfare reform bill to pass. Finally, reform fell victim to the monumental bureaucracy. Too many congressional committees oversee operations of the income security system, and two had enormous power—Senate Finance and House Ways and Means. Add to these the cabinet departments that had some jurisdiction, the state legislators, administrative agencies, and the tortuous route that any reform had to take would be a sufficient obstacle alone. Add to this profession turf considerations and the task seems overwhelmingly difficult.[24]

One problem acknowledged by administration officials in the aftermath was the overburdening of Congress with major bills. The House Ways and Means Committee had three major bills to consider simultaneously—energy, tax reform, and welfare reform. There simply was too much to handle for any of them to emerge in the short time given by the administration. Senator Daniel Patrick Moynihan blamed the failure on economists. The whole process was turned over to technocrats with their models and numbers, but they never understood the wider implications of the process. Economists then turned their work over to bureaucrats, called idiot savants by Moynihan, who never understood the process either and only misrepresented it.[25]

Of course, a good deal of blame for failure must be leveled at the administration. Carter never successfully committed his preferences to the people working on reform, leaving advisers too much room to depart from his desires. Carter failed in his leadership role by again leaving to cabinet heads the responsibility to develop a program. According to some, cabinet officials are not equipped to assume this role, and his staff should have been more responsible. Once the process was started, it became enmeshed in technical details, losing sight of the philosophical and political dimensions. The sense of purpose was lost in the debates over details, cost constraints, and number crunching. When these came under criticism, the administration balked at revisions; when the complex proposal needed clarification, administration officials became almost contemptuous and impatient; when costs seemed to be a problem, and the zero-cost tactic a stumbling block, the administration could have scaled back its proposal to win approval, but it refused until it was too late.[26] In short, the whole process was mishandled in much the same fashion as previous proposals, such as energy programs.

Perhaps no welfare reform proposal would have survived in the climate of the 1970s. The problems were real enough, but the nation was not prepared to deal with them when so many other concerns were clamoring for attention. Welfare expenditures are contentious at any time, but when energy problems, inflation, and foreign affairs were creating feelings of fear and insecurity, thoughts of providing for the less advantaged could not be expected to be given much consideration. Workers were struggling with declining real wages, and sympathy for those who were not working would likely be lacking. Moreover, there was a genuine shift to conservatism, and in such a movement, radical changes in the welfare system, particularly those that might invite more recipients at greater cost, were not apt to gain favor.

As the process of welfare reform dragged on, the Carter administration had less and less credibility. Then when Carter seemed to lose interest in the whole idea of reform, he more or less signaled the demise of welfare reform. While his actions might have been understandable, he may not have considered their consequences. One repercussion of the failure of welfare reform was that all the time and effort put into it appeared to have been wasted, and it would be a long time before politicians would be ready to repeat the process.

NATIONAL HEALTH CARE REFORM

Another Carter campaign promise—to reform the nation's health care system—suffered a fate similar to welfare reform. Once again, everyone acknowledged the need for reform, and once again, little reform was accomplished. Similar scenarios were followed as well: a deeply sincere president made hesitant by cost data and the threat of inflation began to waiver and, facing growing opposition by special interest groups and challenges from within his own party, retreated from the combat and settled for some modest first steps toward reform that satisfied no one.

Admittedly, the health care system in the United States has always been difficult to change. Decades of debate over who should administer the system, how to control health care costs, how to pay for it, and numerous other side issues had failed to resolve these thorny issues. What remained were massive public confusion and misconceptions fostered by hardened positions that were no better than slogans and platitudes. Under these conditions, few politicians were even willing to confront the subject and risk political capital in the effort. Carter's initial willingness to do so demonstrated his sincerity in solving one of the nation's more pressing social concerns and, incidentally, to his commitment to traditional Democratic causes. His slow retreat from the issue once again soured the old-style Democrats, and they began to question his priorities.

Indeed, some of the major challenges to the administration came from within its party and from old nemeses—Senators Russell Long and Edward Kennedy. Senator Long, chairman of the powerful Senate Finance Committee, wanted a plan to cover only catastrophic illnesses. He wanted no part of a comprehensive national health plan. Senator Kennedy had championed a national health care plan for many years and had produced several versions of one. Now he sensed the time was propitious for another attempt, and he badgered the administration to fulfill its promise. When the administration dragged its feet (or so he thought), he produced another bill and held extensive hearings to generate support.[27]

While Kennedy wanted quick action, Carter was willing to delay and conduct further studies of the health care issue. In 1977, the administration debated whether to propose a bill in 1978 or 1979, while Kennedy fumed that no further studies were necessary, and delay was damaging. Carter wanted to postpone action but indicate his commitment to reform by a statement of principles. Briefly these principles included universal coverage; freedom of choice of providers; need for cost controls; financing from a variety of sources, including government, employers, and cost sharing; and implementation in 1983.

As the debates became more heated, the administration was busy preparing several variants of a national health care plan. In April 1978, four plans were available for comment: (1) one based on market forces, relying on the private sector; (2) one federally financed "targeted plan" for catastrophic illness; (3) one that required private employers to provide health insurance in tandem with a public corporation for those who were not able to get private insurance; and (4) a publicly guaranteed plan with federal controls (the Kennedy approach).[28]

Later in the year, only two plans were being considered: the targeted plan for catastrophic illness favored by Sen. Long and the major economic advisors of the administration who feared the costs of a more extensive program, and the comprehensive plan that provided health insurance through employers, which included publicly supported catastrophic insurance and which federalized Medicaid. In the end, the administration fashioned a bill resembling the latter, and it was introduced in September 1979. Neither this bill nor any other health care bill became law.[29] Kennedy orchestrated congressional hearings and gained the support of organized labor, along with the AARP, farmers' groups, and many private citizens. As might be expected, opponents included the AMA, hospital groups, and health insurance agencies.[30]

Continued worry over the costs of a national health care plan and its effect on inflation diminished the administration's fervor that was required to pass such important legislation. After all the delays, the administration's plan did not receive an adequate hearing; it was overshadowed by Kennedy's end run and his growing ambition. Kennedy had the advantage of not having to worry about inflation, but with health care costs escalating, any plan had to confront the implausibility of introducing a major program when inflation was such a serious problem. Health care accounted for 8.8% of GNP in 1978 (estimated to rise to 10% by 1983), spending 12.5 cents out of every federal tax dollar. Indeed, health care was the third largest industry in the United States.

Thus, health care reform was another casualty of inflation in the latter part of the 1970s. Regardless of the merits of any plan, it was perhaps the wrong time to make the attempt and only served to bolster the arguments of the opposition, if one were needed. But Carter was stuck with the campaign promise and pushed by Kennedy to deliver on it. In addition, divisions within the Democratic party were further exacerbated, paving the way for the contentious presidential campaign of 1980.

Hospital Cost Containment

Actually, the first target in the effort to reform the health care system was to contain hospital costs. It is easy to see why: Hospital costs were rising at a rapid rate, approximately 15% annually. Expenses per patient admission rose from $315 dollars in 1965 to $1,311 in 1977. The increases were blamed on unnecessary medical procedures and days spent in the hospital, expensive equipment, unnecessary tests, exorbitant fees of physicians and staff, and, of course, the lack of incentives to curb costs with the current insurance system. Potential savings from more oversight were enormous, and one estimate was $53 billion from 1980–84. As such, the effects on inflation would be 0.5 to 1.2 percentage points lower.[31]

With data like these, the administration was eager to attack what it considered waste in the health care system and demonstrate its drive for efficiency. Accordingly, in April 1977 it proposed to limit hospital charges to a rate of increase of 1½ times that of the CPI instead of the 2½ rate that was occurring. The cap was to be temporary until a more formal system could be put in place.

Of course, the health industry protested at the lid put on their charges and lobbied against any form of mandatory limits. Put on the defensive, it initiated a voluntary effort to limit the increase in hospital costs. To this end, they were successful, as the Senate passed a bill incorporating a voluntary cost containment system, with a mandatory fallback position in the event that the voluntary provisions were not met.[32]

The administration conceded defeat on the strictly mandatory system and adopted a bill similar to the Senate version. In March, it sent up the Hospital Cost Containment Act of 1979 for congressional approval. It required the secretary of HEW (beginning in 1980) to promulgate a national voluntary percentage limit for hospital expenses occurring in the previous year. Taking into consideration past wage increases, prices of goods purchased by hospitals, the percentage increase in U.S. population, and an intensity allowance (cost of additional services, such as new technology, minus savings from productivity increases) of one percent. When costs rose above the standard, mandatory controls would be triggered through a complicated formula.

Despite the rising costs of hospital care and the potential savings for the federal government and everyone else utilizing hospitals, and despite the acknowledged necessity to control these costs, no hospital containment plan managed to get through Congress. Powerful special interests, the distaste for controls of any kind, and the lack of public support combined to defeat the administration's efforts. Once again, what should have been an easy target for the administration failed to elicit the necessary support. Another administration initiative to increase efficiency and reduce costs went unfulfilled. Efficiency was not as important to the public and its representatives as it was to the Carter administration.

TAX REFORM

Everyone recalls Carter's description of the tax code as a national disgrace. Its complexities, special provisions, and loopholes result in widespread confusion as well as huge compliance costs. Carter's criticisms were hardly new, since so many others had complained about the bewildering way the federal government collects income taxes. Still, most of the complainers were not in a position to improve matters very much, but Carter did have that opportunity. It is interesting to examine his proposals to rectify the tax problems.

The tax bills of Carter's administration in terms of their macroeconomic effects have already been described so that we can concentrate on their reform provisions. In 1977, there were no real reform provisions, since the administration was concerned with a stimulus package for the economy. As part of its 1978 tax proposal, however, the administration was prepared to suggest some tax reforms as an integral part of the tax bill. We will not go into a detailed discussion of these reforms, but the case for them was carefully presented by the administration.[33]

The revenue effects of the 1978 tax proposal reduced individual taxes by –$22.5 billion and corporation taxes by –$6.3 billion; these revenue losses were offset by the tax reform proposals for individuals of $4.2 billion and for corporations of $1.1 billion for a net revenue loss of –$25 billion (for FY1979). Clearly, the major emphasis of the tax proposal was tax reduction, not reform, but the reform effort had begun.

For individuals, the main reform items were concentrated in the itemized deduction area. The bill repealed the provisions for deductions for gasoline taxes ($.6 billion), sales taxes ($1.7 billion), miscellaneous deductions ($.4 billion), and political contributions, and limited the medical and casualty deduction ($1.4 billion). In addition, the bill would have taxed unemployment compensation, repealed the capital gains alternative tax method, taxed qualified retirement plans and employee death benefits, and given the states the option of continuing to issue tax-exempt bonds or taxable bonds with a federal subsidy.

For corporations and businesses, the main reform measures were changes in the way in which banks and thrifts calculate reserves for bad debts (provisions for bad debts were overestimated in the past), gradual elimination of the Domestic International Sales Corporation (DISC) that shielded export income from taxation ($.3 billion in 1979), curtailment of entertainment expenses ($.7 billion), limiting the use of industrial development bonds for specific types of uses, and mandating the accrual method of accounting for agricultural corporations.

For an administration that viewed the tax code as a disgrace, these reform measures were not overly ambitious. Others had supplied many reforms that could have been included, and public finance experts had many suggestions to offer.[34] For example, some of the more important reform measures often mentioned were missing: deductions for property taxes and mortgage interest on owner-occupied homes, state and local income taxes, personal interest, as well as capital gains taxation and gains accrued on inherited assets at death that escape taxation. For corporations, the integration of the personal and corporate taxes to escape double taxation, and the restructuring of depreciation rules were ignored.

Perhaps it was wise not to attempt a complete overhaul of the tax code at this time, since Carter's influence was waning somewhat. Many of the reforms were indeed justified and deserved to be seriously considered. Yet, having made a start at it, why not take the time to do a thorough job and reclaim some political capital for having initiated actions that demonstrated the sincerity of his remarks on national television? The administration did claim that the tax bill of 1978 would benefit families with incomes below $30,000 per year more than higher income families. Why not go further with reforms and appeal to the loyal Democratic constituency? Furthermore, the administration claimed its proposal was simplifying the tax code, but that assertion was clearly overstated. Tax simplification was hardly achieved by the elimination of several tax deductions, while leaving in place so many of the provisions that made the tax code incomprehensible.

In short, the administration did not go far enough to warrant the claim that it was correcting tax inequities substantially or simplifying the tax code in any meaningful way. The reason was simply that Congress was in no mood to tackle tax reform at this time. In fact Senator Long asked the administration not to send up tax reform measures, but the administration wanted to satisfy its campaign pledge. So, the administration settled for tax reductions and abandoned its half-hearted efforts at tax reform. In doing so, it once again demonstrated that it was not the crusading administration that it claimed to be, and the media's emphasis on eliminating the expense deduction for the three-martini lunch, only served to convey the impression to the general public that the tax reform proposal was probably insignificant.

REGULATION

The last campaign promise to be covered here is regulatory reform. Carter placed a high value on regulatory reform, since he maintained that regulatory programs had grown steadily in number and scope, but they seldom had been re-examined to ascertain whether they were meeting their missions with minimum burdens. The regulatory system had become unwieldy with ninety agencies issuing rules, but there was little effort to coordinate overlapping rules, and even less to analyze the costs and benefits of proposed rules.

Thus, to remedy these shortcomings, it was necessary to revamp the regulatory process. In January 1978, the Regulatory Advisory Review Group (RARG) was established to review the important new regulations that seriously affect inflation (those costing or likely to cost $100 million). The review group was made up of every cabinet department except defense, state, and treasury, together with leaders from OMB, CEA, and EPA. From this group, an executive committee was selected on a rotating basis. Schultze of the CEA was chairman, and apparently most of the work was done by the CEA and by the staff of the Council on Wage and Price Stability (COWPS).[35]

In March 1978, Carter issued executive order 12044, which required all federal agencies to conduct economic impact studies of proposed regulations whenever their impact on the economy was significant. The order made OMB responsible for compliance, but in practice, the RARG took on the responsibility (only a small number of cases were to be examined, about 10). Finally in October 1978, the president created the Regulatory Council (composed of all executive departments and some independent agencies with regulatory responsibility), which was charged with creating a governmentwide calendar of proposed regulations. The calendar would include a timetable for regulations and objectives and cost estimates for each regulation. With this information, the council could ensure coordination of rules and prevent conflicts and duplication. This entire process was supposed to improve the regulatory system.

The administration was generally pleased with its efforts to rationalize the regulatory process, and its initial successes demonstrated that it was on the right track and further improvements would only make the system better. Outside the administration, however, there was considerable concern over this new system. To some in Congress, the president was regarded as a super-regulator, deciding which regulations were important and which could be delayed. To others, the president was running afoul of the Administrative Procedure Act, which spelled out when amendments could be made to proposed legislation; changes could not be made after public hearings were held, but with the administration's system, further discussion could be held.[36]

Legalities aside, the administration's regulatory process was regarded as significant and innovative. In fact, a similar procedure was adopted by Reagan (with more power to OMB) without acknowledgment to Carter, just as Carter built on the initiatives of the Ford administration. Still, even as the administration was claiming numerous successes[37] with the system, it recognized that further reforms required legislation. (Besides, others in Congress [Senators Charles Percy and Abraham Ribicoff and others] had begun to propose reform legislation, and the administration wanted to be out front on this issue.)

The Regulation Reform Act of 1979 was designed to incorporate the reforms introduced in executive order 12044 and overhaul important provisions of the Administrative Procedure Act. In general, the act required a cost-benefit analysis of each proposal for change in regulations, required a calendar of upcoming rules, provided for public participation in the regulatory process, reduced paperwork requirements, and initiated a sunset provision to examine the effectiveness of regulations in practice. Thus, it sought to institutionalize the system devised by the administration, as well as include the reform changes proposed by the Senate bills being considered at the same time.[38]

The Record

The reform bill never became law. Still, some of the features contained in the reform bill are worth repeating. The main feature was the requirement that cost/benefit analysis be performed for new regulations or changes in them. With economists in charge, it is not surprising that this approach was elevated to prominence over a legalistic approach, which is concerned with the details and procedures of legislation. The economist's approach emphasized justification for regulations, while the legal approach emphasized the compliance features.

The other important feature, found also in the competing Senate bills, was the sunset provision. Every ten years, a congressional review of pertinent regulations was required to ascertain whether the regulation was effective and efficient. Supplementing these innovations were the valuable additions that removed unnecessary paperwork, eliminated nitpicking rules, and established procedures for administrative judges.

While the administration did not achieve all the legislative initiatives it desired and, thus, solidify its approach to regulation, it did manage to introduce some worthwhile concepts and transform the entire controversy over regulations to more rational procedures rather than their justification in a complex world. Yet if this was all that it accomplished, its success would have been still considered a forerunner of the Reagan plan. Actually, the move toward deregulation of important industries was the main achievement of the Carter administration in this area.

Consider some of the results of the administration's efforts:

1977   air cargo was deregulated, and airlines were given the power to set fares

1978   airlines deregulated

      decontrol of natural gas

      OSHA revises nitpicking rules

      CAB is gradually phased out

      EPA starts emissions trading policy

1980   FCC eliminates cable TV regulation

      trucking industry deregulated

      depository institutions law phased out interest rate ceilings; S&Ls given more powers

      Staggers Rail Act allowed railroads to adjust rates and make contracts with shippers

These examples of deregulation, along with future possibilities, gave the administration some credibility in the field of regulation and also gave it some justification for claiming success in this controversial area.

CONCLUSIONS ON REFORM ISSUES

These sketchy accounts of the administration's attempts at various reforms are useful in showing its general approach to reforms and are sufficient to allow for some judgments about the process of seeking reforms.

No one doubted the sincerity of Carter and his aides in pursuing the goal of genuine reform in the areas covered. Welfare, tax, health, and regulatory reforms were high on the list of things the administration wanted to accomplish. Carter's conception of populism alone would have ensured that some effort would be made to recast these institutions into something more effective and efficient, while minding equity concerns.

Yet, Carter's vision of improvements often ran counter to those of more traditional Democrats. It is difficult to achieve fundamental changes in existing arrangements when members of one's own party are challenging one's conceptions and proposing their own versions. Indeed, when genuine changes are being contemplated, support is needed from presumed associates. As shown, this support was lacking, and in the process of defending his policies, Carter created only confusion for the public.

Although some of the failure to achieve reforms lies with the discord within the Democratic Party, Carter must bear some of the blame as well. Planning policies in secret, unwilling and unable to compromise, and abandoning the battle when most needed, Carter helped to ensure that reform efforts would miscarry. Some began to question his commitment to these causes, which only added to the difficulty of convincing reluctant and often resistant members of Congress to push through needed legislation.

One of the main reasons for Carter's withdrawal from promising beginnings was his concern for the costs involved. Whenever policies threatened to exacerbate inflation, Carter backed away. A fiscal conservative at heart, he was not about to aggravate the nation's foremost problem with reforms; they could wait until conditions improved. Some critics, less concerned about inflation, did not choose to postpone action, while opponents to change welcomed the excuse to delay.

Again, it was probably not the right time, if there is one, for the confluence of fiscal conservatism with social reform. Carter felt that his duty was to the nation and all the people, and inflation was a national problem. However desirable social reforms were, they were not on the same plane with the corrosive problem of inflation.

In retrospect, the failure to achieve reforms during this period meant that they would not be seriously considered again for some time, if at all, and the chance for remodeling some institutions was squandered. For a Democratic regime sandwiched between Republican administrations, the abortive attempts at reform would prove particularly disappointing and damaging to the party's future.

NOTES

1. This claim did not go unchallenged. Victor Lasky, a Carter critic, did some investigative work and concluded that while 278 agencies were eliminated, only 66 involved agencies that were important enough to receive funding. He quotes Georgia House Speaker Tom Murphy that instead of a revolution in state government, all Carter did was "a cosmetic rearrangement of the furniture." He further asserts that the reorganization did not save money nor did it decrease the number of state employees. See Victor Lasky, *Jimmy Carter: The Man and the Myth* (New York: Richard Marek Publishers, 1979), 115–117. Whether these claims are true or not is beside the point, but it is ironic to note that the elimination of useless agencies in Georgia was apparently a success. Carter lamented that he failed to do the same for similar federal agencies.

2. A good deal of controversy was created by the administration's provisions for authority to reorganize government. These mainly legal issues are fascinating to students of government but would be inappropriate to pursue here. For those interested, see U.S. Senate, Committee on Government Operations, *To Renew the Reorganization Authority*, 95th Congress, 1st session, February 8, 1977; also U.S. House of Representatives, Committee on Government Operations, *Providing Reorganization Authority to the President*, 95th Congress, 1st session, March 1 and 8, 1977.

3. See the testimony and written reply for additional information of Harrison Wellford in hearings before the U.S. House Committee on Government Operations, *Extend Reorganization Authority of the President*, 96th Congress, 2nd session, February 26, 1980.

4. Jimmy Carter, *Keeping Faith* (New York: Bantam Books, 1982), 71.

5. For an early assessment of civil service reform, see James L. Sundquist, "Jimmy Carter as Public Administrator," *Public Administration Review* (January/February 1979), 3–11. While basically approving the Reform Act, he did call attention to some flaws that would have to be corrected.

6. See Donald A. Marchand, "Carter and the Bureaucracy," in *The Carter Years*, edited by M. Glenn Abernathy, Dilys M. Hill, and Phil Williams (New York: St. Martin's Press, 1984), 192–207. The analysis that follows is based on this work.

7. The interested reader should consult Peter A. Pyhrr, *Zero-Base Budgeting: A Practical Management Tool for Evaluating Expenses* (New York: John Wiley & Sons, 1973); See also Phyrr, "Zero-Base Budgeting," *Harvard Business Review* (November–December 1970), 111–121; for a comprehensive analysis, see Thomas H. Hammond and Jack H. Knott, *A Zero-Based Look at Zero-Base Budgeting* (New Brunswick, N.J.: Transaction Books, 1980). For more on the topic and for the experience of the states, see U.S. Senate, Committee on Government Operations, Subcommittee on Intergovernmental Relations, *Compendium of Materials on Zero-Base Budgeting in the States*, 95th Congress, 1st session, January 1977.

8. For more detail than can be discussed here, see Hammond and Knott, *Zero-Base Budgeting*. The authors examine each phase of the process and discuss the shortcomings in both theory and practice. This text owes much to their thorough analysis of ZBB.

9. Ibid., 45.

10. See the evaluation of George S. Minmier, *An Evaluation of the Zero-Base Budgeting System in Governmental Institutions*, reprinted in the U.S. Senate, Committee on Government Operations, *Compendium of Materials on Zero-Base Budgeting in the States* (Washington, D.C.: United States Government Printing Office), 133–185, where

one finds a statement like this: "The zero-base budgeting system has made only a minor contribution toward the establishment of a control budgeting system in the State of Georgia." However, the report goes on to suggest recommendations for improvement.

11. Ibid., 144.

12. Laurence E. Lynn, Jr., and David deF. Whitman, *The President as Policymaker: Jimmy Carter and Welfare Reform* (Philadelphia: Temple University Press, 1981), 40–41. This is the most complete source for tracing the evolution of welfare reform during the Carter administration.

13. Government-sponsored experiments using the NIT in selected areas to study work disincentives had just become available and suggested that work reduction did occur with NIT, but they were rather modest. High income guarantees and high tax rates did, however, discourage work effort. For a summary of these studies, see U.S. Senate, Committee on Finance, Hearings before the Subcommittee on Public Assistance, *President's State on Principles of Welfare Reform*, 95th Congress, 1st session, May 1977, 34–39.

14. Lynn and deF. Whitman, *The President as Policymaker*, 43. See also the *Economic Report of the President, 1978*, 221–232, for an early discussion of welfare reform by the administration.

15. Joseph A. Califano, Jr., *Governing America* (New York: Simon and Schuster, 1981), 325. Califano supplies an insider's view of the process of welfare reform in this work and provides a glimpse into the workings of the administration in this and other areas.

16. Lynn and deF. Whitman quote Frank Raines, a member of the Domestic Policy Staff helping to guide the process on this point: "The president understood there was no real political gain in proposing welfare reform. He didn't see this as a centerpiece of how it was going to help him out politically. Welfare was just one of those problems—one of those nasty problems—that ought to be solved, and he was a problem-solver president" in *The President as Policymaker*, 91.

17. In his statement, Carter reaffirmed his belief that the present welfare system had to be scrapped and established the following goals:

1. No higher initial cost than the present systems.
2. Under this system every family with children and a member able to work should have access to a job.
3. Incentives should always encourage full-time and part-time private sector employment.
4. Public training and employment programs should be provided when private employment is unavailable.
5. A family should have more income if it works than if it does not.
6. Incentives should be designed to keep families together.
7. Earned income tax credits should be continued to help the working poor.
8. A decent income should be provided also for those who cannot work or earn adequate income, with federal benefits consolidated into a simple cash payment, varying in amount only to accommodate differences in costs of living from one area to another.
9. The programs should be simpler and easier to administer.
10. There should be incentives to be honest and to eliminate fraud.

11. The unpredictable and growing financial burden on state and local governments should be reduced as rapidly as federal resources permit.

12. Local administration of public job programs should be emphasized.

Taken from the U.S. Senate, *President's Statement on Principles of Welfare Reform*, 86.

18. See the testimony of Henry Aaron, assistant secretary for Planning and Evaluation, HEW, before the U.S. House of Representatives, Committee on the Budget, *President Carter's Welfare Proposals*, 95th Congress, 1st session, October 1977, 2–30.

19. For more on job creation, see the testimony of F. Ray Marshall, secretary of labor, in U.S. Senate, Committee on Finance, Subcommittee on Public Assistance, *Welfare Reform Proposals*, 95th Congress, 2nd session, part 1, February 1978, 136–180. These hearings, in five parts, are the most complete regarding welfare reform.

20. Congressional Budget Office, *The Administration's Welfare Reform Proposal: An Analysis of the Program for Better Jobs and Income*, April 1978, 40. These costs might still appear large to some but when considered against the cost of welfare programs with the current system in 1982, they show a large reduction. The cost of the existing system would have been $74.9 billion with the federal cost alone rising at an annual rate of 7.2% (pp. 38–39).

21. The details of cost estimates rapidly get complex, and there is no need to repeat them here. For more on costs, see the study of Robert Haveman and Eugene Smolensky, "The Program for Better Jobs and Income: An Analysis of Costs and Distributional Effects," in U.S. Senate, *Welfare Reform Proposals*, Part 2, 259–272.

22. Joseph Califano has written, "Any possible reform effort has to have constant, persistent, almost stubborn support from the President and the Congress. Jimmy Carter, as it turns out, was no more willing than Richard Nixon to commit the necessary political capital. Perhaps he never had it to commit" in Califano, *Governing America*, 366. Lynn and deF. Whitman characterized the effort as follows: "Carter, in contrast [to Roosevelt] was relatively passive and inflexible. Once he had decided on the process he wanted followed, he took little personal interest in following through and showed little resilience when his advisers ran into difficulties or sought his help" in Lynn and deF. Whitman, *The President as Policymaker*, 275.

23. For a description of these, see Lynn and deF. Whitman, *The President as Policymaker*, 241.

24. Califano, *Governing America*, 364–366.

25. Quoted in Lynn and deF. Whitman, *The President as Policymaker*, 260.

26. More searching criticisms of the Carter administration's handling of its welfare proposal can be found in Lynn and deF. Whitman, *The President as Policymaker*, 227–280.

27. For one view of the contest between the administration and these leading senators, see Califano, *Governing America*, 88–135.

28. Ibid., 104.

29. For those interested, the two major health plan competitors—the administration and Kennedy—are outlined in U.S. House of Representatives, Committee on Interstate and Foreign Commerce, *National Health Insurance*, 96th Congress, 1st session, November 1979.

30. See U.S. Senate, Committee on Human Resources, *National Health Insurance, 1978*, 96th Congress, 1st session, October–December, 1978, parts 1 and 2.

31. Califano, *Governing America*, 144. See also U.S. House of Representatives, Committee on Interstate and Foreign Commerce, *Hospital Cost Containment*, 96th Congress, 1st session, 1979.

32. The arguments of the hospital industry are interesting but not of particular concern to this discussion. They can be found in the hearings of the U.S. House of Representatives, Committee on Ways and Means, *President's Hospital Cost Containment Proposal*, 96th Congress, 1st session, March 1979, particularly part 2 of the 2-part hearings.

33. See the statement of Treasury Secretary Blumenthal in hearings before the U.S. House of Representatives, Committee on Ways and Means, *The President's 1978 Tax Reduction and Reform Proposals*, 95th Congress, 2nd session, part 1 of 9, January–February 1978, 43–93, or in the more detailed treasury department review, pp. 160–486. See also the *Economic Report of the President, 1978*, 216–221, for an early discussion of the administration's views.

34. See, for instance, David F. Bradford, *Blueprints for Basic Tax Reform*, 2nd ed. (Arlington, Virg.: Tax Analysts, 1984); the original edition was issued in 1977. Also see the leading scholar at the time on tax matters, Joseph A. Pechman, *A Citizen's Guide to the New Tax Reforms* (Totowa, N.J.: Rowman & Allanheld, 1985) that summarizes the views of several public finance experts on the subject.

35. Susan J. Tolchin, "Presidential Power and the Politics of RARG," in *Regulation* (July/August 1979), 44–49. See also the *Economic Report of the President, 1979*, 85–91.

36. For the administration's view on the regulatory system, see *Economic Report of the President, 1981*, 99–115; hearings were held on the Administrative Procedure Act, for instance, by the U.S. House of Representatives, The Committee on Rules, *Regulatory Reform and Congressional Review of Agency Rules*, parts 1–3, 96th Congress, 1st session, 1980. Also note this observation by Tolchin, "It is apparent that, through the RARG process, the President hopes to establish hegemony over the regulatory actions of disparate agencies. It is equally clear that the process has been arranged to shield the President from political controversy by leaving the formal responsibility for particular decisions with the agency heads themselves," Tolchin, "Presidential Power," 45.

37. Carter claimed that HEW had eliminated 300 pages of rules; OSHA voided 1,000 rules; the FCC rewrote its rules; EPA revised its procedures and saved millions of dollars; and pension regulations were reorganized, eliminating duplication and reducing paperwork. In addition, many other initiatives were underway in 1979, when the reform legislation was being considered. See the President's reform message to Congress in support of the Regulation Reform Act of 1979, reprinted in U.S. Senate, Hearings before the Committee on Governmental Affairs, *Regulatory Reform Legislation*, 96th Congress, 1st session, March–May 1979, 161–169.

38. For more on the competing bills, see U.S. Senate, *Regulatory Reform Legislation*, parts 1 and 2.

Part III
The Legacy

Chapter 9

Economic Issues
in the 1980 Campaign

It was not a propitious time for Jimmy Carter to run for reelection: The year 1980 was not a good one for the economy. In the first half of the year, the economy was in a short, sharp recession. In the second half of the year, the economy grew at a slow rate, with the seemingly perennial stagflation. With the unemployment rate hovering around 7.4%, and the CPI growing at a rate of about 12%, the misery index (the combination of the two) was close to 20%—a record high. There was nothing to be cheerful about, and appeals to the fact that the U.S. economy was doing better than that of some of its trading partners offered little solace to an embattled and bewildered public.

We already have seen that the administration refused to fight the recession through economic stimulation, deferring instead to the fear of exacerbating inflation. It reduced government spending by $14 billion; tightened its wage and price standards; imposed credit controls; proposed an oil import surcharge; and tried vainly to increase productivity. But as the economy foundered, the Carter administration not only had to respond to growing discontent from within its own ranks, but also had to respond to the increasingly strident criticisms of its Republican opponents—mainly Ronald Reagan.

Finally in August, after watching its credibility steadily diminish and facing mutiny from Senate Democrats who were ready to make their own tax proposals, the administration responded to the pressure and offered its economic revitalization program. When announcing his program, Carter answered his critics by eschewing political repercussions, "Now, in the heat of an election year, is not the time to seek votes with ill-considered tax cuts that would simply steal back in inflation in the future the few dollars that the average American taxpayer might get. . . . America needs to build muscle, not fat, and I will not accept a pre-election bill to cut taxes." This was in response to the massive tax cuts advocated by Representative Jack F. Kemp (R-N.Y.) and Senator William V. Roth, Jr. (R-Del.) and adopted by candidate Ronald Reagan.

The administration's tax cut proposals were much more modest and weighted toward business. It proposed a $27.3 billion total gross tax reduction for 1981, with $15.5 billion for business and $11.8 billion for individuals. Table 9.1 outlines the administration's tax and spending plans. The tax features would not affect the economy in 1980, and thus it could

Table 9.1

Tax Reductions and Expenditure Increases in the Economic Revitalization Program

Item	Revenue Loss or Cost in 1981 (bill.)
Tax reductions	
Business tax cuts	
Liberalized depreciation	$ 6.3
Investment tax credit	2.4
Reduced payroll taxes	6.6
Special targeted investment tax credit	0.2
Total business tax reductions	$ 15.5
Individual tax redictions	
Social Security tax credit	6.2
Earned income tax credit	0.9
Marriage tax penalty removal	4.7
Total individual tax cuts	$ 11.8
Total tax reductions	$ 27.3
Expenditure increases (in mill.)	
Economic and regional development	$ 31.0
Science and technology	165.0
Transportation	90.0
Energy security	255.0
Human resources	130.0
Supplemental employment benefits	1,385.0
Countercyclical revenue sharing	500.0
Total expenditure increases	$ 2,556.0
Total estimated budgetary effect FY 1981 (bill.)	$ –(6.0–7.5)

Source: White House paper, *Economic Growth for the 1980's*, August 1980, reprinted in U.S. House of Representatives, Committee on the Budget, *President's Economic Revitalization Program*, 96th Congress, 2nd session, September, 1980, 6–30, and 66, 92.

be maintained that they were not proposed for political purposes, or to affect stagnation in 1980 and thus risk inflation. To fend off critics, the tax cuts could be presented as evidence that the administration was interested in a tax bill in 1980. After all, Carter had to contend not only with challenges from within his party, mainly from Senator Kennedy, but also from an unexpected serious challenge from without, mainly from Reagan. The unknown affect of the third-party candidate John Anderson only added to his woes. Since all were advocating tax cuts and spending initiatives, and since members of his own party were waffling on support-ing Carter's re-election, some economic policy had to be advanced to retain any following at all.

In general, the White House paper for an economic blueprint for the 1980s attempted to respond to two fundamental concerns: for the short term, to keep the economic recovery going without "rekindling" inflation; and for the longer term, to address the problems plaguing the economy for some time—inflation, energy dependence, low investment and productivity growth, and the challenge of industrial competitiveness. As for the short-run horizon, the administration did not expect action on the tax cuts until 1981 and only hoped for action in the remaining months of 1980 on the energy proposals, supplemental unemployment benefits, and countercyclical revenue-sharing parts of the president's program. None of the other elements of the plan would even be submitted to Congress until January 1981.[1] In 1980, restraint was still the byword for this administration.

The spending increases in Table 9.1 certainly attest to the modesty on the expenditure side. Only a $2.6 billion increase was proposed for 1981 (but an increase in budget authority of $4.8 billion). The economic development component was designed to stimulate investment in dis-tressed areas and for industrial development programs. Only a small sum was expected to be spent in 1981—$31 million—but a potential increase in budget authority of up to $1 billion was possible for future spending in 1981 ($2 billion in 1982).

To increase innovation and foster technological advances, the admini-stration planned to spend $165 million in 1981 but had proposed an increase in budget authority of $300 billion in both 1981 and 1982. The aim was to stimulate research in universities and encourage cooperation among government, universities, and industry in research projects and in basic research.

In addition to the large outlays already allotted, more funding was deemed necessary to meet the requirements of the nation's highways. An additional $90 million was requested for 1981 with $600 million in increased budget authority. Another $255 million was requested in 1981 for energy security of conservation programs, the Solar and Energy Conservation Bank, efficiency improvements in federally owned power plants, and for weatherization programs. Over $1 billion in authorization was requested for 1981 and 1982.

For human resources, the plan called for an increase of an additional $130 million in 1981 for training under CETA to provide jobs for the disadvantaged and the unemployed. Extending unemployment compensation to the long-term unemployed for an additional thirteen weeks would cost an additional $1.4 billion in 1981.

Finally, the last part of the plan was a countercyclical revenue-sharing program of $500 million to "help ensure that harmful temporary reductions in service levels do not take place" in communities undergoing problems due to the recession. This $500 million represented an additional allocation to the already requested $500 million for an increase in budgetary authority of $1 billion. So even here, there was no net addition to the 1981 budget request, only a transfer of an item already included in the 1981 budget request. Any additional spending in this category would affect the economy in later years.

To summarize, the revitalization program was, in CEA chairman Schultze's words, "relatively cautious and prudent." That is certainly an understatement as far as the spending component goes. Most of the increase in expenditures can be found in unemployment compensation extensions, a program hardly designed to aid in the recovery but rather to mitigate against its effects. Again, the fear of inflation blocked a more aggressive program, and at least, the program could be viewed as the administration doing something, even if that something was modest indeed. We turn now to the more extensive proposals on the tax and revenue side of the plan.

As part of its tax policy, the administration hoped to "offset rising individual tax burdens in ways that do not rekindle inflation." Accordingly, the administration sought to lessen the tax burden for individuals by allowing a Social Security tax credit equal to 8% of taxes paid. There was a scheduled increase in Social Security taxes to take effect in January, and this program would have reduced the burden of these increases. It was a two-year program with the first-year revenue loss put at $6.2 billion.

The second part of tax relief for individuals was designed to reach low-income taxpayers. An increase in the earned income tax credit to 12% (from 10%) was proposed, which would phase out at income levels from $7,000 to $11,000, up from a range of $6,000 to $10,000. The first-year cost was estimated at $900 million.

Finally, Carter proposed to relieve the penalty on couples who file joint returns and pay a heavier tax than single people with the same incomes would pay. The remedy was a special tax deduction equal to 10% of the lower earning spouse's earnings, up to a maximum of $30,000. The revenue loss for the first year was estimated at $4.7 billion, rising to $8.9 billion in the fifth year of operation.

The longer term goals of the administration are more clearly visible in its tax plans for business. In its White House paper, it made the case quite clear, "We will encourage private investment and expand public investment to revitalize America's economy—so we can produce more, export more, invent more, and employ more." Revitalization of American industry would require, however, a new spirit of cooperation among government, business, and labor. To facilitate this cooperation and deal with the complex issues of an emerging industrial policy, Carter's program provided for a new institution: The President's Economic Revitalization Board. The board would have the responsibility for developing funding for industrial development, for providing assistance to areas of the nation undergoing transition problems, for coordinating development operations now carried out by separate units of government, for seeking ways to upgrade the skills of workers, for examining regulations and their impact, and for dealing with industrial dislocation problems in communities.

To aid in this grand revitalization program, the administration proposed tax policies designed to encourage real investment. With the increased share of the national output devoted to real investment, the growth of labor productivity was anticipated to grow. One of the causes of the decline in the growth of labor productivity was thought to be the slow rate of capital accumulation over the recent past.

The first of the tax proposals was a liberalized depreciation allowance. The depreciation rates were increased and simplified in order to encourage firms to expand investment spending. The loss of revenue in the first year was thought to be about $6.3 billion, rising to over $24 billion in the fifth year.

The second tax proposal was for a refundable investment tax credit that would cost $2.4 billion in 1981 and beyond. The refundable tax credit was designed for firms that qualified for the normal investment tax credit but that had limited or no tax liability; thus, the credit offered them little benefit. The administration proposed to remedy this problem by granting such firms a refund of the earned but unused investment tax credit up to 30% (with carry-forward provisions for the remainder).

A special investment tax credit of 10% would be made available for investment projects that were undertaken in economically distressed areas of the nation. This targeted investment would also be eligible for the refunding provisions. The first-year cost was estimated to be only $200 million, but the administration envisioned authorizing about $1 billion per year thereafter for such projects.

To reduce labor's costs (and combat inflation) and to aid labor-intensive firms for whom the investment tax credit is not important, the administration decided to provide firms with a Social Security tax credit for two years as it did for individuals. The cost would be $6.6 billion in 1981 alone.

These are the main provisions of the administration's economic policy. Also mentioned were future plans to aid small business, offer more assistance to distressed areas, pursue regulatory reforms, and explore new ways of combating inflation with the cooperation of business and labor. Perhaps new forms of incomes policies could be developed to control inflation.

Thus, the administration, true to its word, eschewed political gains from immediate economic policies that could have won votes and looked for longer term solutions to the vexing economic problems confronting the nation. The plan was released around Labor Day, the traditional start of serious presidential campaigns, and obviously, there was more than an eye given to the coming election.

Not surprisingly, this program was ignored by Congress. By this time, the Carter campaign was in serious trouble, and challengers were getting most of the public's attention. In addition, Carter was losing the support of his own party, and his endorsement for a second term was decidedly halfhearted. This will become evident later in the chapter, when we review the economic programs of his rivals from within and without his party.

OTHER MACROECONOMIC VIEWS OF THE ADMINISTRATION

To complement the economic program just outlined, it might be useful to reveal some of the other approaches that might have been considered had Carter won the election. In its *Economic Report of the President, 1981*, published after the election, the CEA shared its views on the problems facing the nation and on the solutions the Carter administration would presumably have proposed to solve them. Acknowledging the persistent problem of inflation, it cogently outlined the other problems that

Are themselves closely related to inflation, either as a cause or as consequence. Our nation's productivity growth has virtually halted in recent years. The era of cheap energy has ended, the world has grown vulnerable to supply disruptions, and the course of domestic inflation and unemployment has become closely dependent on economic and political developments in the oil-rich but politically unstable Middle East. Meanwhile, the struggle to find a proper balance between a clean, healthy, and safe environment, on the one hand, and satisfactory economic growth with lower inflation on the other, will continue. All of these developments, together with the growing interdependence of the world economy, have set in motion major changes in economic structure, occupational skill requirements, and industrial location that will continue to pose sizable adjustment problems to many industries, communities, and workers.[2]

This concise delineation of the nation's economic ills was easier to relate than to prescribe. Since inflation was identified as the major problem, it received a great deal of attention. Without attempting a full discussion of inflation-related issues, a few comments on what might have become of the administration's policies may be in order. The CEA maintained that restraining aggregate demand policies were still useful, but it acknowledged that they might not be as powerful as before, now that wages and prices no longer responded (i.e., fell) in the face of restraint; output and employment fell instead, imposing costs on the society, which could become intolerable. Therefore, macroeconomic policy should be directed at the long-run reduction in GNP, while trying to minimize employment and production decreases. The long-run policy of macro restraint might, however, conflict with short-term responses; these short-run policies would have to be carefully monitored to avoid threatening the credibility of the longer run policy of restraint. Finally, the proper response to outside shocks should not be to accommodate them and thus risk inflation, but to continue the policy of restraint to prevent the indirect effects of inflation via increases in wages and prices that might follow.

Still, to prevent a wage-price spiral, an incomes policy may be required. The rational would be to modify the usual reactions of workers and firms to inflation and change their behavior. By forcing workers and firms to accept lower increases than might have been forthcoming, an incomes policy could work to reduce inflation and encourage positive economic growth. The administration favored voluntary incomes policies over mandatory ones and in its final two years proposed one such variant. The administration claimed that its voluntary program worked to reduce wage demands (by 1 to 1½ percentage points in 1979) and hence inflation, while it was in operation, but it candidly admitted that the current program could not be expected to work for much longer. Leaving aside for now the claim that the current program was effective, what kind of program would replace it?

It appears that the administration was moving toward a tax-based incomes policy (TIP). Under a pay TIP, the government would set a pay standard (or price standard) and either reward workers for complying with the standard or penalize them (or the firm) for failure to do so. The reward system would favor voluntary cooperation and was the preferable one to the administration. Under such a system, those workers who agreed to pay increases below the standard would receive a tax credit; if a penalty system were chosen, those who were not in compliance would pay a tax penalty. In either case, it was the average pay change that was the measure of compliance, and thus there was flexibility built into the system, as firms were permitted to pay more to some individuals and still be in compliance. There were, however, many administrative problems to solve before such a system could be made operational, and many administrative costs to be incurred.[3] Still, if the system worked, the macro policies of restraint would be shifted more to limiting wage and price increases and away from output and employment reductions.

The final element in the CEA's macroeconomic approach was the need to increase investment. One of the main reasons for the decline in productivity was the failure of investment to grow by enough to meet the requirements of a growing labor force. The capital stock that labor has to work with, that is, the capital/labor ratio, K/N, remained constant over the last five years, after growing at a rate of 3% per year. In order to restore the old capital/labor ratio and increase productivity lost for this reason, investment would have to increase its share of GNP by 1 to 2% (from a base of 10 to 12%). If this analysis were correct, then the question would shift to how to increase the share of output devoted to capital accumulation, and since GNP growth would be restrained due to inflationary pressures, how to increase investment's share of GNP while discouraging consumption and government expenditures.

The answers have already been revealed in the President's Revitalization Program: decreases in business taxes. Decreases favored by the administration were liberalized depreciation allowances and expansion and simplification of the investment tax credit. The decreases were seen as more effective reductions in the corporate income tax rates. Reductions in personal income taxes to increase saving were also viewed as less effective and possibly counterproductive if they increased consumption.

FURTHER ADMINISTRATION SUGGESTIONS

Energy

If the Carter administration had won the election, and the CEA retained its influence (Schultze was regarded as the chief economic spokesman by Carter), some further ideas on the economy might have received a trial.

Foremost among the problems envisioned by the CEA was energy usage and availability. At the time, the nation was acutely aware that the United States was heavily dependent on oil-producing countries and that supply disruptions could cripple the economy. To minimize the effect of disruptions, the administration hoped to increase the flexibility of producers and consumers. The ability to switch fuel use from oil to coal and natural gas, for example, would lessen the shock of supply limitations. (In economic terms, one would hope to increase the elasticity of demand and supply of energy.) Another way to lessen vulnerability to supply shocks would be to build on the strategic reserve concept and accumulate inventories of fuel supplies. A longer term program might envision the accumulation of capital stock that would be capable of greater flexibility in the choice of fuel or greater efficiency in its use.

On the whole, the administration favored the use of the market whenever possible to allocate resources. The market was seen as the best vehicle to ensure efficient use of scarce resources. Equity concerns, however, may require public intervention to prevent severe hardships and adverse income transfers from consumers to suppliers. Some compromise between efficiency and equity must be found, and thus, the market could not be used exclusively.

The only plan in existence to meet supply shortages was a gasoline rationing scheme and a standby price control authority. While the rationing scheme might lead to greater equity in allocating gasoline, it would interfere with fuel-switching possibilities and thwart efficiency goals, not to mention the bureaucratic jungle that might be created. Thus, the existing plans had major faults and were rejected, as was the reverse—complete reliance on the marketplace to determine the allocation of energy supplies. Also rejected were schemes that allowed the market to allocate resources but tax the windfall profits and rebate them to consumers; import fees were also found wanting as too uncertain in practice. Both might create bureaucratic nightmares.

Thus, the CEA was drawn back to some simple and straightforward elements of an energy policy: (1) to use the market whenever possible to allocate resources; (2) to use stockpiles to counter shortages; and (3) to develop contingency plans to meet situations that threaten to overwhelm the market solutions.[4] After discussing the energy problem and its solutions, these policy suggestions seem lame indeed.

Regulation

Federal regulations have always been the subject of criticism, sometimes legitimate, sometimes self-serving. Federal regulations do impose costs on the society—actual dollar costs, burdens on small businesses, interference with or unduly influencing technological change, and limitation of the flexibility of an industry to respond quickly to changing conditions. It was the latter consequence of regulations that worried the CEA.[5]

Proud of the administration's record of deregulation, the CEA was less pleased with attempts to smooth the transition from regulation to free market. To cushion the shock of deregulation, a great deal of emphasis had been put on easing the transition in hopes of shielding consumers and workers from sudden changes and protecting them from severe dislocations. However desirable such goals might be, they limit the flexibility of the deregulated industry to respond to changes in the external environment. For example, sharp changes in energy prices made the transition in the deregulated natural gas industry unreasonable—external prices rose faster than permitted in the Natural Gas Policy Act so that the new price of natural gas was soon sharply less than the decontrolled market price. How to close the gap between the two without serious disruption shows the problem of transition that is evident in all deregulatory instances to some degree. Sharp increases in energy prices also affected the transition in the airline and railroad industries.

The lesson is clear: "Inflexible transition paths are likely to encounter problems, particularly if the period preceding deregulation is stretched out to protect the economic positions of workers, shareholders, or consumers. Flexible transition paths, on the other hand, can allow industries to weather even large unanticipated shocks by permitting innovation."[6]

The same flexibility is necessary in the case of social regulation. Efforts to protect the environment and to protect the safety of workers and consumers were still necessary, but more thought should have been given to the design of these regulations that also considered efficiency and flexibility. The administration claimed it was making a start at more realistic regulations by its establishment of institutions that would oversee the entire process.

Federal agencies were already required to consider the economic consequences of their new regulations, sometimes using cost-benefit analysis, and submit their proposals to The Regulatory Analysis Review Group (RARG) for review. Further efforts along these lines could lead to more rational, more efficient, and more reasonable regulations in the future.

Finally, the administration was hoping to institute what it called "smarter" regulations. One of these was the "bubble concept." The bubble concept would allow the EPA to determine the permitted pollution over an industrial area but allow private decision-makers to decide how to meet the EPA requirements; there would be no standard for a specific source or type of emission—the costs of these emissions would govern how to meet the standards at the lowest costs.

Another possibility might have been the use of marketable permits to emission rights. Once a determination of the allowable emission had been made, firms could buy and sell their allotted portion of the emission by dealing in the rights. Firms that were efficient and emitted less than they were permitted could sell these rights to other, less efficient firms. Thus, the marketplace would replace direct control and penalize the less efficient operators.

Other regulatory improvements might have been found to reduce the burden on smaller businesses by exempting them from some of the adverse effects, by constantly reviewing and eliminating regulations that were not necessary, and simply approaching the whole idea of government regulation by looking at alternatives to the old method of "command and control" regulation.

The CEA generally approved of the recent trends in banking deregulation as contained in the Depository Institutions Deregulation and Monetary Control Act of 1980 and the development of new monetary instruments by the financial marketplace. Not all of the effects of deregulation were apparent yet, and some problems remained, of course, but areas were identified as ready for further liberalization. Geographical expansion by commercial banks, for instance, would create competition and promote efficient operations. Prohibited since the 1930s, geographical restrictions may no longer be necessary in the changing financial world. Similarly, thrift institutions should be permitted to make more business loans, and in essence become more like commercial banks. Finally, restrictions on stock holdings and other market assets, also prohibited since the 1930s, may also be obsolete.

Acknowledging that the thrifts were facing difficulties in the world of rising interest rates, the CEA rejected solutions that would simply allow them to fail or those that would subsidize them, and chose instead to advocate mergers and consolidations. In general, the CEA again favored letting the market determine the shape of the financial world, since it could be relied upon to reach the most efficient solutions, but providing just enough regulation and safeguards to preserve the soundness of financial institutions—a delicate balance indeed. (The same general approach was applied in the case of agriculture, that is, more reliance on the marketplace for efficiency reasons, while ensuring price stability and the availability of supplies.)

Industrial Policy

The challenge of global competition, and the necessity of planning in an era of restrained growth, led many experts to advocate an industrial policy whereby government would guide, help, or subsidize the development of U.S. industry. Other countries had aided their industries in various ways, and now these industries had grown sufficiently to challenge their U.S. counterparts. As a result, several key industries were declining, and various areas of the nation were distressed. Many voices were heard stating that government had an obligation to prevent the decline in the U.S. industrial base and the disappearance of jobs, many of them high-paying ones.[7]

The CEA rejected government intervention into areas previously reserved for private decisionmakers. Throughout its discussion of government regulations, the CEA pointed out that government frequently reduced efficiency and adaptability when it intervened in the market. An industrial policy offered another opportunity for government to make things worse while attempting to make things better. It argued that government would be involved in "picking winners" whenever it began to intervene to guide the development of some industries and neglecting others. It would be presumptuous for government to pick winners among industries in a dynamic economy, and even if it tried, some firms within the industry would fail. The result, according to the CEA, is that government would not allow firms to fail and would end up supporting many marginal firms, while gaining a few successful ones. Moreover, decisions would become politicized, centralized, and far removed from the original purpose of the policy.

Better, said the CEA, to use government indirectly by altering tax policies, by regulating sensibly, and by using trade policies to encourage and stimulate industries in ways that would not decrease efficiency or unduly interfere with the marketplace. The call for government to do something may be understandable, but interventions are successful only when they are necessary. "The danger [of government intervention] lies in the unwise manipulation of policy variables designed for one set of purposes to attain goals which can be better achieved by the private market."[8]

DEMOCRATIC RIVALS

It is not customary for party members to challenge an incumbent president, but Carter was perceived as so weak and vulnerable that Democrats feared an electoral disaster if he were to run for re-election. Carter's approval rating dropped to an all-time low of 28 percent in June 1980, and few thought he had the answers to or the leadership qualities for addressing the nation's pressing problems. The economy was floundering, inflation was continuing, gasoline was in short supply, Iran had seized American hostages, and Russia had invaded Afghanistan.

These and other issues encouraged the idea of challenging the president. Many people were suggested, many feelers were put out, and many discussions ensued. In the end, only two Democrats remained as serious contenders. Without examining their platforms in detail, it is useful to see how they differed from Carter on economic matters.

Jerry Brown

Governor Edmund G. Brown, Jr., of California emerged as a challenger. The quixotic Brown ran on a slogan of "protect the earth, serve the people, and explore the universe." Critics charged him with vagueness, brashness passing for boldness, and flightiness as he turned to one issue after another. Brown challenged political and economic institutions and in the process hoped to attract constituents from the full array of political beliefs. He attacked government bureaucracies; questioned the government's ability to meet all demands of special interests; called for limits on traditional New Deal programs; appealed for a new sense of community values in families, neighborhoods, schools; championed a balanced budget amendment; and supported conservative ideas on crime. This conservative agenda showed one side of this mercurial politician.

On the other hand, Brown favored strict environmental measures, sought to bring in more minorities and women into public life, advocated a federal energy agency (not private oil companies) to explore and develop energy resources from public lands, proposed an import authority to import oil instead of oil companies, wanted to restore organized labor's power in the bargaining process, opposed nuclear energy, and so on. Many liberals could identify with these ideas.

Still, these general proposals are basically conflicting, and attempts to reach out to both liberals and conservatives and mold a coalition appears in retrospect to be fanciful. Brown was unable to shake the perception of opportunism in the attempt, and many came to regard him as a "flake" or, in terms similar to what the Californians called him, "governor moonbeam." After causing an initial excitement as a gadfly, he faded rapidly from the political scene. His failure to attract a following was also a consequence of having to share the spotlight with another challenger.

Edward Kennedy

Edward M. Kennedy presented Carter with a more formidable opponent. The personification of a liberal, Kennedy was more closely identified with the traditional values of the Democratic Party and, thus, appealed to the party faithful who welcomed his entrance into the race. The popular senator from Massachusetts threatened to reverse the brand of fiscal conservatism associated with Carter and pursue a more active agenda. Basically, however, leadership was the issue that Kennedy stressed, a wise decision since Carter was vulnerable with the public on that score.

Kennedy took exception to the fiscal constraints imposed by the Carter administration in that the budget cuts affected "the poor, the black, the sick, the young, and the unemployed" disproportionally. Here Kennedy was appealing to the traditional strengths of his party. He also advocated a comprehensive and costly national health care system run by the federal government. He was opposed to oil and gas deregulations and was lukewarm on nuclear energy. Kennedy's own energy program stressed conservation and incentives to industry to increase efficiency. On inflation, he proposed a system of wage and price controls.

To illustrate Kennedy's strength in the party, many of his programs were adopted in the party platform, and while platform items are often vague and simply showpieces, they do indicate some notion of party direction. Carter was forced to accept a $12 billion antirecession bill, a promise not to take budgetary actions that would increase unemployment, or pursue policies that would use high interest rates as anti-inflationary policies that would harm the truly needy. Moreover, the party adopted Kennedy's idea to spend more on alternative energy sources and accepted his rejection of federal agencies overriding state environmental, health, or safety laws.[9]

There are a few examples of the concessions Carter was forced to make, although he had the necessary primary victories to ensure his nomination.

These concessions pushed the party back toward the left and away from the brand of fiscal conservatism that Carter wanted to employ. Thus, even as the Kennedy campaign began to falter, he cast a long shadow over the Democratic Party and over its standardbearer, Jimmy Carter, who was now grudgingly accepted.[10]

THE OPPOSITION

John B. Anderson, Independent

Representative John Anderson (R-Ill.) became a leader of the liberal Republicans with his espousal of social programs and civil rights causes. A serious, articulate man, Anderson moved from a typical midwestern conservative to a liberal Republican in large part because of his religious beliefs. While being on the left in the Republican Party may not be saying much, he still bothered the party with his championing of causes not considered orthodox by his conservative colleagues. For example, he voted for open housing legislation, supported busing to force integration, urged ratification of the Equal Rights Amendment, opposed the development of new weapons, supported the Panama Canal Treaty and the SALT II treaty, pushed for campaign financing reform, and advocated and sponsored environmental programs. Clearly, these issues alienated him from his more conservative colleagues, and his popularity among them faded with each position he took.

Disillusion with Nixon's imperial presidency and the Watergate scandal finally pushed Anderson into the decision to run as an independent. Unhappy with his current position as a member of the House of Representatives, but unable or unwilling to advance in either the House or the Senate, he chose instead to run for the presidency.

Anderson considered himself more in the mainstream when it came to fiscal matters, but even here, he demonstrated the willingness to challenge traditional approaches. His economic program, carefully spelled out, attracted many who found his ideas appealing. Among his ideas were the following: a plan for tax-based wage-price standards; youth and retraining programs for the unemployed; indexing of the tax code; administration power (subject to congressional approval) to vary the tax rates by ±10%; liberalization of IRAs and expansion of dividend and interest exclusion from taxation to encourage saving; a refundable investment tax credit; reduction of the regulatory burden; the encouragement of energy conservation by tax credits and by taxing gasoline at 50 cents a gallon; adoption of an industrial policy; proposals to remove barriers to exports; and a promise to work to strengthen international economic cooperation.[11]

With the lack of financing, Anderson's campaign was limited, and while he created a political stir by his entrance into the race, he finished with only 6.6% of the popular vote and did not act as a "spoiler" for Carter.[12] His economic views are included here as a contrast to the right wing of the Republican party, which was in ascendance at the time.

The Republicans

The 1980 presidential campaign saw a host of hopefuls on the Republican side. Sensing Carter's vulnerability, many contenders decided to run against him, including Senator Howard H. Baker (R-Tenn.), George Bush, an experienced public official, John B. Connally, former governor of Texas and official in the Nixon administration, Representative Phillip M. Crane (R-Ill.), Senator Robert Dole (R-Kan.), and Ronald Reagan, former actor and governor of California. It is not necessary to review the economic positions of all of these hopefuls, for they contain many similarities and there is little to differentiate them. It is better to concentrate on the most passionate, and most conservative, of them, and the eventual winner, Ronald Reagan.

Ronald Reagan

Ronald Reagan, ex-radio announcer, ex-movie actor, ex-Democrat, and ex-governor, turned his sights to the highest office in 1976. His loss of the presidential nomination to Gerald Ford did not deter him, and he again sought the presidency in 1980. This time Ford was not in the race, and he bested the men listed above to win the nomination.[13]

Reagan gained notoriety following a speech made in 1964 on behalf of Barry Goldwater. This speech and various derivatives was used on countless occasions and was modeled after a series of talks he gave around the country on behalf of General Electric, which had sponsored his television program "Death Valley Days." The speech stressed the benefits of free enterprise and the evils of big government. Government was blamed for most of the nation's ills, ranging from inflation, education, and social welfare, to the decline of U.S. industry through over-regulation. The problems were simple to understand and simple to fix: reduce government involvement in the economy and transfer whatever legitimate functions exist to state and local governments. The federal government's role would be reduced to that in Adam Smith's world where national defense, justice, and general government would be appropriate government functions and just about everything else would be left to local governments.

The ideas expressed in this speech are, of course, traditional beliefs of conservative politicians. Nevertheless, spoken by the personable Reagan, the old beliefs sounded fresh and straightforward and appealed to many who were longing for a simpler world after the pessimism generated by Carter. Reagan rejected the notion that the nation's problems were complex and that there were no simple answers. He believed there were simple answers. The nation was ready to succumb to anyone who promised a better future by way of simple changes and to anyone who promised to return pride to the nation and restore patriotism and traditional values to their rightful places.

Thus, the transformation of Ronald Reagan from Democrat to conservative Republican was complete, but would not have attracted much attention if the nation had not been so disillusioned with Carter, and the set of ideas had not been packaged so well. In addition, Reagan added something to the traditional conservative beliefs that made his economic program irresistible: a massive tax cut. Under the old conservative economics of Goldwater, cuts in government spending would reduce the size of government, but when practiced resulted in a recession. Spending cuts would have reduced the deficit, regarded as inherently evil, and then after a time, taxes could be reduced as well. This root canal economics was then generally rejected by the voters who did not care for the pain involved in scaling down the public sector.

Thanks to supply-side economics, this scenario was no longer necessary. Taxes could be cut first, regardless of what happened to government expenditures, without incurring any problems with the deficit. Tax reductions, it was held, would increase the incentives of people to work and invest, and their efforts would increase the national income, create jobs, increase productivity, and eventually increase tax revenues for the government to cover in large part or in whole the loss of revenue from the original tax cuts. Apparently the government tax rates were too high, thus discouraging productive efforts. According to supply-siders, led by Arthur Laffer,[14] the reduction in tax rates would bring in more revenue and not increase the deficit significantly, even if government expenditures remained the same.

This free-lunch economics had enormous appeal to politicians and the public. Reagan was slow to adopt this supply-side ideology, but once he did, it became a cornerstone of his economic program. With his communicative skills, he added it to the rest of his conservative program. In brief, his economic program included the following:

1. A reduction in government spending and reductions in the involvement in private affairs. In the campaign, such reductions were to eliminate waste in government.

2. A 30% reduction in individual tax rates over three years. This is the Kemp-Roth tax proposal that had been circulating since 1978.

3. An increase in national defense spending to meet any foreseeable challenge. The United States was perceived as weak thanks to past administrations policies.

4. Reduction in inflation, relying on the monetary authorities to do the job.

5. Deregulation of the economy. Government was too involved in U.S. industry, adding to their costs and hurting their competitiveness.

6. Balancing the federal budget by 1983.

This was Reagan's basic agenda as he evolved into a conservative politician. His economic program was not as detailed as some of the other candidates' and relied mainly on the grand scheme design and on agreeable rhetoric. Reagan's personal charm and sincerity were summoned to carry the day, not a blueprint for economic action. That came after the victory celebration.[15] His personal knowledge of economics was minimal, and during the campaign he relied on anecdotes, one-liners, and sarcasm as he blasted away at some of his favorite themes: the welfare cheats, the bureaucrats, and the costly unnecessary government programs.

Against such a formidable personal campaign, Carter looked irresolute and indecisive. Against such an attractive economic program, Carter's looked tenuous and anemic. While many questioned Reagan's economic plan, it was bold and uncomplicated. Huge deficits would result if adopted, said Charles Schultze, and the CBO concurred.[16] Others thought that elements of the program were contradictory and could not be achieved at the same time. Still others thought inflation would result as aggregate demand exceeded supply. Criticism appeared from all quarters, and not many economists agreed with the entire package. Even George Bush labeled it "voodoo economics."

No matter how many criticisms were leveled at the program, the public found it exciting and innovative. It needed hope and confidence, and Reagan promised both.

CONCLUSION

While Reagan stumped the nation and harangued the administration, Carter employed the Rose garden strategy. He kept to the White House, ostensibly to be near if and when word of the hostages in Iran arrived. The hostage crisis in Iran and the Russian invasion of Afghanistan hurt Carter as much or more than the economic condition of the nation. Daily reminders of these events seemed to diminish the stature of the United States and certainly that of the impotent Carter. The promise of more of the same or even marginal improvement was not sufficient to entice the public to overcome whatever reservations it had about Reagan. On the economic issues, Reagan outpolled Carter by substantial margins, while on the social issues, Carter was deemed to be far superior. Clearly, in this campaign the economic issues weighed more heavily on the voters' minds. Reagan cleverly hammered away at the economic issues and the quality of leadership. In the debates, he asked the question, "Are you better off than you were four years ago?" Many could answer no, and those who were better off did not feel as though they were.

A general feeling of uneasiness pervaded the 1980 presidential campaign, one that was not easily recognized or understood. It was too vague to comprehend, but it was there. Carter was identified as a good man, honest and sincere, but not up to the job of reviving the nation. It was time to try something different.

Out of the 54.0% voter turnout, Reagan received 50.8%, Carter received 41.0% and all others received 8.2%. Reagan thus received the support of just over 27% of the voters, hardly a mandate to try something new, but that is what he and his followers claimed.

NOTES

1. Testimony of OMB director, James T. McIntyre, Jr., before U.S. House Budget Committee, *President's Economic Revitalization Program*, 96th Congress, 2nd session, September 1980, 57.

2. *Economic Report of the President, 1981*, 29.

3. See the discussion in Ibid., 57–68.

4. Ibid., 97–99. The energy problem is discussed on pages 90–99.

5. Ibid., 99–107.

6. Ibid., 102.

7. Among the many voices, see Robert Reich, *The Next American Frontier* (New York: Times Books, 1983).

8. *Economic Report of the President, 1981*, 130.

9. See also Michael J. Malbin, "The Conventions, Platforms, and Issue Activists," in *The American Elections of 1980*, edited by Austin Ranney (Washington, D.C.: American Enterprise Institute, 1981); other contributions in this volume are also pertinent to this analysis. See also the Congressional Quarterly's *Candidates '80* (Washington, D.C.: Congressional Quarterly, January 1980) for succinct profiles of the candidates and their backgrounds and positions. On page 17, the following quote is attributed to Carter

assessing Kennedy, "Sen. Kennedy is much more inclined toward the old philosophy of pouring out new programs and new money to meet a social need. I'm much more inclined to try to make existing programs work efficiently and start up new programs only when it's absolutely necessary." These two sentences illustrate concisely the differences between the two men and the rift within the Democratic Party.

10. For an insider's view of the problems the Carter administration faced with regard to Sen. Kennedy, see Jody Powell, *The Other Side of the Story* (New York: William Morrow, 1984), 182–208.

11. Clifford W. Brown, Jr., and Robert J. Walker, comp. *A Campaign of Ideas: The 1980 Anderson/Lucey Platform* (Westport, Conn.: Greenwood Press, 1984), 351–361.

12. See the analysis by William Schneider, "The November 4 Vote: What Did It Mean?" in *The American Elections of 1980*, edited by Austin Ranney (Washington, D.C.: American Enterprise Institute, 1981), 223.

13. There are many books on Ronald Reagan and his administration. Books from within the administration include William A. Niskanen, *Reaganomics* (New York: Oxford University Press, 1988); Murray Weidenbaum, *Rendezvous with Reality* (New York: Basic Books, 1988); David Stockman, *The Triumph of Politics* (New York: Harper and Row, 1986). From outside the administration, Benjamin M. Friedman, *Day of Reckoning* (New York: Brown Brothers Harriman, 1988); and Anthony S. Campagna, *The Economy in the Reagan Years: The Economic Consequences of the Reagan Administrations* (Westport, Conn.: Greenwood Press, 1994).

14. For an explanation of the tax cuts and supply-side economics, see Jude Wanniski, *The Way the World Works* (New York: Simon & Schuster, 1978), and Paul Craig Roberts, *The Supply-Side Revolution* (Cambridge, Mass.: Harvard University Press, 1984).

15. See the White House Paper, *A Program for Economic Recovery*, February 18, 1981.

16. Schultze estimated that Reagan's tax package would reduce revenues by $280 billion—"about $180 billion more than is needed to keep the economy growing on . . . a prudent path." See Schultze's testimony before the U.S. House of Representatives, Committee on the Budget, *President's Economic Revitalization Program*, 96th Congress, 2nd session, September 1980, 69. See also the Congressional Budget Office, *An Analysis of the Roth-Kemp Tax Cut Proposal* (Unpublished, 1978).

Chapter 10

Conclusions and Legacy

The Carter administration has been characterized (or dismissed) as ineffectual and judged as a failure. Such a conclusion is easy to reach given its legislative record and administrative ineptitude. Were the times so challenging that the nation was ungovernable, as some have alleged? Was Carter a trustee of the public welfare, making unpopular decisions? Was Carter pursuing what was right, spurning special interests requiring that he be above politics as usual? His defenders answer yes to these questions and ask that the Carter administration be viewed in this revised light.

After assessing these questions, however, Burton Kaufman, a Carter biographer, reluctantly concludes that attempts to reassess the Carter administration are flawed and sums up his analysis as follows: "The events of his four years in office projected an image to the American people of a hapless administration in disarray and of a presidency that was increasingly divided, lacking in leadership, ineffective in dealing with Congress, incapable of defending America's honor abroad, and uncertain about its purpose, priorities, and sense of direction."[1] The original and immediate assessments of this administration were, in the end, closer to the truth than the revisionists' portrayal.

It is difficult to quarrel with this concise appraisal of the Carter administration, and in this book, there are numerous examples and references that support such a conclusion. In general, then, I would agree with this assessment of the administration in its *totality*. We must now inquire if the same indictment can be applied to the economic policy-making of the administration.

As applied solely to Carter's domestic economic policy-making, the Kaufman quote is generally accurate, but a bit harsh and in need of qualification. It is too sweeping a statement when applied to an area as volatile as economics. Simple, straightforward, and uncontroversial answers to economic problems are seldom found in practice, so that some degree of vacillation and ambivalence is to be expected. What may appear as indecision may actually be prudence in disguise.

With this admonition in mind, we can look at the question of leadership. Carter, as we have seen, assigned policy formation to others with only minimal direction. The reform and energy proposals are examples of this behavior. Whether one regards this procedure as good leadership depends upon one's concept of leadership. Many would regard this as an example of good leadership: Delegating authority to subordinates is often viewed as commendable and desirable. Others might interpret this as an abrogation of authority and demand more involvement by the leader. Without entering into the pros and cons of these extreme positions, it is clear that Carter put much faith in his chosen associates and elected to give them a good deal of autonomy.

The trouble comes when the leader backs away from the issue either because it is or becomes unpopular or too controversial and leaves the subordinate without oversight or support. When the policy comes under attack or is critized severely, it is then time for more direction, not less. Yet less is apparently what Carter gave, as illustrated by his actions in the reform areas. So it seems he was good at giving general directions, but not as good in following through once the issue became messy. This has more to do with the setting of priorities, to be sure, but he often left subordinates dangling when he withdrew support for his policies.

Contrast this assessment with another criticism often leveled at Carter: He was too immersed in details. Obviously, this was not true in economic areas and may be overstated in other areas as well. According to one observer, "He liked to make decisions, had confidence in his capacity to make good ones and was inclined to make more decisions than he should. This was not getting bogged down in details but rather is an analogue to his tendency to place more issues on the public policy agenda than could be handled easily."[2] Perhaps the details on economic matters bored him, or more likely, there were too many variants presented to him, and he found them confounding and was willing to leave to others the difficult task of sorting them out.

Few would quarrel with the judgment that Carter was ineffective with Congress. Again numerous examples illustrate, for example, the tax rebate that pulled the rug out from under congressional leaders and the energy policies developed in secret. His reluctance to consult with Congress, his unwillingness to compromise, and his failure to play even the simple games of politics, surely alienated him from members who could have served him better.

It is true, of course, that several factors worked against a comfortable relationship with Congress. First, Carter was not highly regarded; he was after all an outsider who had promised to clean up the mess in Washington. Even members of his own party were not impressed with his ability. Second, Congress was flexing its muscles and asserting independence. Following Nixon, Congress was ready to exert its powers and defy the executive branch. Third, party allegiance was breaking down. Carter was the first president to suffer the consequences of party disintegration. Thus, it was a difficult time to govern, and anyone would have had trouble with these circumstances, especially an untried outsider.

Nevertheless, this is precisely the time when the quality of leadership is most necessary. Carter was not the leader for these times; perhaps in another time, under different circumstances, he would have proved an acceptable if not a celebrated one. Nor was it a good time to be a Democratic president. Traditional Democrats pulled one way, conservative Democrats pulled another way, and Carter tried to reconcile the differences with his own philosophy. He did not succeed, and the failure was costly, for him and for his party.

Finally, did the administration act without purpose in economics? Did it fail to establish priorities? It is here, more than anywhere else, that harsh criticism must be tempered. Carter did not create the problems that haunted his administration, but he did acknowledge them and tried to confront them.

Most of the economic problems facing the Carter administration can be traced to its predecessors. The energy crisis, tax cuts vs. reforms, the welfare mess, the health care dilemma, and the controversy over government regulation did not emerge in 1977, but all had a long history of unfilled promises and partial solutions. Unfortunately for Carter, some persistent problems now demanded more action, such as energy, and some neglected ones, from a traditional Democratic view, demanded attention, such as national health care. It was not a happy time for economists because the more important issues were mutually exclusive: solving one aggravated another. To steer a steady path under these circumstances would have required an omniscience that no one, in or out of government, possessed.

Economic problems at the time seemed intractable, for instance, the problems caused by stagflation. The Phillips curve that was designed to show the trade-off between inflation and unemployment now seemed a cruel hoax. Stagflation, the worst of both worlds, presented the economy with no ready solutions; fighting inflation made unemployment worse and vice versa. With these conditions, what is the meaning of setting priorities? Which is worse: unemployment or inflation? Economists did not or could not answer the question definitively, leaving the answer to politicians, who often followed political and economic power rather than unbiased analyses.

Since no one had the solutions to stagflation, Carter, a fiscal conservative from the beginning, was thrown back to his personal bias and chose to elevate inflation to the nation's most pressing problem. In so doing, he indeed set a priority, one that perhaps did not sit well with his more liberal cohorts, but he can hardly be faulted for his political decision. He sacrificed the liberal agenda in the process and was well aware of the political consequences. More radical solutions to stagflation, such as direct wage and price controls or voluntary wage freezes to halt the wage/price spiral, were not thought to be socially acceptable. So, in the end the administration acquiesced to monetary stringency and watched its tenure recede.

Inflation thus muddled Carter's desire to bring reforms to the forefront of the nation's concerns. The administration was well aware of where it wanted to take the nation but also recognized that it was not possible to realize these aims. It had a purpose, but sacrificed it to the exigencies of the times, perhaps hoping for a second term to accomplish it.

These factors may be responsible for the observation that the administration failed to promote its policies. It did not mobilize the effort in many economic policies that it did in, for example, the Panama Canal Treaty or energy matters. The halfhearted promotion may be explained by the sense of futility in receiving enough support to accomplish what it wanted. Perhaps in a second term, when economic conditions changed, more might have been accomplished.

Thus, the administration was forced to select a priority by events it could not control and address problems it could not solve. Inflation was wreaking havoc in the society, whether justified or not, and the political response was to acknowledge that concern and appear to address it. This is not to defend the administration's policies, but to point out that it did identify its main economic enemy and after some hesitation decided to combat it. The administration's lack of success in its efforts should not be misconstrued as lack of a purpose in economic affairs. However, retreat from its much heralded reforms caused the perception of incoherence and indecision to develop, which was the fault of the administration.

LEGACY

As mentioned previously, Carter occupied a rather curious place in the history of presidential administrations. The conservative movement had been gaining strength since the election of Richard Nixon, and Carter's election represented a continuation in its development. To many, Carter represented a return to liberalism, but in reality no such reversal occurred, or was likely to occur. Carter was more conservative than people realized when they elected him. On the other hand, neither was he from conservatism's far right. His brand of Southern populism prevented him from aligning himself with their more draconian solutions to the nation's problems.

To gauge Carter's place in the conservative movement, one has only to look at him as a forerunner of Reagan. The Reagan administrations regarded themselves as revolutionary, making over the role of government in the economy. However, a glance at the economic policies of the Carter administration reveals that Reagan just continued the policies of Carter. A list of the important policies begun by the Carter administration and continued by the Reagan administrations shows not only that Carter was a precursor to Reagan, but also reveals the place of Carter in the conservative trend.

1. Monetary policy—monetarism continued into 1982.
2. Deregulation—policy continued and basic administrative framework adopted by the Reagan administration.
3. National defense spending increased and social program spending reduced.
4. Tax reductions continued from Carter and Ford administrations.
5. Inflation regarded as number one problem while unemployment was given secondary consideration.
6. Balance budget as a goal.

The list is sufficient to illustrate that Carter anticipated Reagan's program and promoted considerable elements of the conservative agenda.[3] Of course, the Reagan camp learned a good deal from Carter, such as the following:

1. Employ a different management style—leave details to others, just set the agenda.
2. Surround the president with loyal advisors who share the vision of the chief.
3. Concentrate on a few major policies, for example, defense increases, tax cuts, and fighting inflation, letting other goals languish.
4. Fight for (3) and promote policies directly to public.
5. Bring campaign for re-election to the people—staying in the White House wins few votes.

No doubt there were other lessons learned from Carter's example. Reagan benefited from Carter's mistakes and managed to achieve some of his goals; Bill Clinton, the next Democratic president, did not learn from either and had a great deal of difficulty in accomplishing his ambitious agenda.

Finally, all of the qualifications that have been mentioned do not overrule the basic conclusion that the Carter administration failed to accomplish its economic goals. It did not stick to them, promote them, or revise them sufficiently to ensure passage. The difficulty of the economic problems is not disputed, and easy answers were not readily available. The Carter administration tried some intricate balancing acts in the effort to solve these problems, but in the end it lacked the political finesse to pull them off. It often made bold proposals, elevating expectations, only to retreat from them when the battle got rough. As a result, it earned the label of incompetence, and while not always deserved, it stuck, and Carter was regarded as ineffectual.

This assessment of Carter as an individual has undergone some revision since he left office. His efforts on behalf of the poor helped to demonstrate his sincerity and humanity; his Center for Peace in Atlanta clearly shows his concern for a more just and peaceful world in which disputes can be settled rationally; and his personal efforts in observing elections and mediating disputes in Haiti, North Korea, and Bosnia have revealed him to be a respected world leader whose integrity is unquestioned. His stature has grown since leaving office and the label of incompetence has disappeared. Perhaps this is one more testament to the observation that he took office at the wrong time, when his ideals and visions did not and could not receive a fair hearing.

NOTES

1. See Burton I. Kaufman, *The Presidency of James Earl Carter, Jr.* (Lawrence, Kans.: University of Kansas Press, 1993), 3. In the preceding pages, Kaufman gives a brief characterization of revisionist views.

2. Erwin C. Hargrove, *Jimmy Carter as President* (Baton Rouge, La.: Louisiana State University Press, 1988), 28.

3. For more on this claim, see Anthony C. Campagna, *The Economy in the Reagan Years: The Economic Consequences of the Reagan Administrations* (Westport, Conn.: Greenwood Press, 1994), 24–29.

Select Bibliography

Abernathy, M. Glenn, Dilys M. Hill, and Phil Williams, eds. *The Carter Years: The President and Policy Making*. London: Frances Pinter, 1984.

Aaron, Henry J., and Michael J. Boskin, eds. *The Economics of Taxation*. Washington, D.C.: The Brookings Institution, 1980.

Blinder, Alan S. *Economic Policy and the Great Stagflation*. New York: Academic Press, 1979.

Brown, Clifford W., and Robert J. Walker, comp. *A Campaign of Ideas: The 1980 Anderson/Lucey Platform*. Westport, Conn.: Greenwood Press, 1984.

Califano, Joseph A. *Governing America*. New York: Simon and Schuster, 1981.

Calleo, David, P. *The Imperious Economy*. Cambridge, Mass.: Harvard University Press, 1982.

Campagna, Anthony S. *The Economy in the Reagan Years: The Economic Consequences of the Reagan Administrations*. Westport, Conn.: Greenwood Press, 1994.

———. *U.S. National Economic Policies, 1917–1985*. New York: Praeger, 1987.

Carter, Jimmy. *Keeping Faith*. New York: Bantam Books, 1982.

———. *Why Not the Best?* Nashville, Tenn.: Broadman Press, 1975.

Congressional Budget Office. *The Disappointing Recovery*. Washington, D.C.: Government Printing Office, 1977.

———. *Employment Subsidies and Employment Tax Credits*. Washington, D.C.: Government Printing Office, 1977.

———. *Overview of the 1978 Budget: An Analysis of President Carter's Revisions*. Washington, D.C.: Government Printing Office, 1977.

———. *Overview of the 1978 Budget: An Analysis of President Ford's Proposals*. Washington, D.C.: Government Printing Office, 1977.

———. *President Carter's Energy Proposals: A Perspective*. Washington, D.C.: Government Printing Office, 1977.

———. *An Analysis of the Roth-Kemp Tax Cut Proposal*. Unpublished, 1978.

———. *CETA Reauthorization Issues*. Washington, D.C.: Government Printing Office, August 1978.

———. *The Administration's Welfare Reform Proposal: An Analysis of the Program for Better Jobs and Income*. Washington, D.C.: Government Printing Office, 1978.

Congressional Quarterly. *Candidates '80.* Washington, D.C.: Congressional Quarterly, 1980.

———. *Energy Policy.* Washington, D.C.: Congressional Quarterly, 1981.

Eckstein, Otto. *Core Inflation.* Englewood Cliffs, N.J.: Prentice-Hall, 1981.

Energy Resources Committee to the National Resources Committee. *Energy Resources and National Policy.* Government Printing Office, 1939.

Executive Office of the President. Office of Energy Policy and Planning. *The National Energy Plan.* Washington, D.C.: Government Printing Office, April 1977.

———. *Energy Policy and Planning the National Energy Plan: Summary of Public Participation.* Washington, D.C.: Government Printing Office, no date.

Fallows, James. "The Passionless Presidency." *Atlantic Monthly.* May and June, 1979.

Franklin, Grace A., and Randall B. Ripley. *CETA: Politics and Policy, 1973–1982.* Knoxville, Tenn.: University of Tennessee Press, 1984.

Fromm, Gary, ed. *Tax Incentives and Capital Spending.* Washington, D.C.: The Brookings Institution, 1967.

General Accounting Office. *Investment Tax Credit: Unresolved Issues.* Washington, D.C.: General Accounting Office, 1978.

Goodwin, Craufurd D., ed. *Energy Policy in Perspective: Today's Problems Yesterday's Solutions.* Washington, D.C.: The Brookings Institution, 1981.

Hall, Robert E., ed. *Inflation: Causes and Effects.* Chicago: University of Chicago Press, 1982.

Hammond, Thomas H., and Jack H. Knott. *A Zero-Based Look at Zero-Base Budgeting.* New Brunswick, N.J.: Transaction Books, 1980.

Hargrove, Erwin C. *Jimmy Carter as President.* Baton Rouge, La.: Louisiana State University Press, 1988.

Hargrove, Erwin C., and Samuel A. Morley. *The President and the Council of Economic Advisors: Interviews with CEA Chairmen.* Boulder, Colo.: Westview Press, 1984.

Hibbs, Douglas A. *The American Political Economy: Macroeconomics and Electoral Politics.* Cambridge, Mass.: Harvard University Press, 1979.

Johnson, Haynes. *In the Absence of Power.* New York: Viking Press, 1980.

Kaufman, Burton I. *The Presidency of James Earl Carter Jr.* Lawrence, Kans.: University of Kansas Press, 1993.

Kraus, Sidney, ed. *The Great Debates: Carter vs. Ford, 1976.* Bloomington, Ind.: Indiana University Press, 1979.

Laffer, Arthur B., and Jan P. Seymour. *The Economics of the Tax Revolt.* New York: Harcourt Brace Jovanovich, 1979.

Lasky, Victor. *Jimmy Carter: The Man and the Myth.* New York: Richard Marek, 1979.

Levitan, Sar A., and Garth L. Mangum, eds. *The T in CETA.* Kalamazoo, Mich.: W. E. Upjohn Institute for Employment Research, 1981.

Lynn, Laurence E., and David deF. Whitman. *The President as Policymaker: Jimmy Carter and Welfare Reform.* Philadelphia: Temple University Press, 1981.

Mirengoff, William, Lester Rindler, Harry Greenspan, and Charles Harris. *CETA: Accomplishments, Problems, Solutions.* Kalamazoo, Mich.: W. E. Upjohn Institute for Employment Research, 1982.

National Commission for Manpower Policy. *CETA: An Analysis of the Issues.* Washington, D.C.: Government Printing Office, Special Report 23, May 1978.

Powell, Jody. *The Other Side of the Story*. New York: William Morrow, 1984.

Pyhrr, Peter A. *Zero-Base Budgeting: A Practical Management Tool for Evaluating Expenses*. New York: John Wiley & Sons, 1973.

Ranney, Austin. *The American Elections of 1980*. Washington, D.C.: American Enterprise Institute, 1981.

Schapsmeier, Edward L., and Frederick H. Schapsmeier. *Gerald R. Ford's Date with Destiny*. New York: Peter Lang, 1989.

Schram, Martin. *Running for President 1976: The Carter Campaign*. New York: Stein and Day, 1977.

Schultze, Charles. *Memos to the President*. Washington, D.C.: The Brookings Institution, 1992.

Shoup, Laurence H. *The Carter Presidency and Beyond*. Palo Alto, Calif.: Ramparts Press, 1980.

Snedeker, Bonnie B., and David M. Snedeker. *CETA: Decentralization on Trial*. Salt Lake City, Utah: Olympus Publishing Company, 1978.

Stein, Herbert. *Presidential Economics*. Washington, D.C.: American Enterprise Institute, 1988.

terHorst, Jerald F. *Gerald Ford and the Future of the Presidency*. New York: The Third Press, 1974.

Thompson, Kenneth W., ed. *The Ford Presidency*. New York: University Press of America, 1988.

Tolchin, Susan J. "Presidential Power and the Politics of RARG," *Regulation* (July/August 1979).

Tufte, Edward R. *Political Control of the Economy*. Princeton, N.J.: Princeton University Press, 1978.

U.S. Congress. House. Committee on the Budget. *President Carter's Welfare Proposals*. 95th Cong., 1st sess., October 1977.

——— . House. Committee on the Budget. *Economic Outlook at Mid-Summer*. 95th Cong., 2nd sess., July 1978.

——— . House. Committee on the Budget. *Outlook and Budget Levels for Fiscal Years 1979 and 1980*. 96th Cong., 1st sess., January 1979.

——— . House. Committee on the Budget. *Recommendations for the Second Concurrent Resolution of the Fiscal Year 1981 Budget*. 96th Cong., 2nd sess., November 1980.

——— . House. Committee on Government Operations. *Providing Reorganization Authority to the President*. 95th Cong., 1st sess., March 1977.

——— . House. Committee on Interstate and Foreign Commerce. *National Health Insurance*. 96th Cong., 1st sess., November 1979.

——— . House. Committee on Interstate and Foreign Commerce. *Hospital Cost Containment*. 96th Cong., 1st sess., 1979.

——— . House. *The Presidential Campaign 1976*. 3 vols. Washington, D.C.: United States Government Printing Office, 1979.

——— . House. Committee on Rules. *Regulatory Reform and Congressional Review of Agency Rules*. 96th Cong., 1st sess., 1980.

——— . House. Committee on Ways and Means. *Tax Aspects of President Carter's Economic Stimulus Program*. 95th Cong., 1st sess., February 1977.

————. House. Committee on Ways and Means. *Panel Discussion on the President's Economic Stimulus Program.* 95th Cong., 1st sess., February 1977.

————. House. Committee on Ways and Means. *The President's 1978 Tax Reduction and Reform Proposals.* 95th Cong., 2nd sess., January, February 1978.

————. House. Committee on Ways and Means. *President's Hospital Cost Containment Proposal.* 96th Cong., 1st sess., March 1979.

U.S. Congress. Senate. Committee on the Budget. *Briefing on Proposed Revisions to the Federal Budget for Fiscal Years 1977 and 1978.* 95th Cong., 1st sess., April 1977.

————. Senate. Committee on the Budget. *First Concurrent Resolution on the Budget-Fiscal Year 1979.* 95th Cong., 2nd sess., July 1978 and February 1979.

————. Senate. Committee on Finance. *President's Statement on Principles of Welfare Reform.* 95th Cong., 1st sess., May 1977.

————. Senate. Committee on Finance. *Welfare Reform Proposals.* 95th Cong., 2nd sess., February 1978.

————. Senate. Committee on Government Operations. *Compendium of Materials on Zero-Base Budgeting in the States.* 95th Cong., 1st sess., January 1977.

————. Senate. Committee on Government Operations. *To Renew the Reorganization Authority.* 95th Cong., 1st sess., February, 1977.

————. Senate. Committee on Governmental Affairs. *Regulatory Reform Legislation.* 96th Cong,. 1st sess., March-May, 1979.

————. Senate. Committee on Human Resources. *National Health Insurance.* 96th Cong., 1st sess., October-December 1978.

————. Senate. Joint Hearings of the Committee on Finance and the Select Committee on Small Business. *Jobs Tax Credit.* 95th Cong., 2nd sess., July 1978.

U.S. Department of Labor. Office of the Assistant Secretary for Policy Evaluation and Research. *Conference Report on Evaluating the 1977 Economic Stimulus Package.* Washington, D.C.: Government Printing Office, 1978.

Wooten, James. *Dasher.* New York: Summit Books, 1978.

Index

About the Author

ANTHONY S. CAMPAGNA is the John H. Converse Professor of
Economics at the University of Vermont. He is the author of *The Economy
in the Reagan Years* (Greenwood, 1994), *The Economic Consequences of
the Vietnam War* (Praeger, 1991), and *National Economic Policies, 1917–
1985* (Praeger, 1987).

ISBN 0-313-29568-9

EAN

9 780313 295683

HARDCOVER BAR CODE